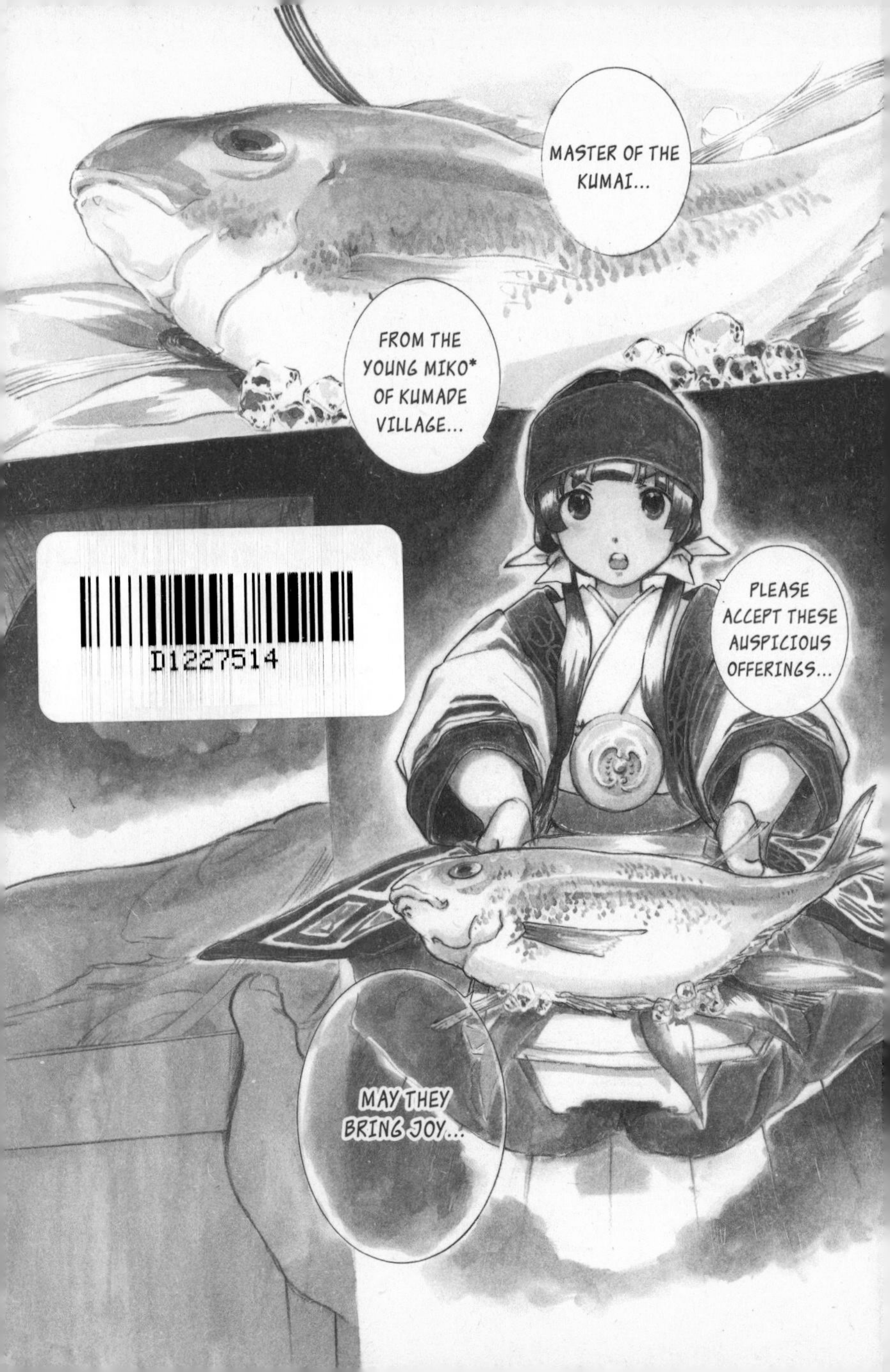
MASTER OF THE KUMAI...
FROM THE YOUNG MIKO* OF KUMADE VILLAGE...
PLEASE ACCEPT THESE AUSPICIOUS OFFERINGS...
MAY THEY BRING JOY...

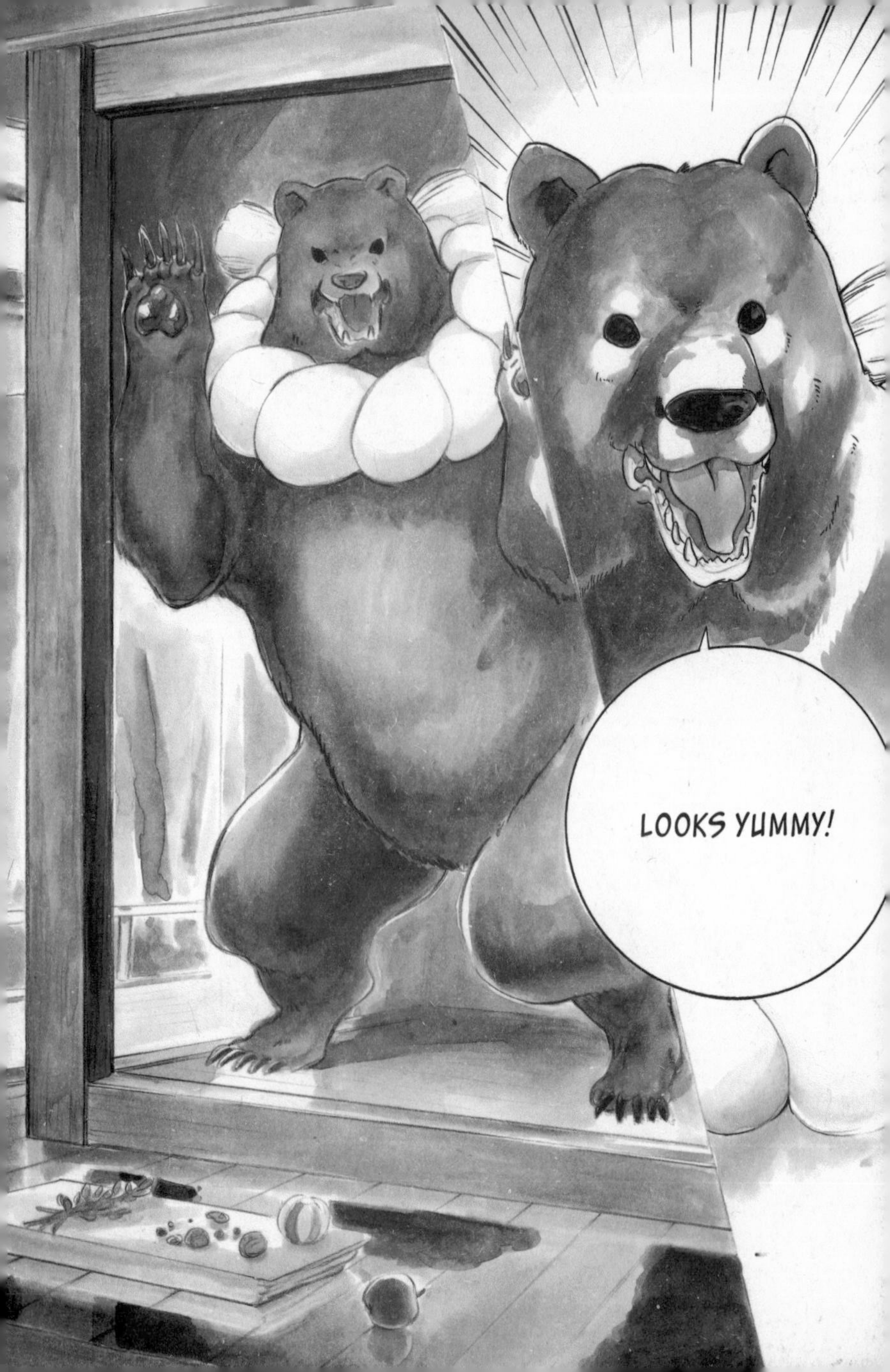
LOOKS YUMMY!

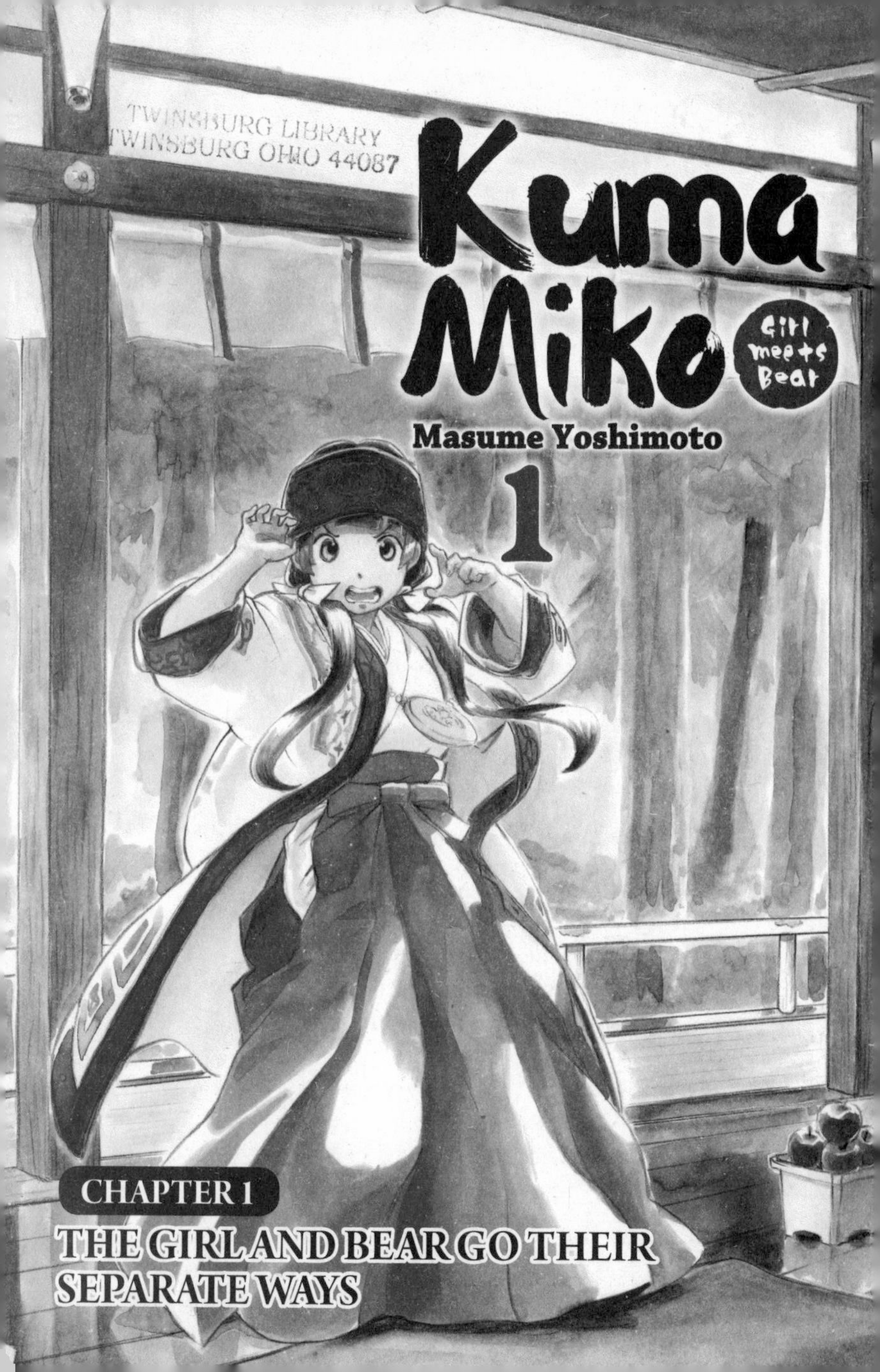
TWINSBURG LIBRARY
TWINSBURG OHIO 44087
Kuma Miko
Girl meets Bear
Masume Yoshimoto
1
CHAPTER 1
THE GIRL AND BEAR GO THEIR SEPARATE WAYS

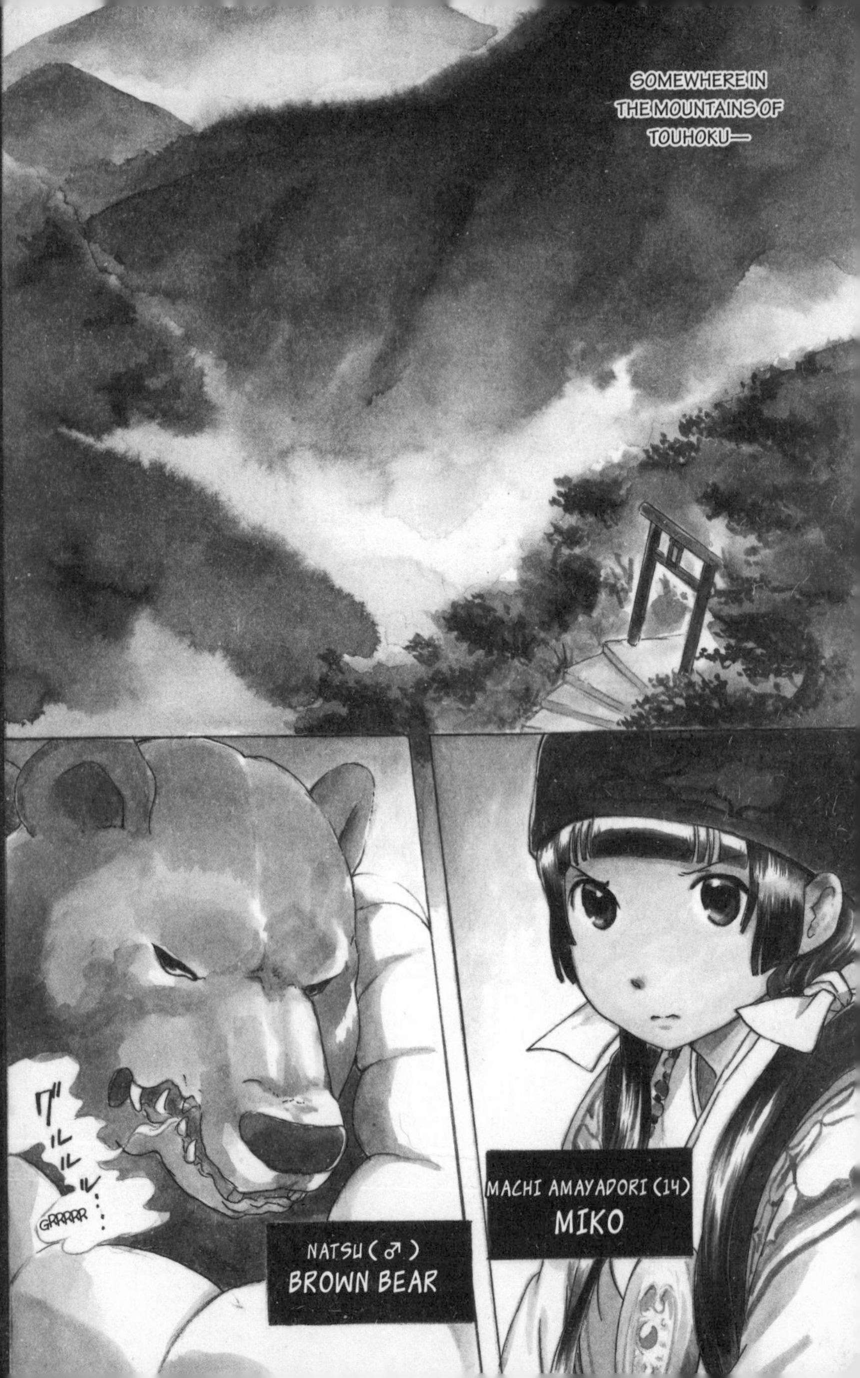
SOMEWHERE IN THE MOUNTAINS OF TOUHOKU—
MACHI AMAYADORI (14)
MIKO
グルルル…
GRRRRR
NATSU (♂)
BROWN BEAR

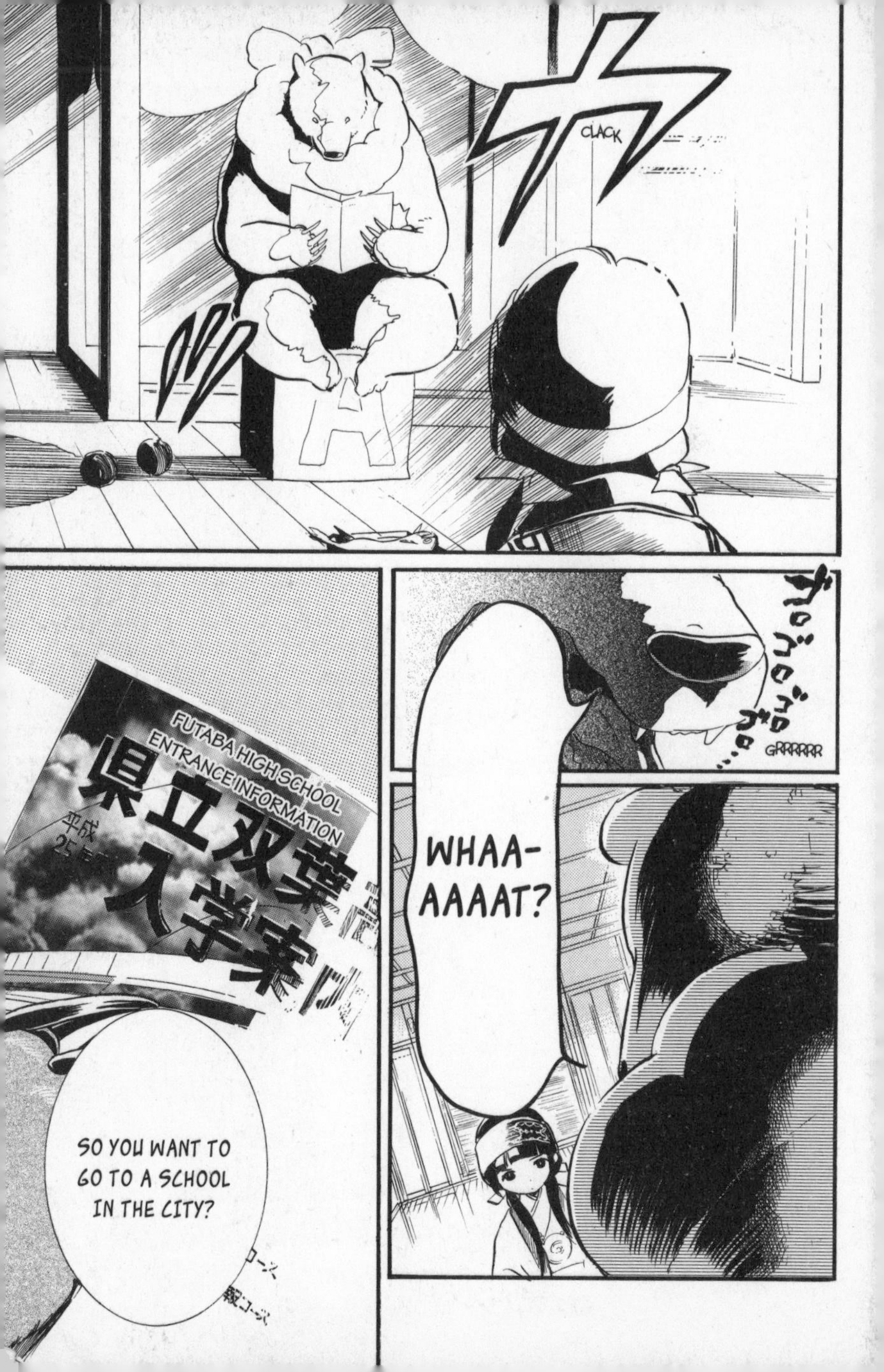
CLACK
GRRRRR
WHAA-AAAAT?
FUTABA HIGH SCHOOL ENTRANCE INFORMATION
県立双葉入学案内
SO YOU WANT TO GO TO A SCHOOL IN THE CITY?

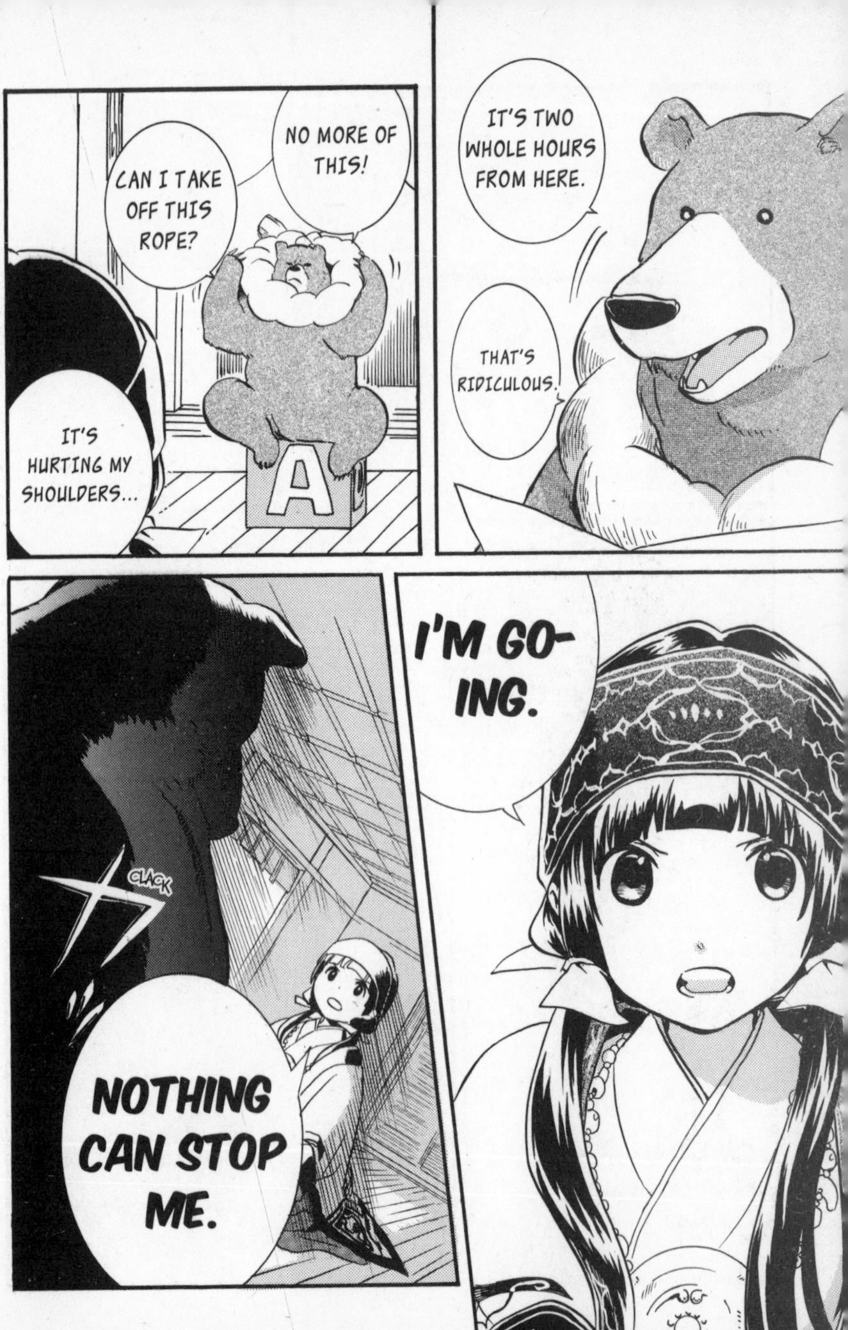
IT'S TWO WHOLE HOURS FROM HERE.
THAT'S RIDICULOUS.
NO MORE OF THIS!
CAN I TAKE OFF THIS ROPE?
IT'S HURTING MY SHOULDERS...
I'M GO-ING.
CLACK
NOTHING CAN STOP ME.

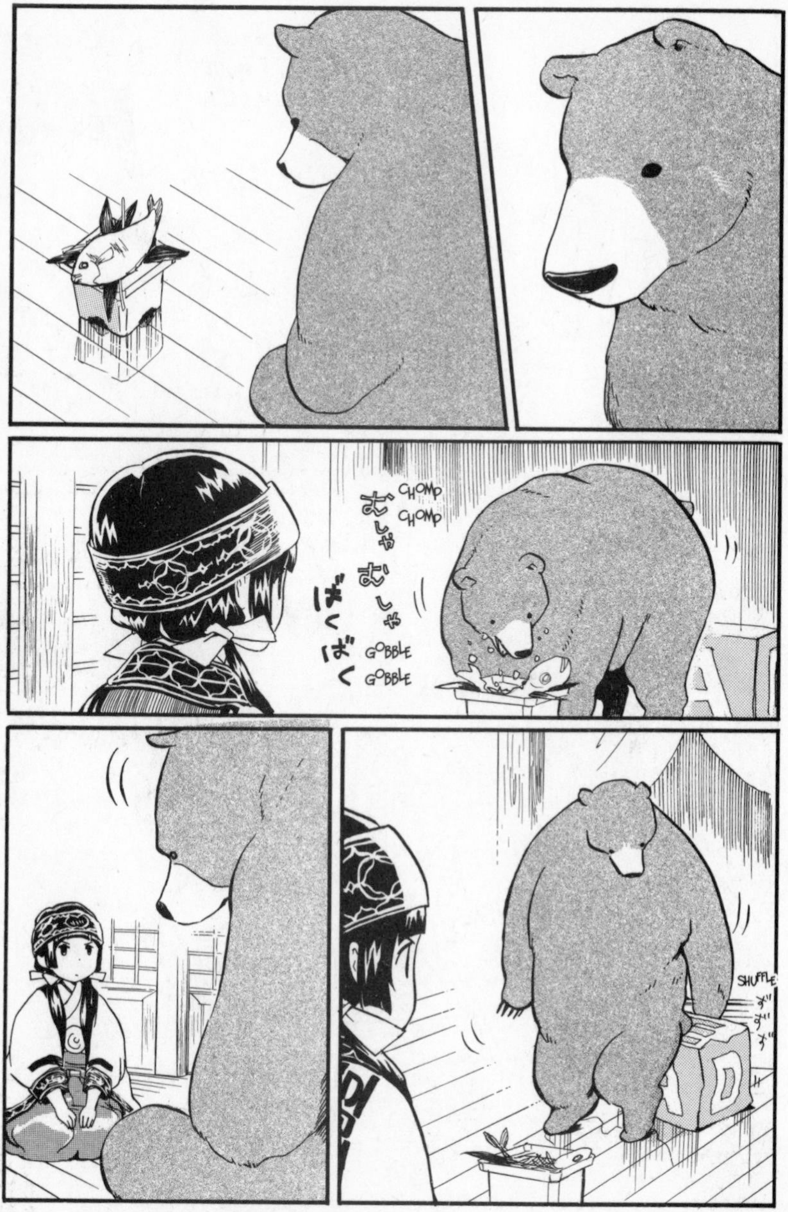
むしゃむしゃ
CHOMP CHOMP
ばくばく
GOBBLE GOBBLE
SHUFFLE
ずずず

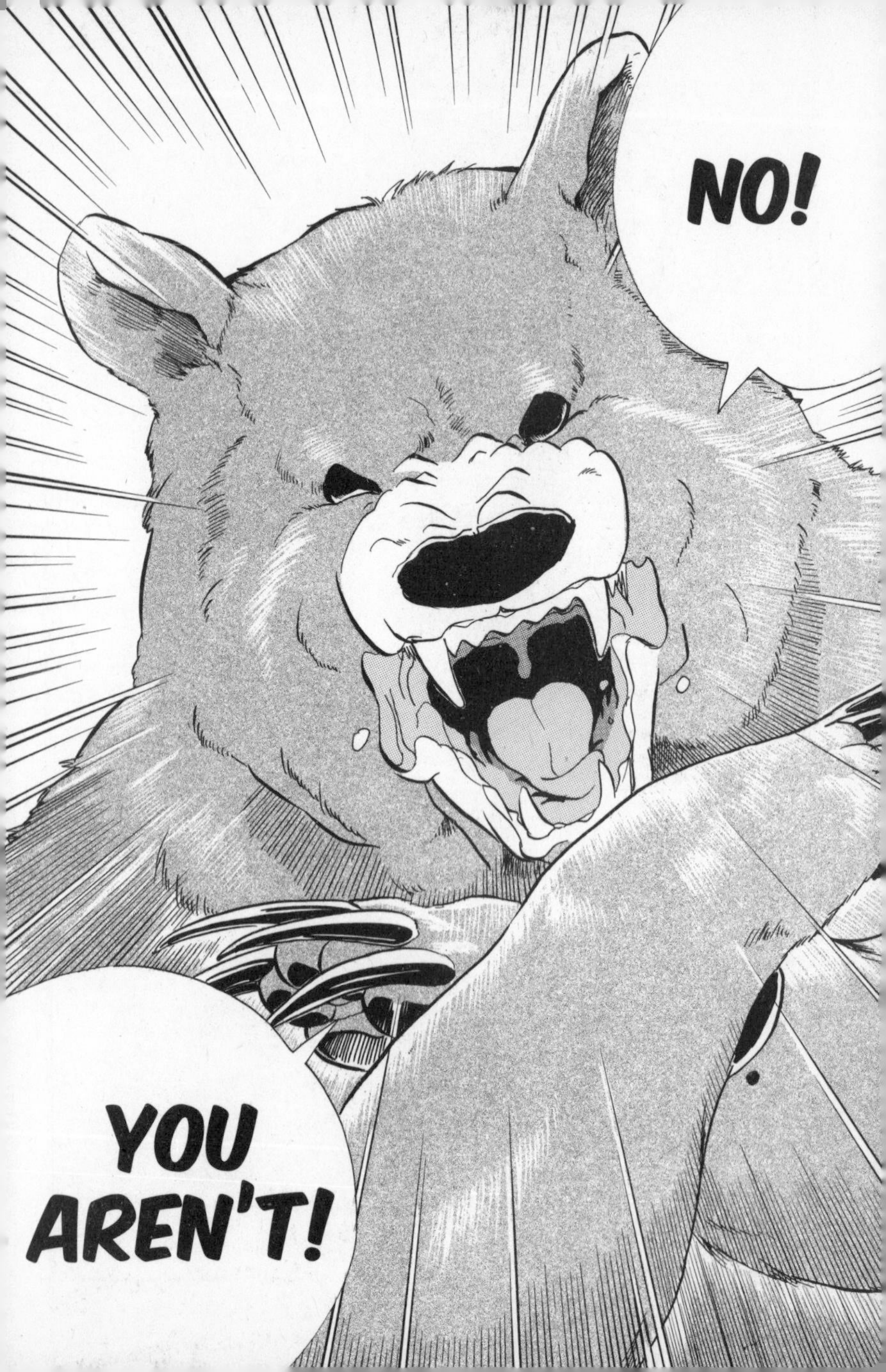
NO!
YOU AREN'T!

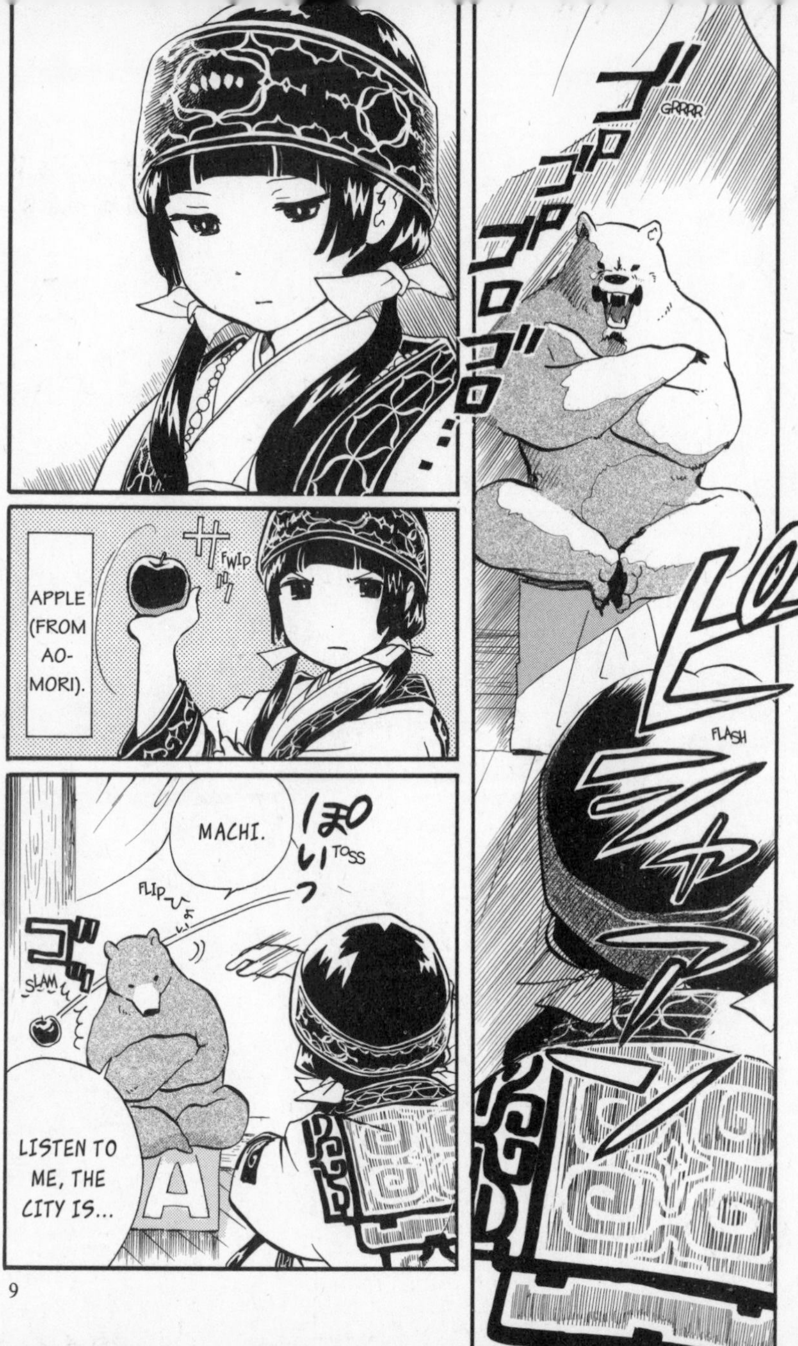
GRRRR
FLASH
APPLE (FROM AO-MORI).
FWIP
MACHI.
TOSS
FLIP
SLAM
LISTEN TO ME, THE CITY IS...

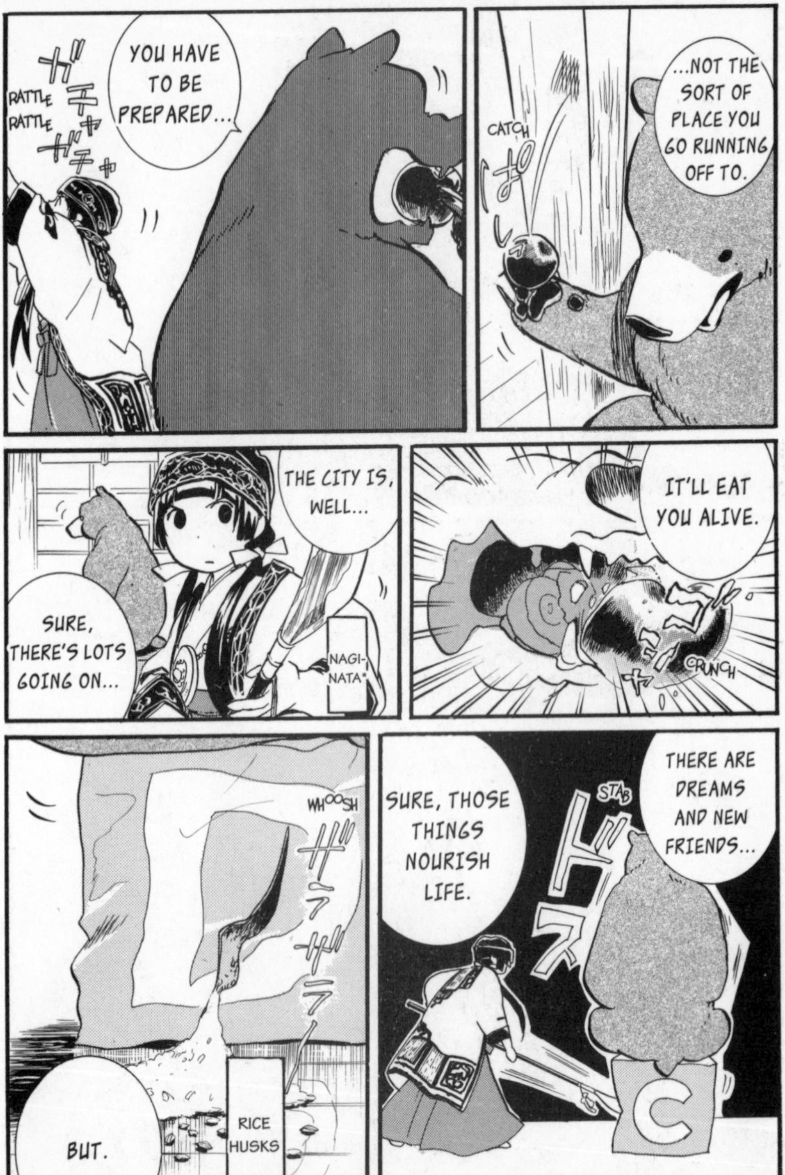
...NOT THE SORT OF PLACE YOU GO RUNNING OFF TO.
CATCH
YOU HAVE TO BE PREPARED...
RATTLE RATTLE
IT'LL EAT YOU ALIVE.
CRUNCH
THE CITY IS, WELL...
NAGI-NATA*
SURE, THERE'S LOTS GOING ON...
THERE ARE DREAMS AND NEW FRIENDS...
STAB
SURE, THOSE THINGS NOURISH LIFE.
WHOOSH
RICE HUSKS
BUT.

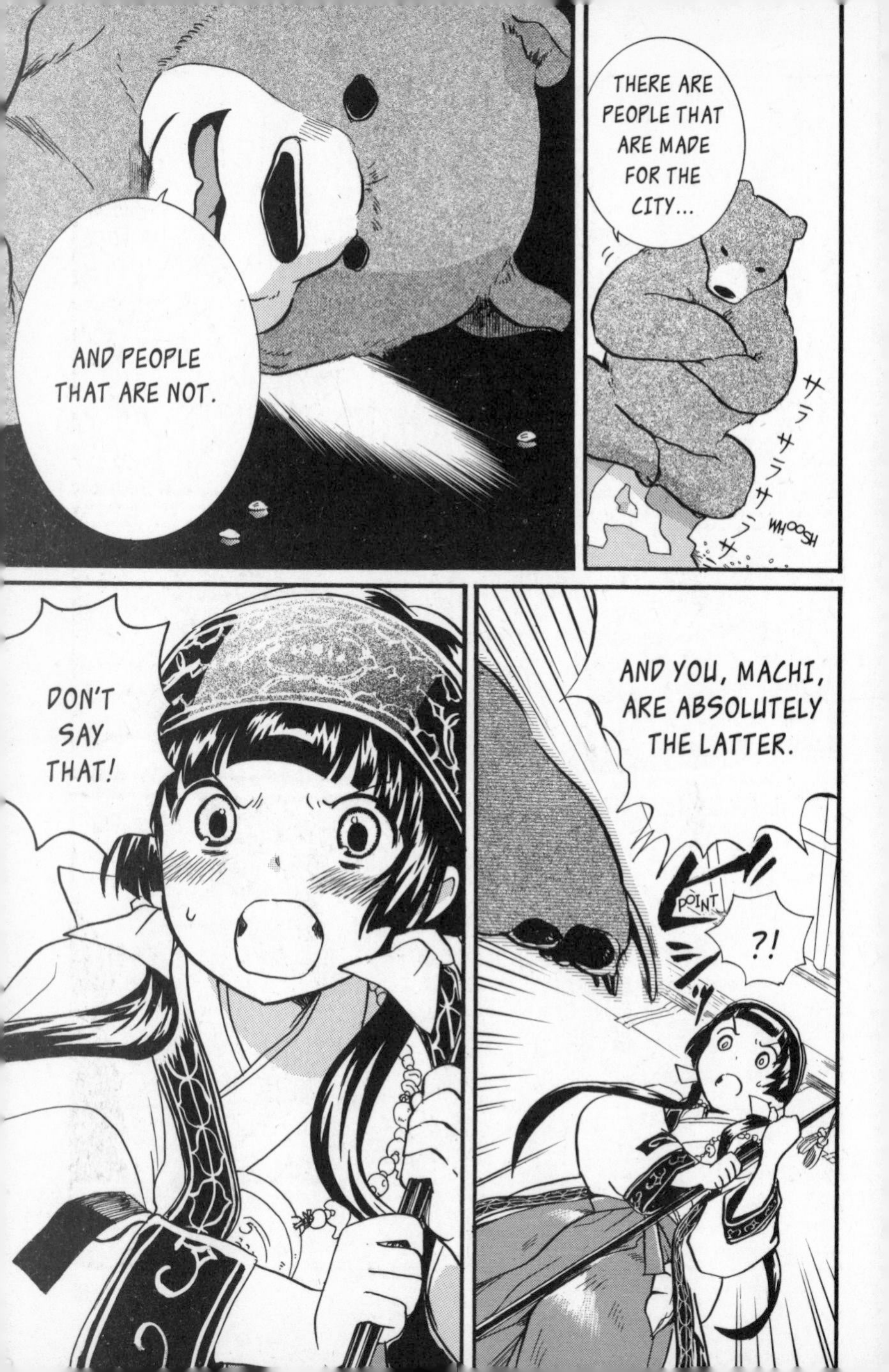
THERE ARE PEOPLE THAT ARE MADE FOR THE CITY...
サラサラサラサ
WHOOSH
AND PEOPLE THAT ARE NOT.
AND YOU, MACHI, ARE ABSOLUTELY THE LATTER.
POINT
?!
DON'T SAY THAT!

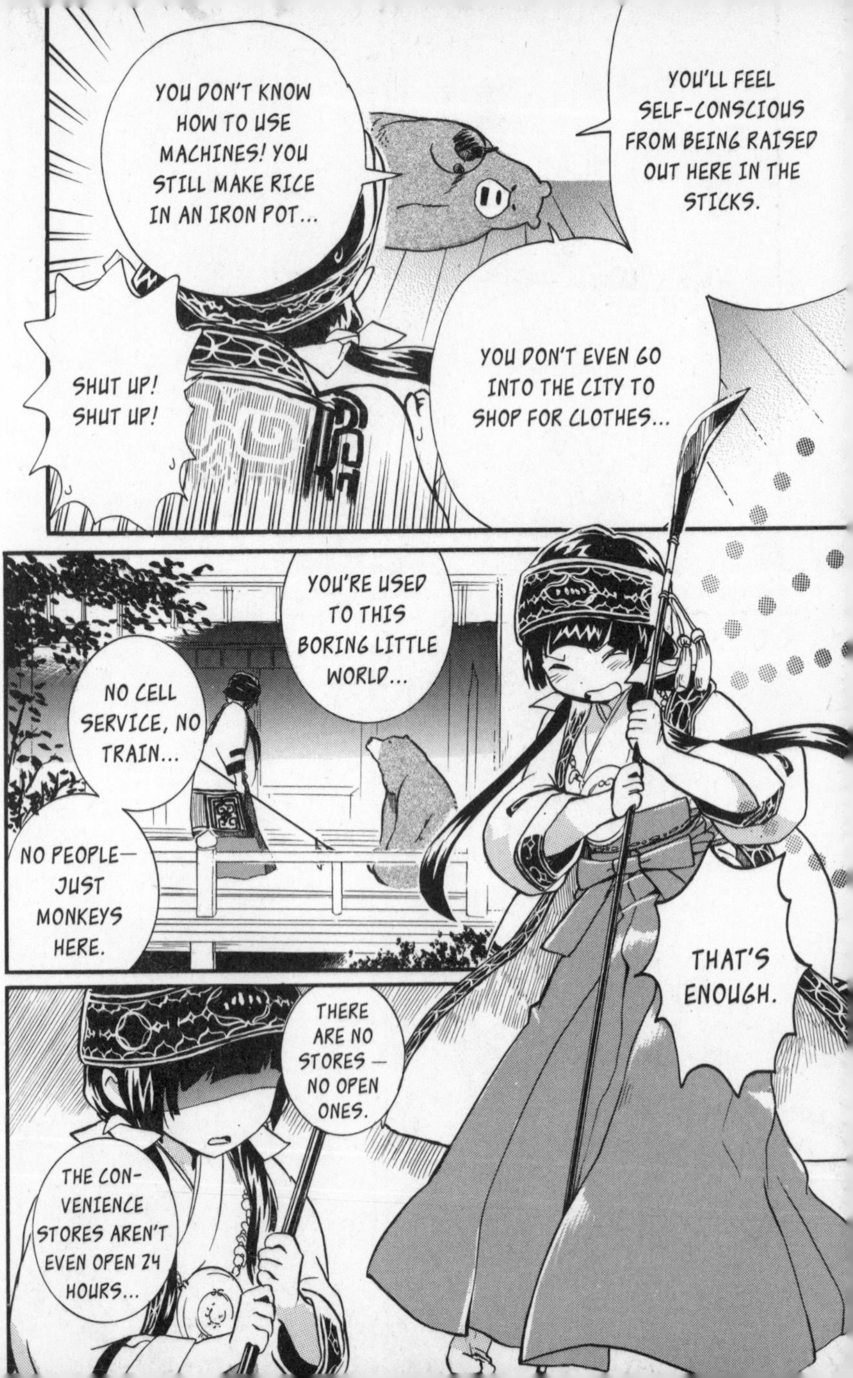
YOU'LL FEEL SELF-CONSCIOUS FROM BEING RAISED OUT HERE IN THE STICKS.
YOU DON'T KNOW HOW TO USE MACHINES! YOU STILL MAKE RICE IN AN IRON POT...
YOU DON'T EVEN GO INTO THE CITY TO SHOP FOR CLOTHES...
SHUT UP! SHUT UP!
YOU'RE USED TO THIS BORING LITTLE WORLD...
NO CELL SERVICE, NO TRAIN...
NO PEOPLE—JUST MONKEYS HERE.
THERE ARE NO STORES — NO OPEN ONES.
THE CON-VENIENCE STORES AREN'T EVEN OPEN 24 HOURS...
THAT'S ENOUGH.

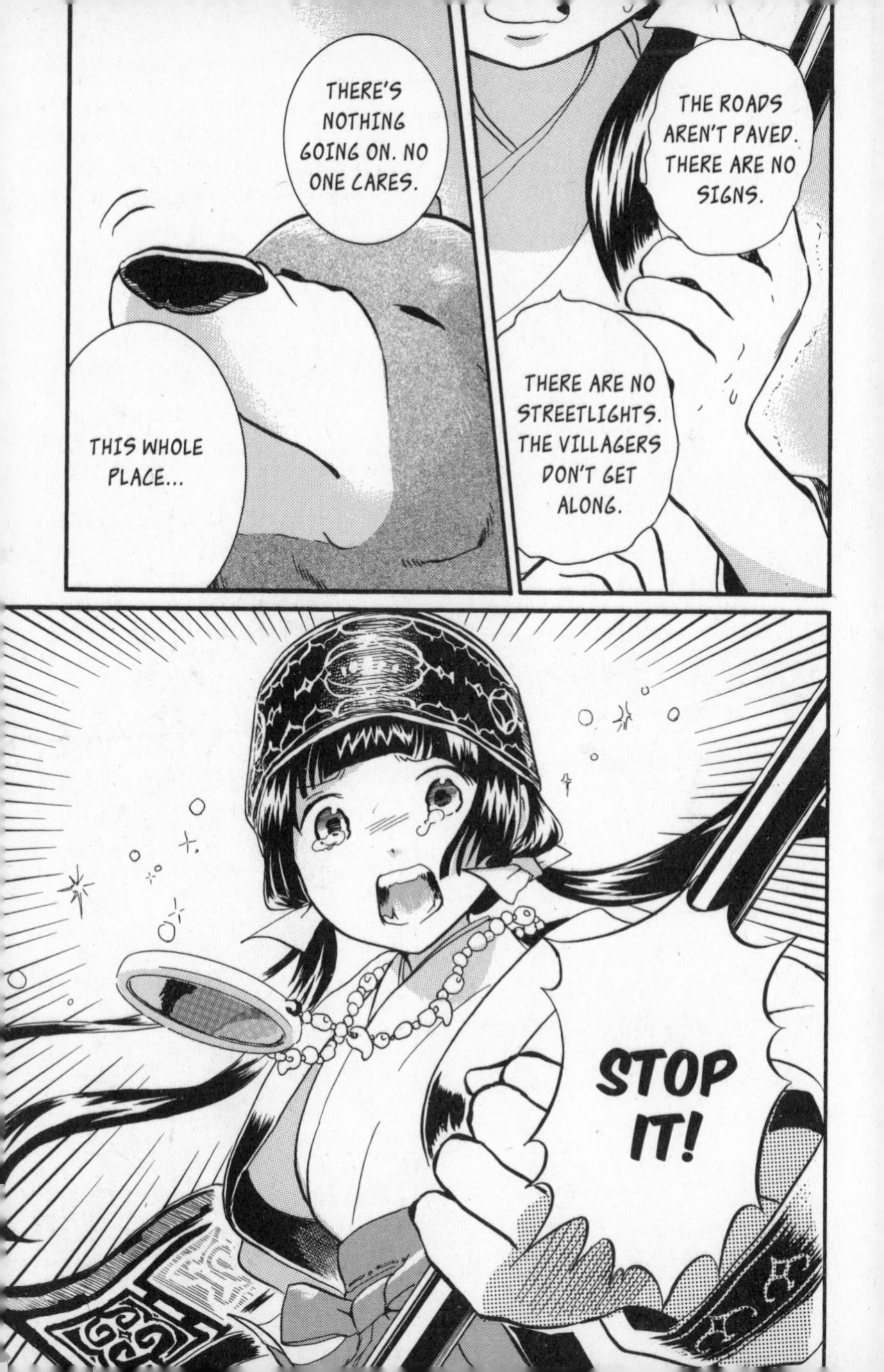
THE ROADS AREN'T PAVED. THERE ARE NO SIGNS.
THERE ARE NO STREETLIGHTS. THE VILLAGERS DON'T GET ALONG.
THERE'S NOTHING GOING ON. NO ONE CARES.
THIS WHOLE PLACE...
STOP IT!

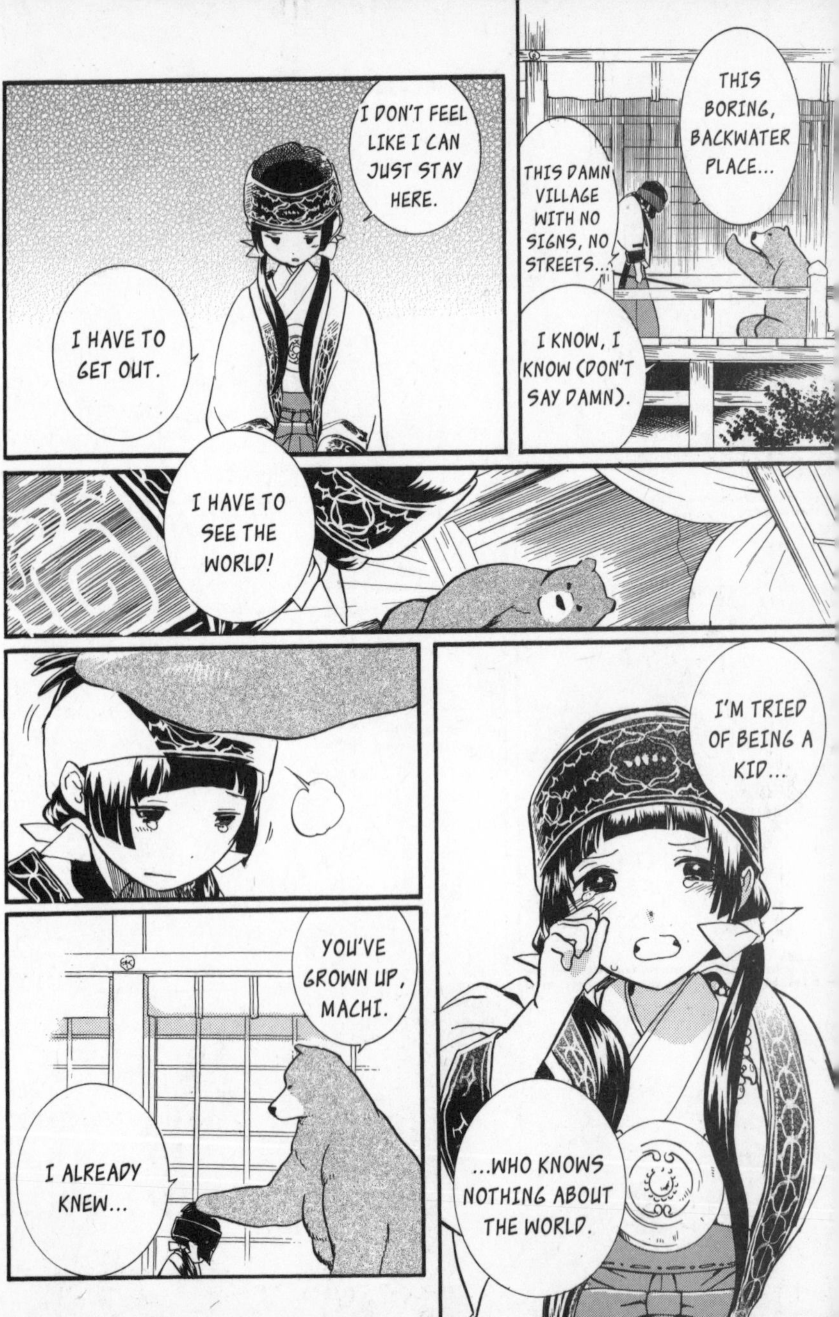
THIS BORING, BACKWATER PLACE...
THIS DAMN VILLAGE WITH NO SIGNS, NO STREETS...
I KNOW, I KNOW (DON'T SAY DAMN).
I DON'T FEEL LIKE I CAN JUST STAY HERE.
I HAVE TO GET OUT.
I HAVE TO SEE THE WORLD!
I'M TRIED OF BEING A KID...
...WHO KNOWS NOTHING ABOUT THE WORLD.
YOU'VE GROWN UP, MACHI.
I ALREADY KNEW...

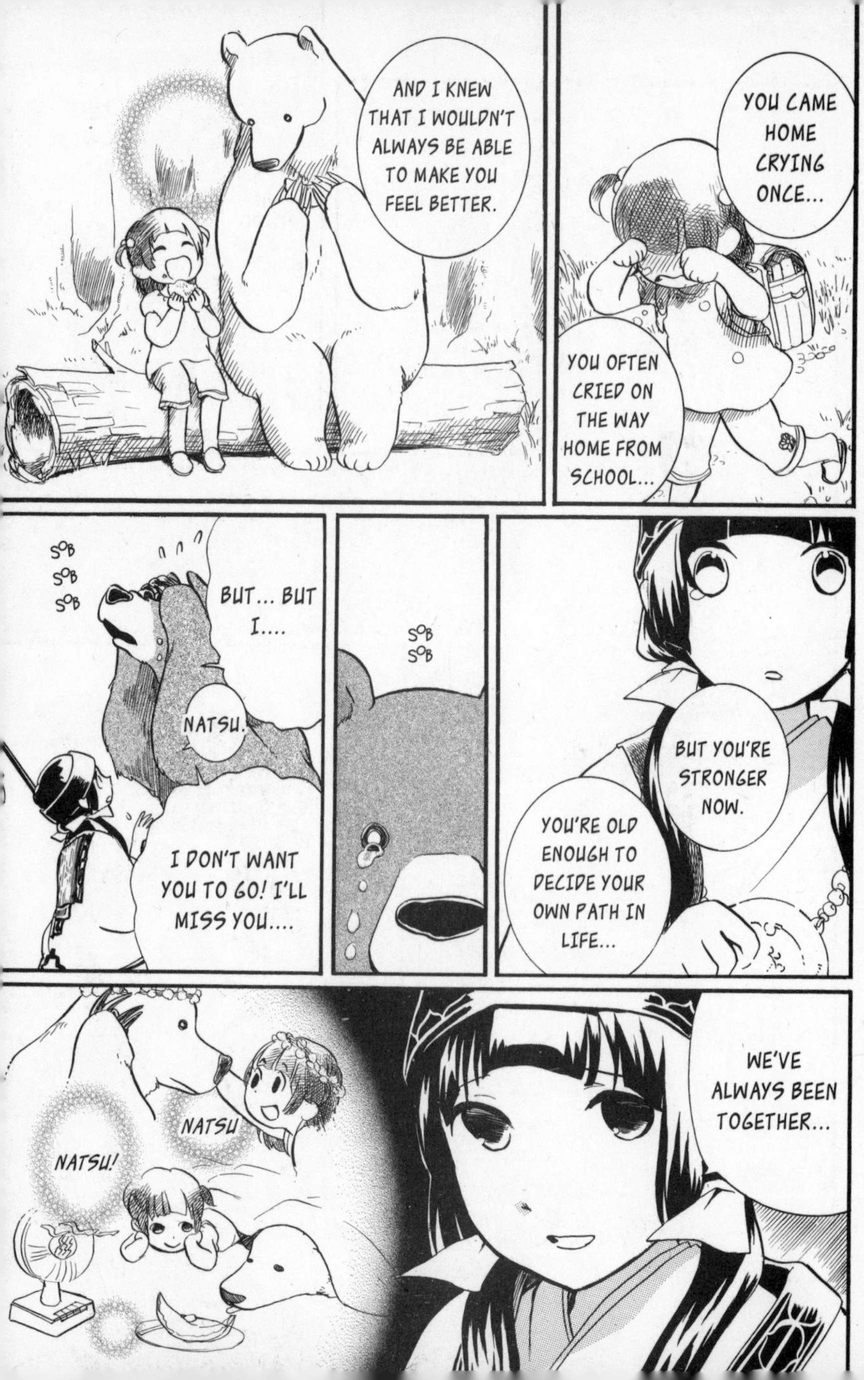
YOU CAME HOME CRYING ONCE...
YOU OFTEN CRIED ON THE WAY HOME FROM SCHOOL...
AND I KNEW THAT I WOULDN'T ALWAYS BE ABLE TO MAKE YOU FEEL BETTER.
BUT YOU'RE STRONGER NOW.
YOU'RE OLD ENOUGH TO DECIDE YOUR OWN PATH IN LIFE...
SOB SOB
BUT... BUT I....
SOB SOB SOB
NATSU.
I DON'T WANT YOU TO GO! I'LL MISS YOU....
WE'VE ALWAYS BEEN TOGETHER...
NATSU
NATSU!

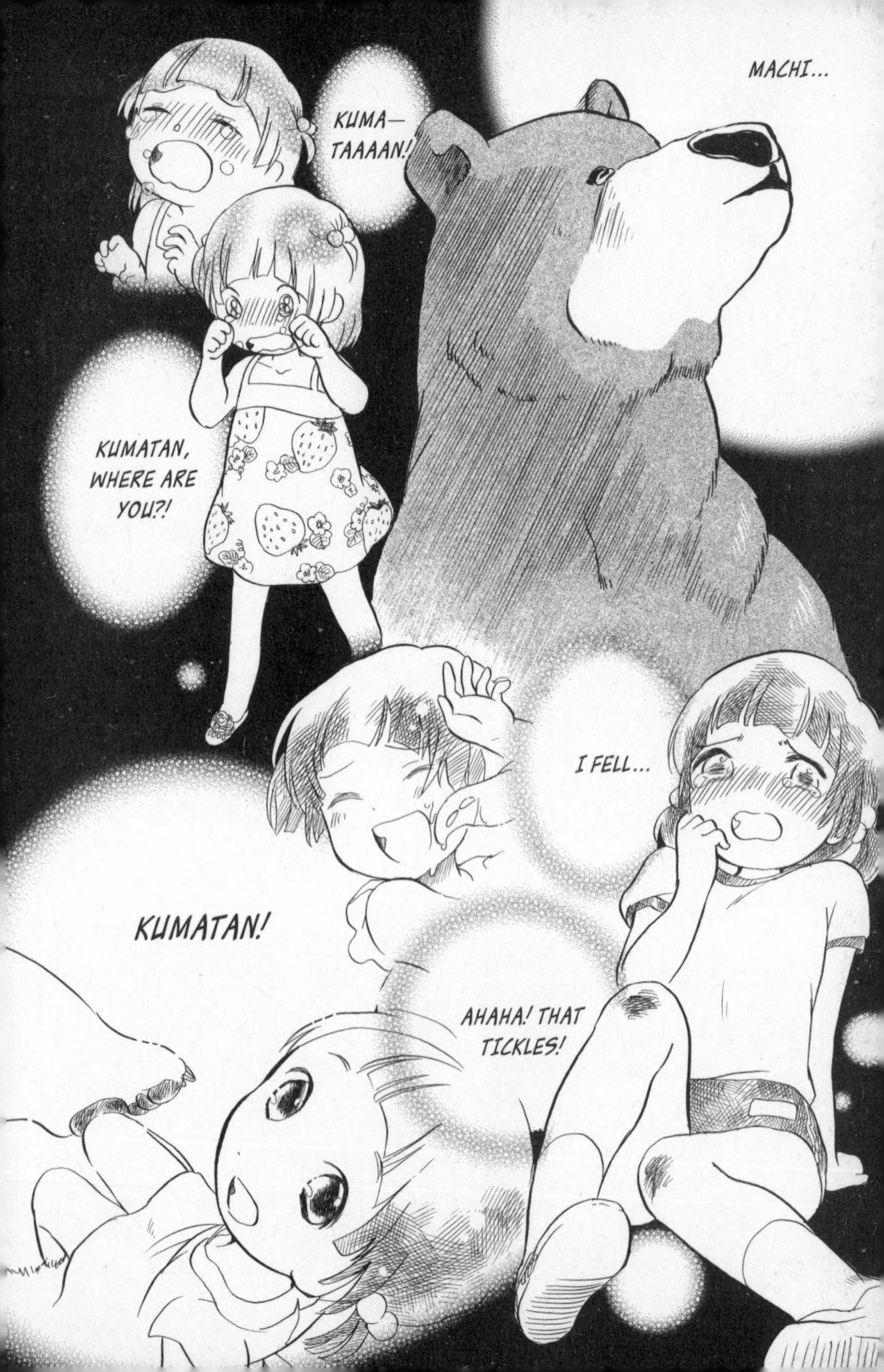
MACHI...
KUMA—TAAAAN!
KUMATAN, WHERE ARE YOU?!
I FELL...
KUMATAN!
AHAHA! THAT TICKLES!

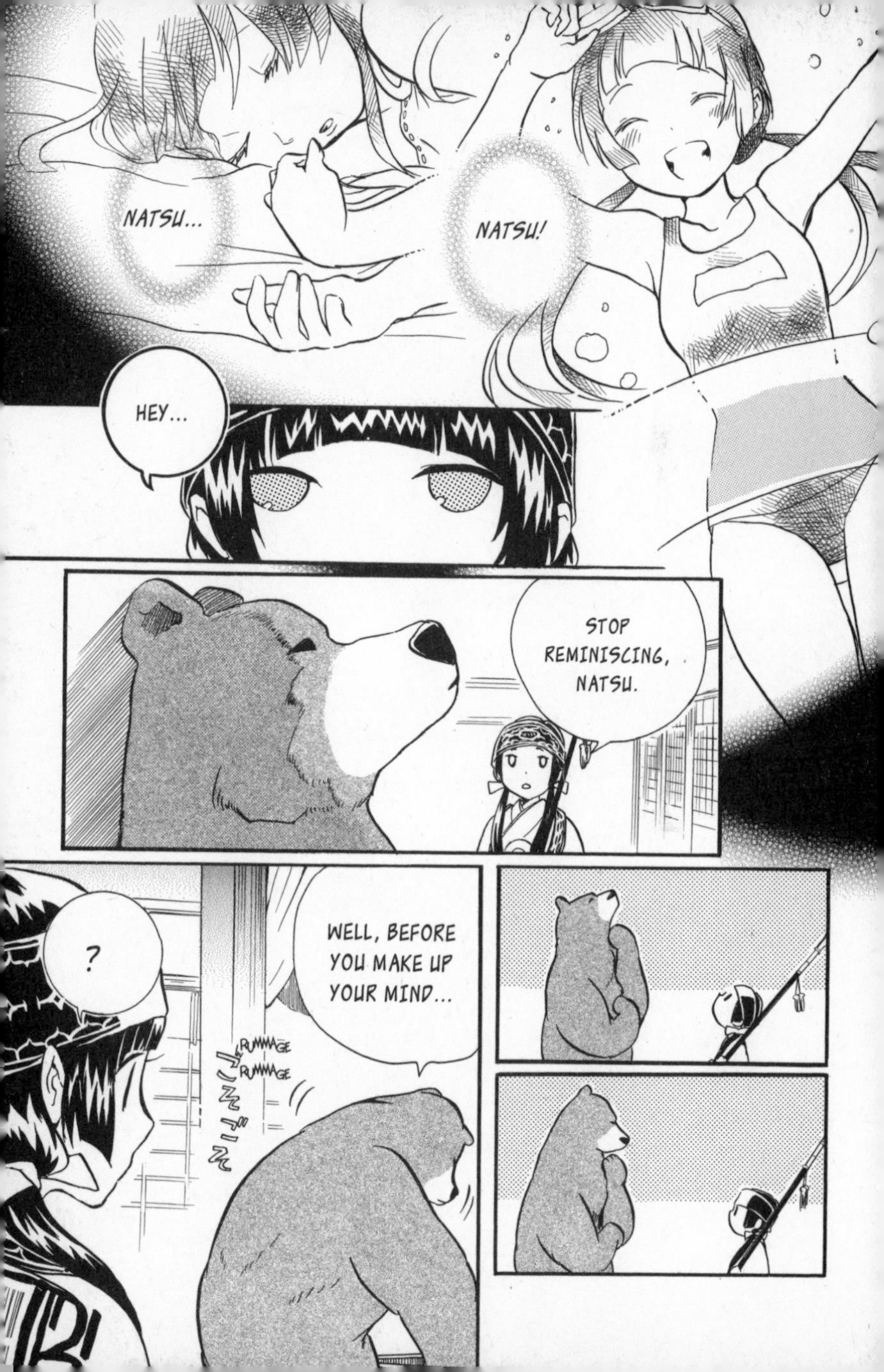
NATSU!
NATSU...
HEY...
STOP REMINISCING, NATSU.
WELL, BEFORE YOU MAKE UP YOUR MIND...
?
RUMMAGE RUMMAGE

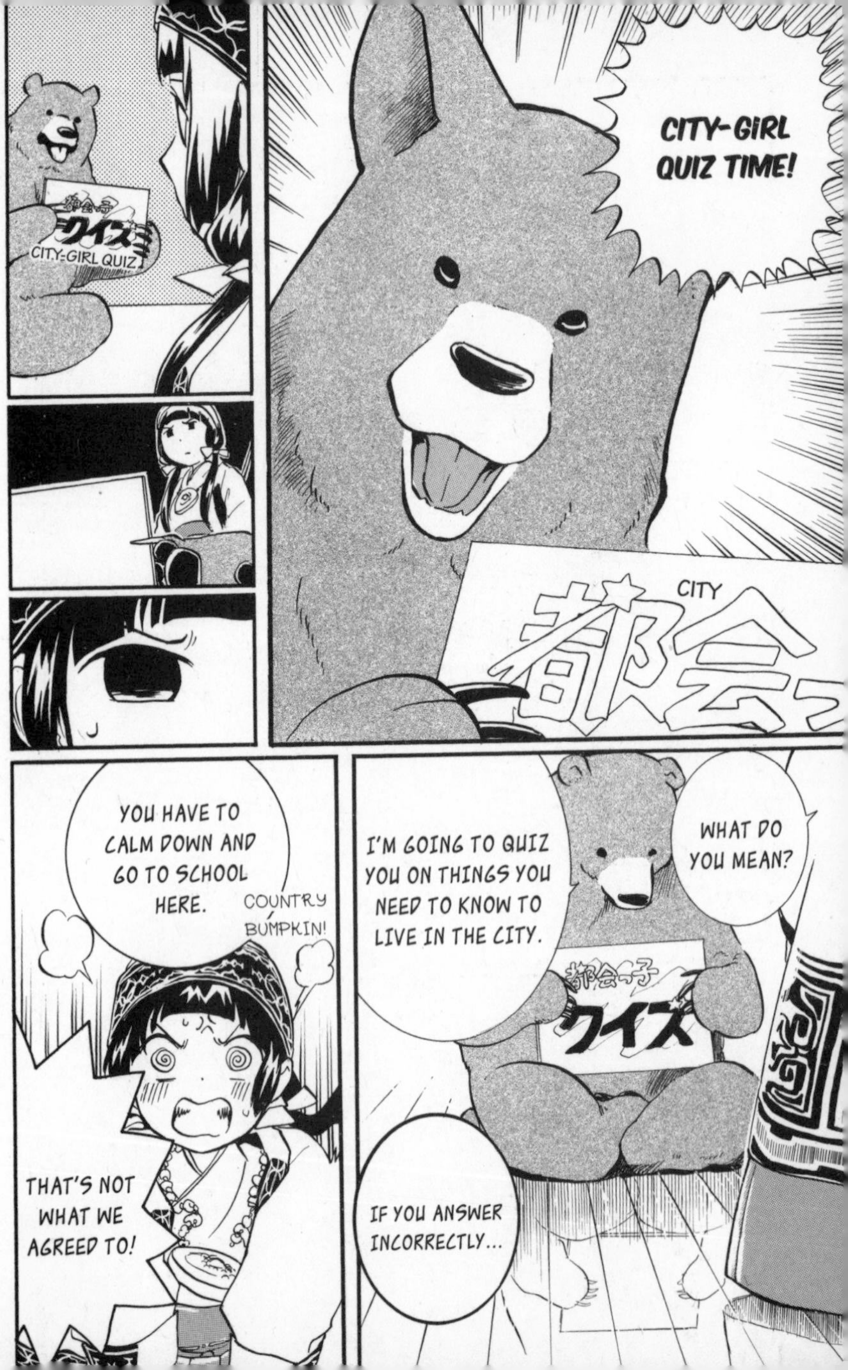
CITY-GIRL QUIZ TIME!
CITY
都会っ
CITY-GIRL QUIZ
WHAT DO YOU MEAN?
I'M GOING TO QUIZ YOU ON THINGS YOU NEED TO KNOW TO LIVE IN THE CITY.
都会っ子 クイズ
IF YOU ANSWER INCORRECTLY...
YOU HAVE TO CALM DOWN AND GO TO SCHOOL HERE.
COUNTRY BUMPKIN!
THAT'S NOT WHAT WE AGREED TO!

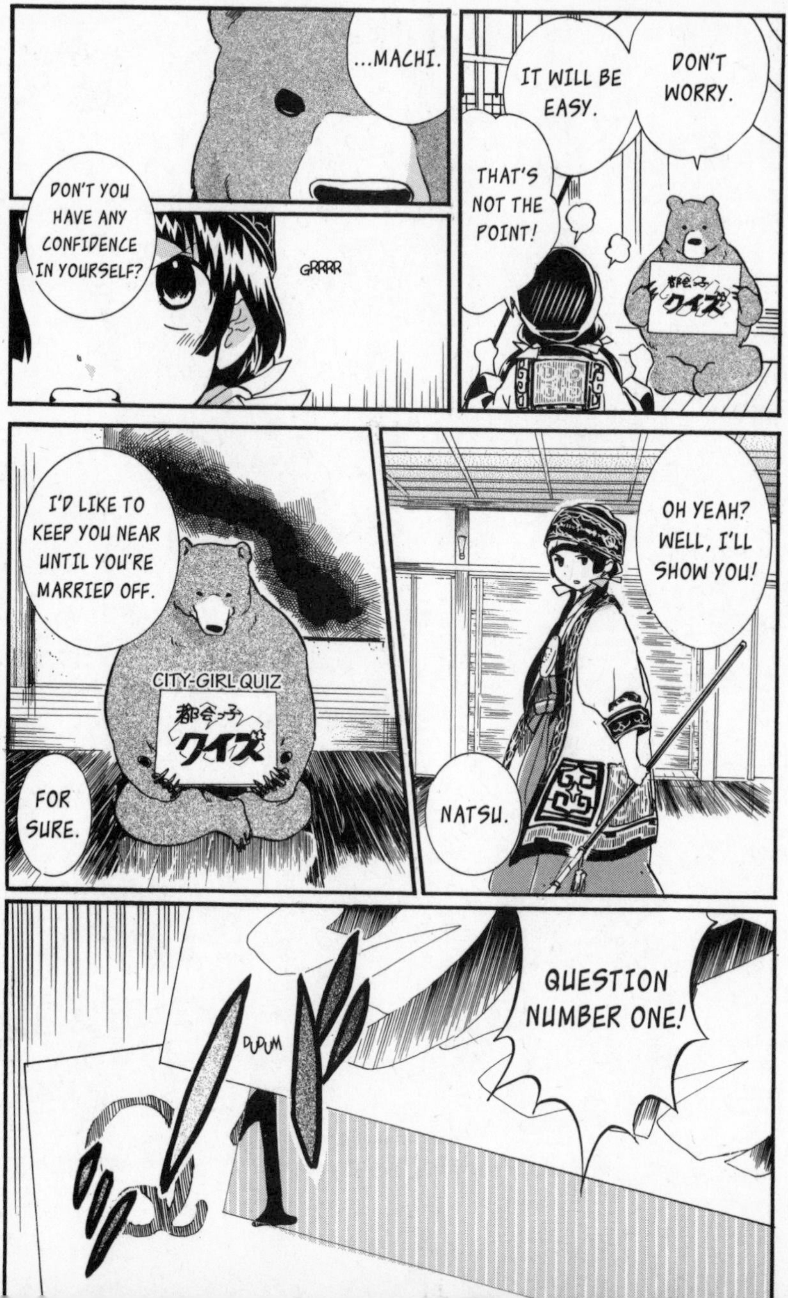
DON'T WORRY.
IT WILL BE EASY.
THAT'S NOT THE POINT!
都会っ子クイズ
...MACHI.
DON'T YOU HAVE ANY CONFIDENCE IN YOURSELF?
GRRRR
OH YEAH? WELL, I'LL SHOW YOU!
NATSU.
I'D LIKE TO KEEP YOU NEAR UNTIL YOU'RE MARRIED OFF.
CITY-GIRL QUIZ
都会っ子クイズ
FOR SURE.
QUESTION NUMBER ONE!
DUDUM

WHAT DO YOU USE TO GET THROUGH THE TICKET GATES AT THE TRAIN STATION?

1 えきのじどうかいさつ 何(なに)を使(つか)うととおれる？

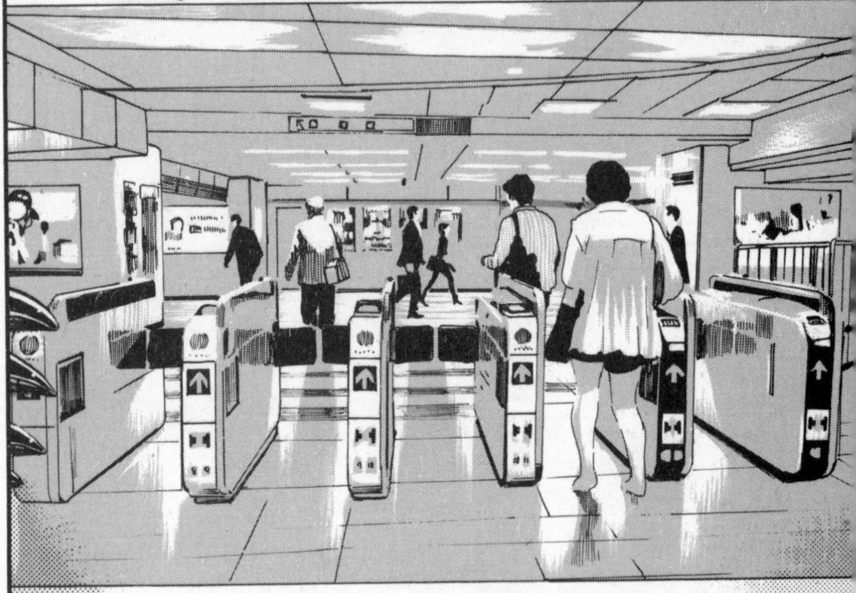

1)SUICA* 2) APPLES 3) BANANAS

① Suica (すいか) ② りんご ③ バナナ (ばなな)

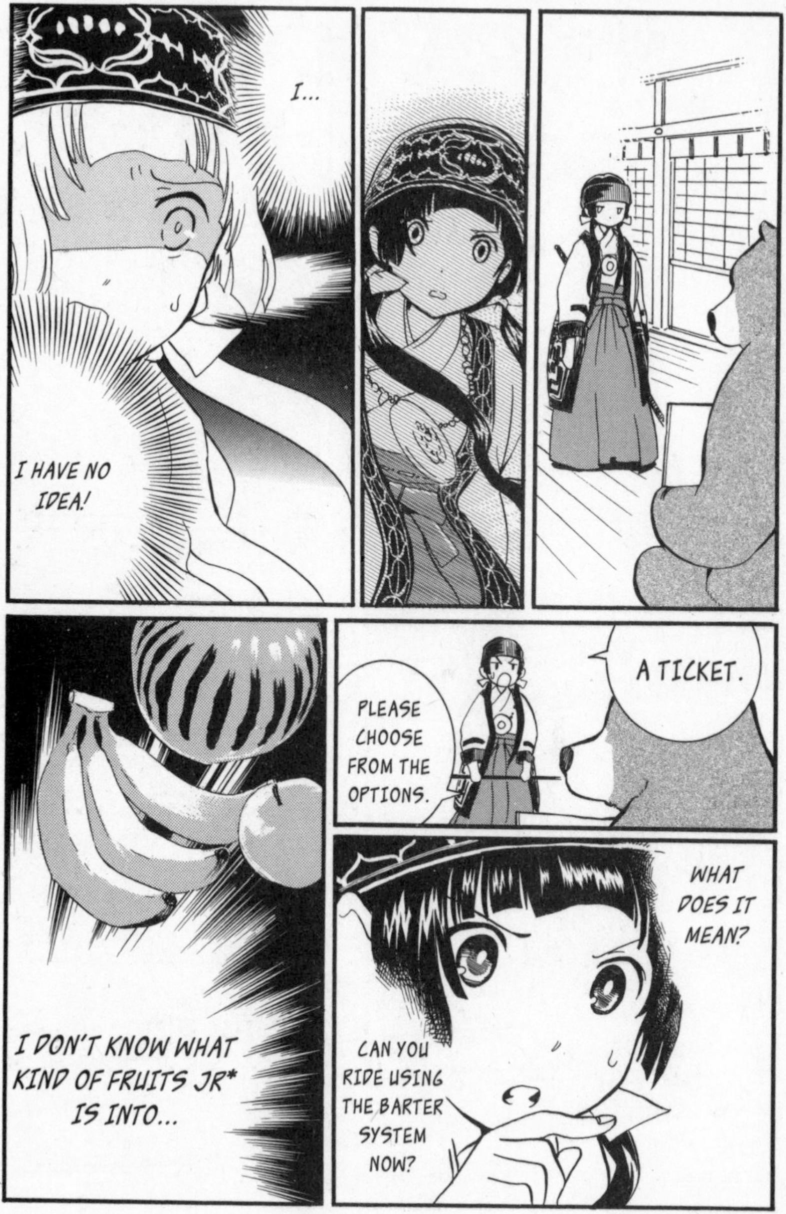
I...
I HAVE NO IDEA!
A TICKET.
PLEASE CHOOSE FROM THE OPTIONS.
WHAT DOES IT MEAN?
CAN YOU RIDE USING THE BARTER SYSTEM NOW?
I DON'T KNOW WHAT KIND OF FRUITS JR* IS INTO...

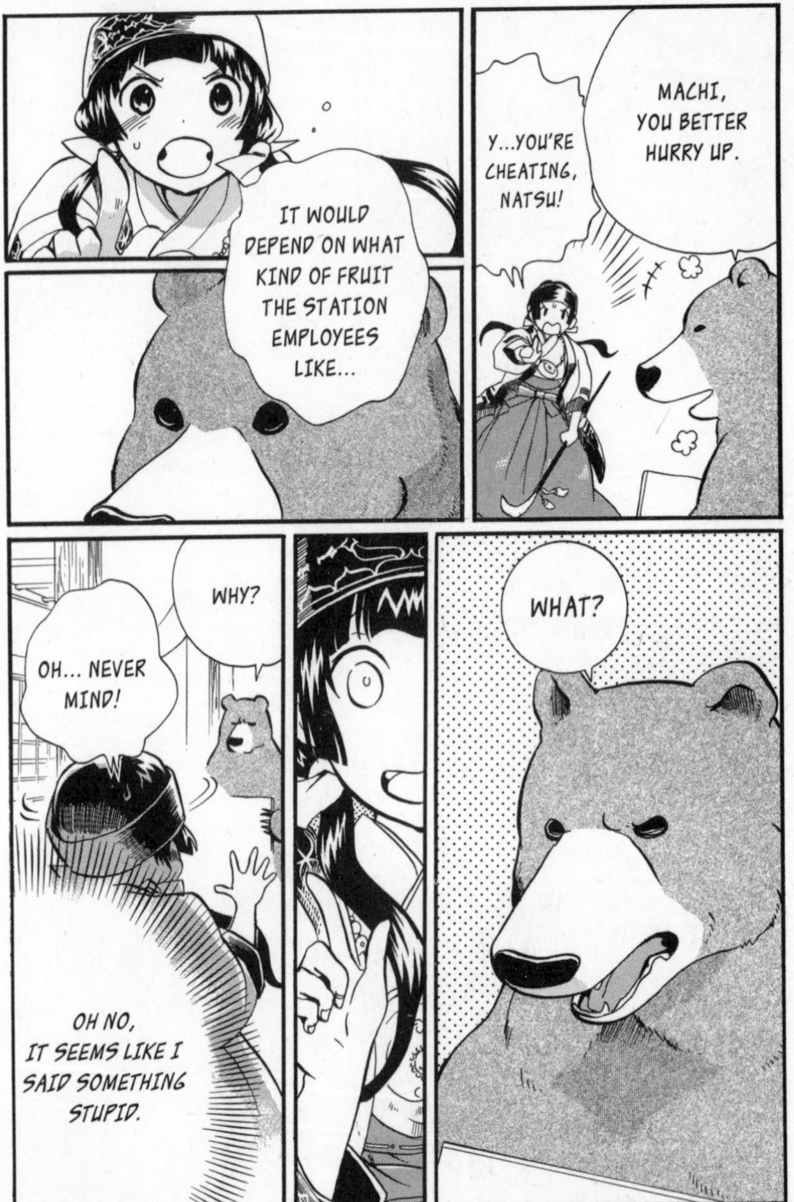
MACHI, YOU BETTER HURRY UP.
Y...YOU'RE CHEATING, NATSU!
IT WOULD DEPEND ON WHAT KIND OF FRUIT THE STATION EMPLOYEES LIKE...
WHAT?
WHY?
OH... NEVER MIND!
OH NO, IT SEEMS LIKE I SAID SOMETHING STUPID.

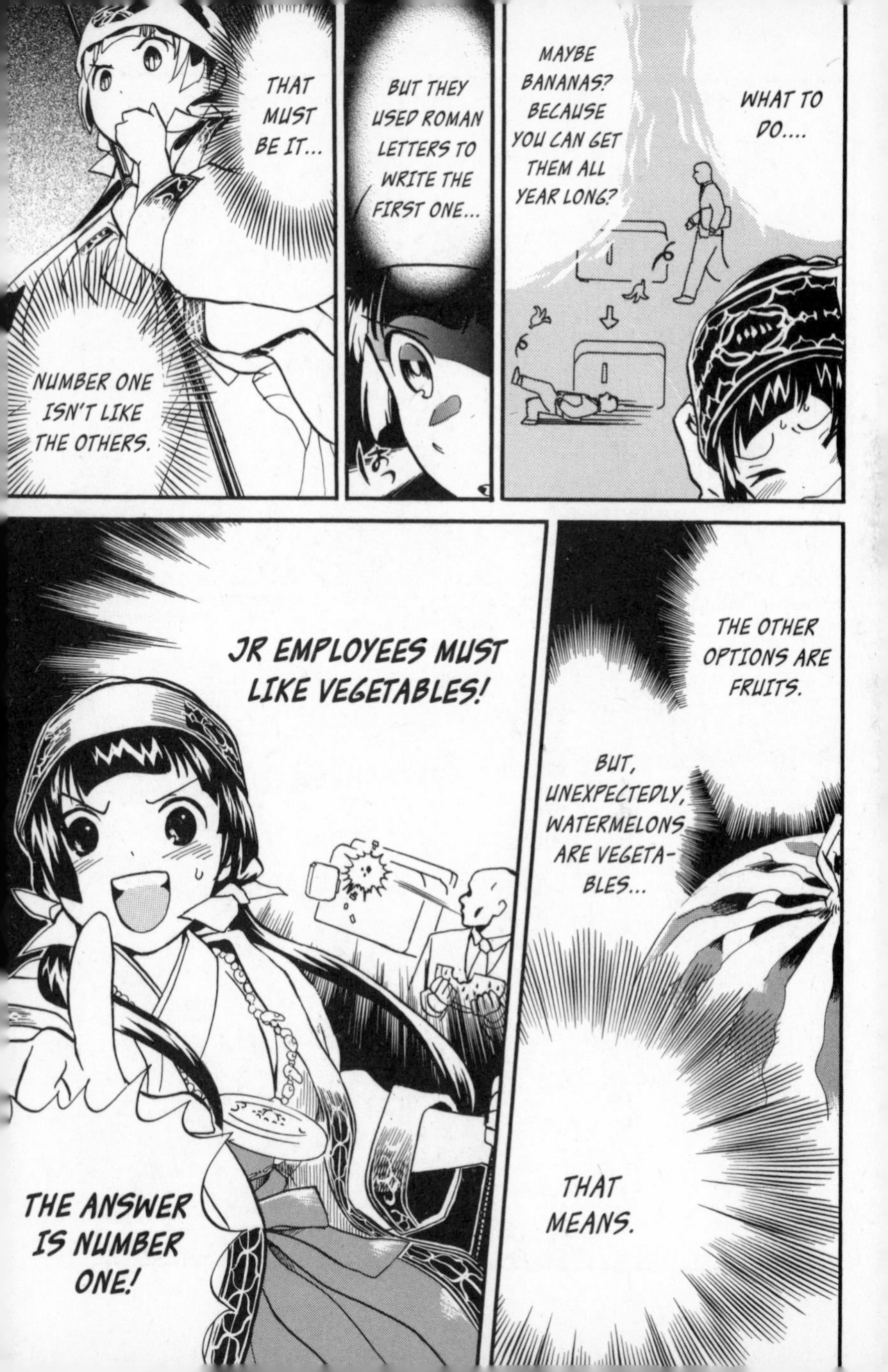
WHAT TO DO....
MAYBE BANANAS? BECAUSE YOU CAN GET THEM ALL YEAR LONG?
BUT THEY USED ROMAN LETTERS TO WRITE THE FIRST ONE...
おっ
THAT MUST BE IT...
NUMBER ONE ISN'T LIKE THE OTHERS.
THE OTHER OPTIONS ARE FRUITS.
BUT, UNEXPECTEDLY, WATERMELONS ARE VEGETA-BLES...
THAT MEANS.
JR EMPLOYEES MUST LIKE VEGETABLES!
THE ANSWER IS NUMBER ONE!

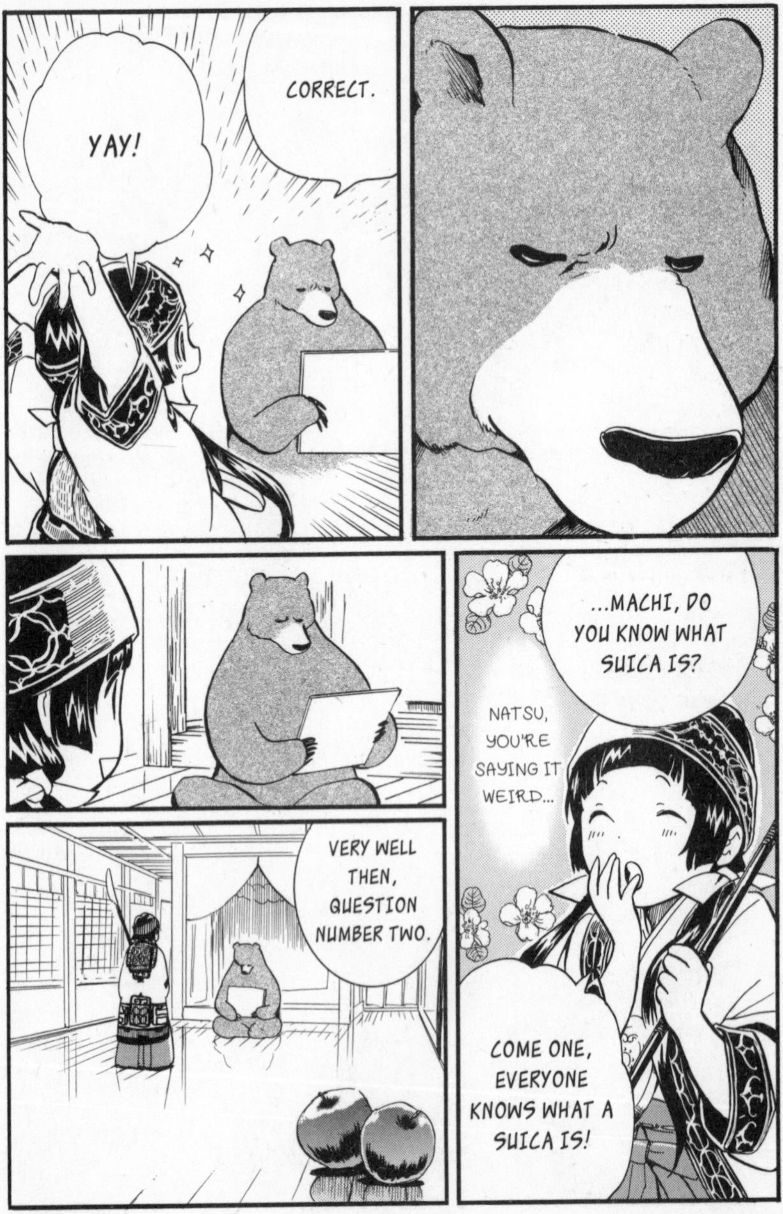
CORRECT.
YAY!
...MACHI, DO YOU KNOW WHAT SUICA IS?
NATSU, YOU'RE SAYING IT WEIRD...
COME ONE, EVERYONE KNOWS WHAT A SUICA IS!
VERY WELL THEN, QUESTION NUMBER TWO.

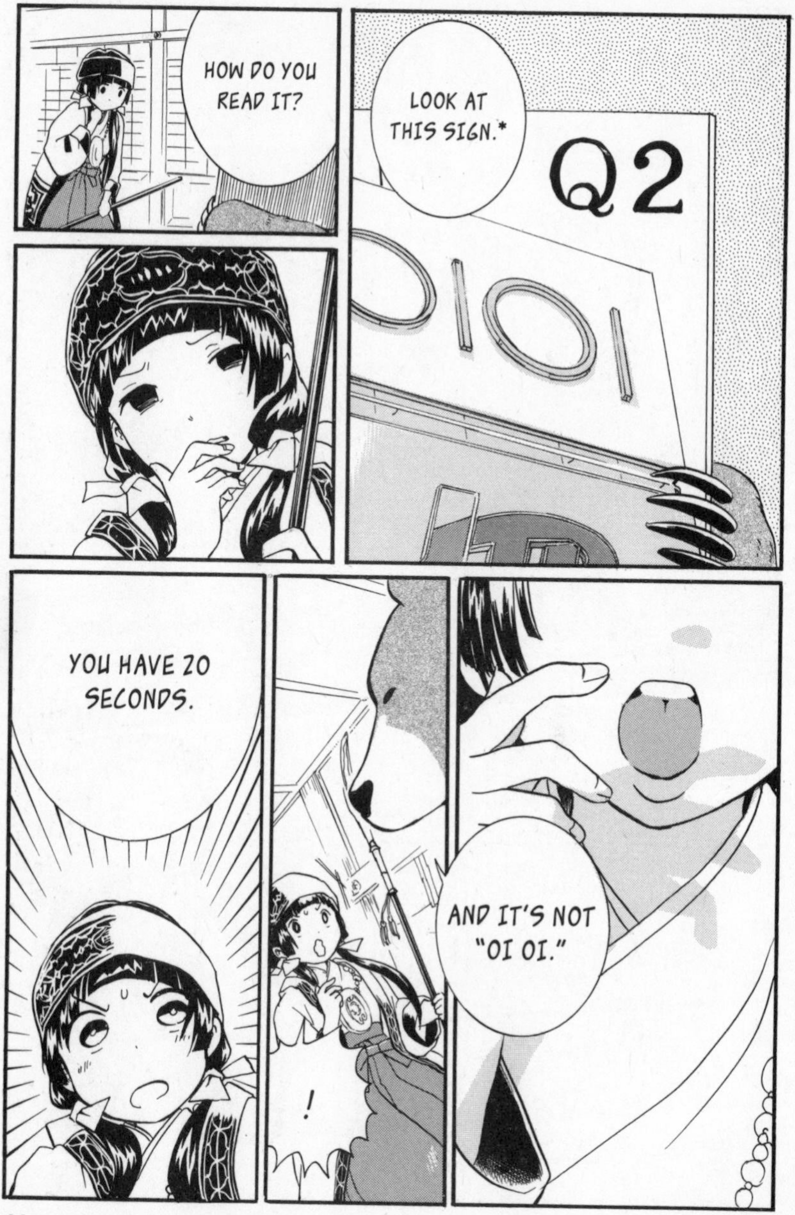
LOOK AT THIS SIGN.*
Q2
OIOI
HOW DO YOU READ IT?
AND IT'S NOT "OI OI."
!
YOU HAVE 20 SECONDS.

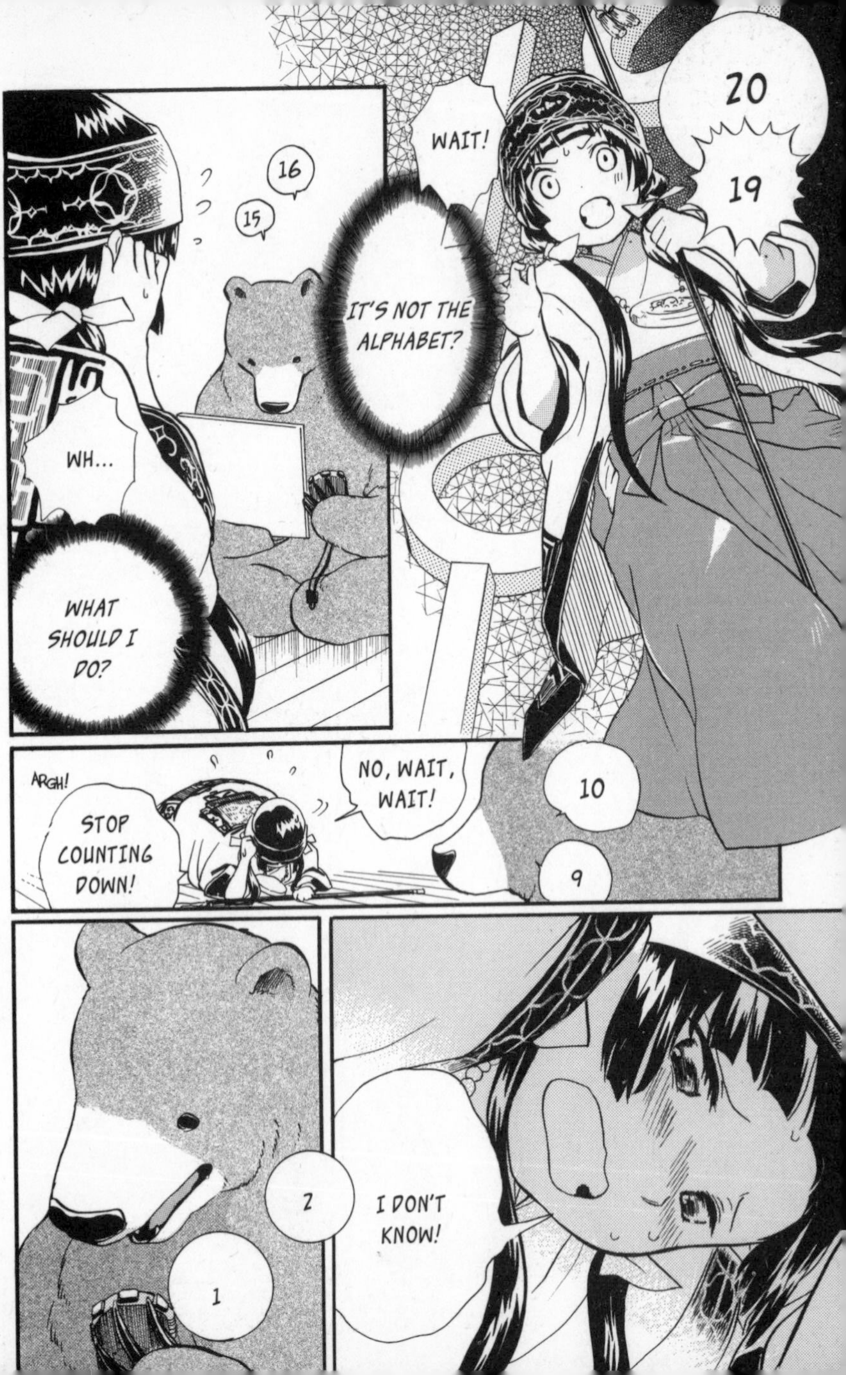
20
19
WAIT!
IT'S NOT THE ALPHABET?
16
15
WH...
WHAT SHOULD I DO?
10
9
NO, WAIT, WAIT!
ARGH!
STOP COUNTING DOWN!
I DON'T KNOW!
2
1

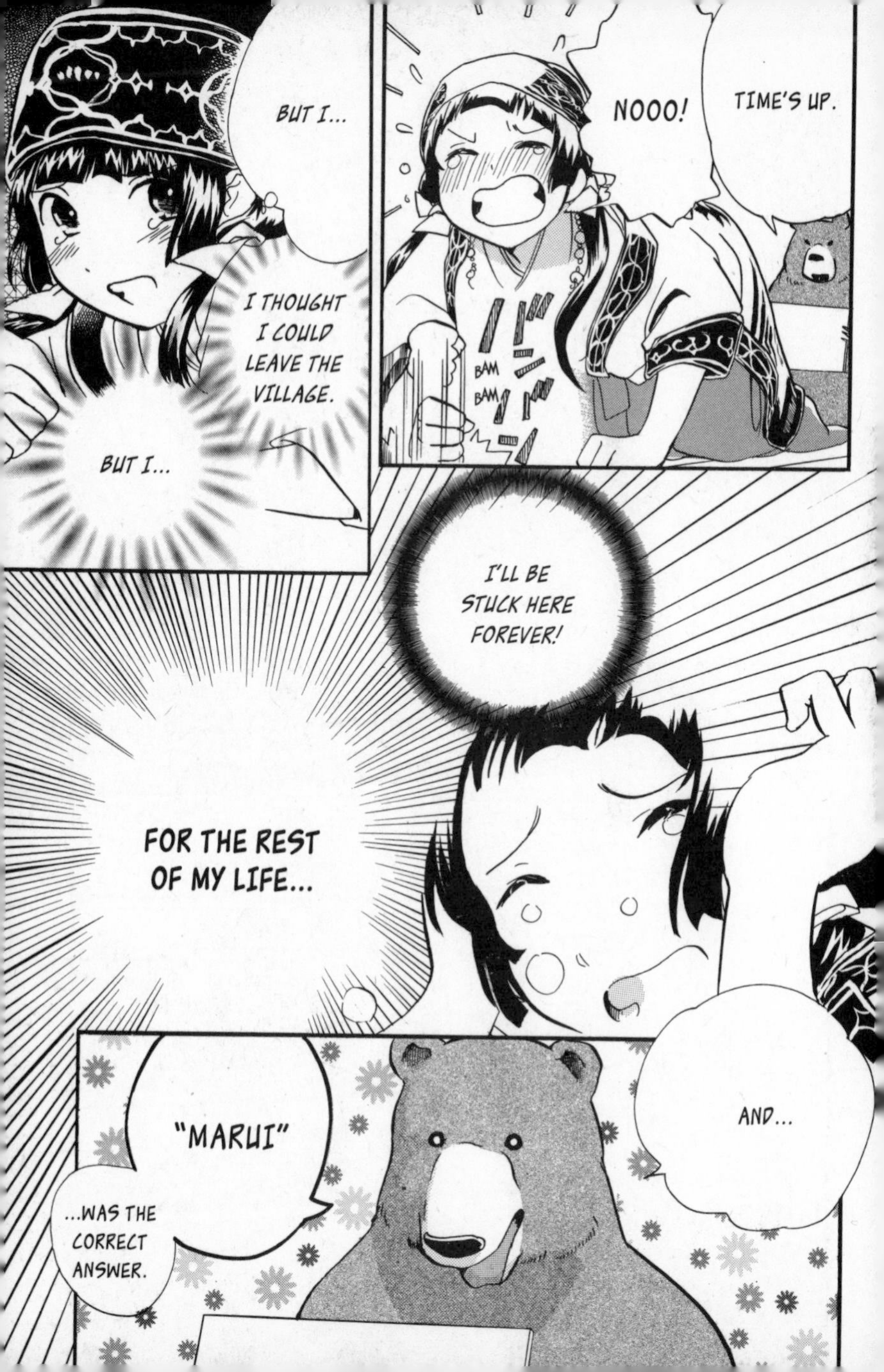
TIME'S UP.
NOOO!
BAM BAM
BUT I...
I THOUGHT I COULD LEAVE THE VILLAGE.
BUT I...
I'LL BE STUCK HERE FOREVER!
FOR THE REST OF MY LIFE...
AND...
"MARUI"
...WAS THE CORRECT ANSWER.

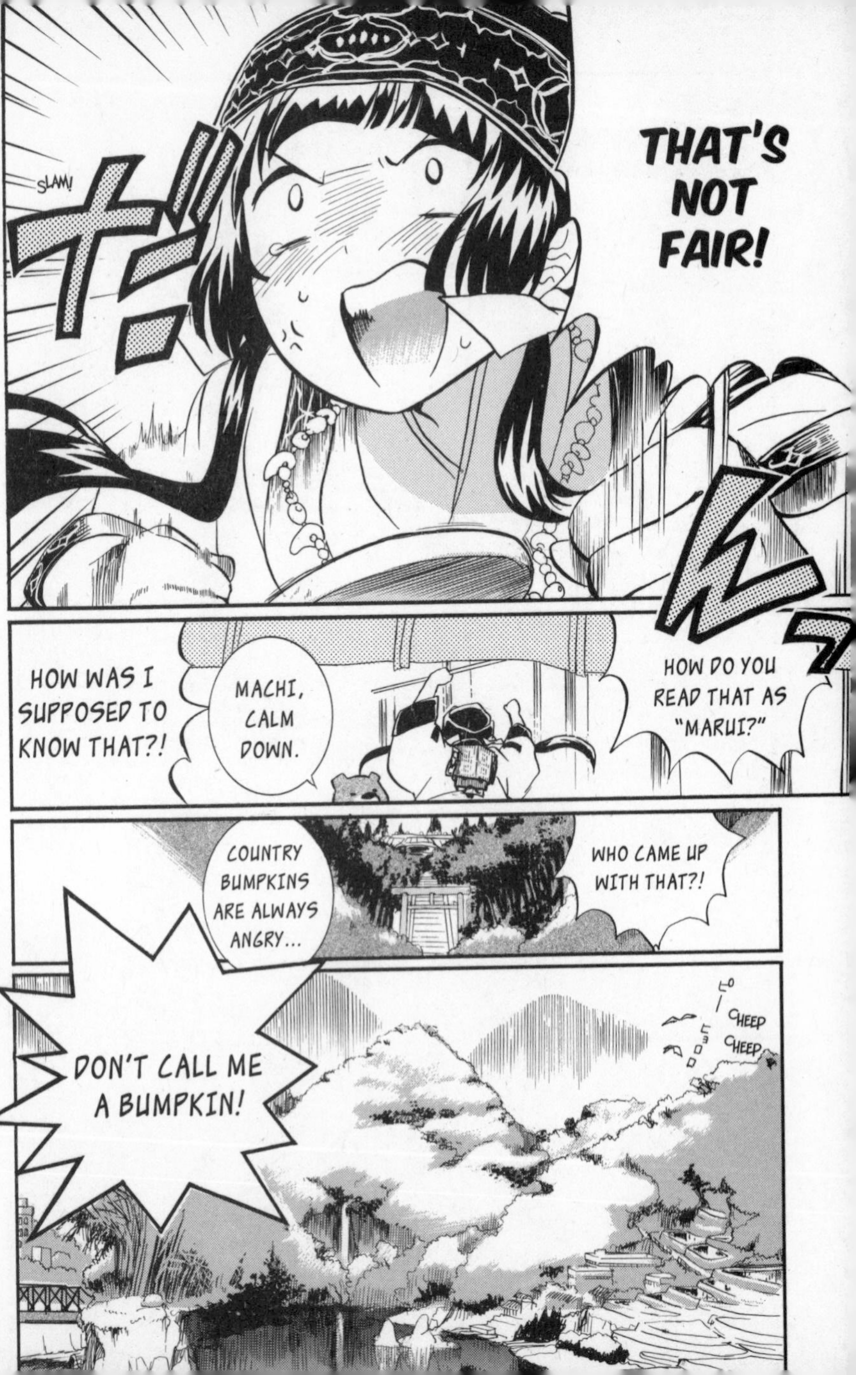
THAT'S NOT FAIR!
SLAM!
HOW DO YOU READ THAT AS "MARUI?"
MACHI, CALM DOWN.
HOW WAS I SUPPOSED TO KNOW THAT?!
WHO CAME UP WITH THAT?!
COUNTRY BUMPKINS ARE ALWAYS ANGRY...
CHEEP CHEEP
DON'T CALL ME A BUMPKIN!

CHAPTER 2 VILLAGE LEGENDS

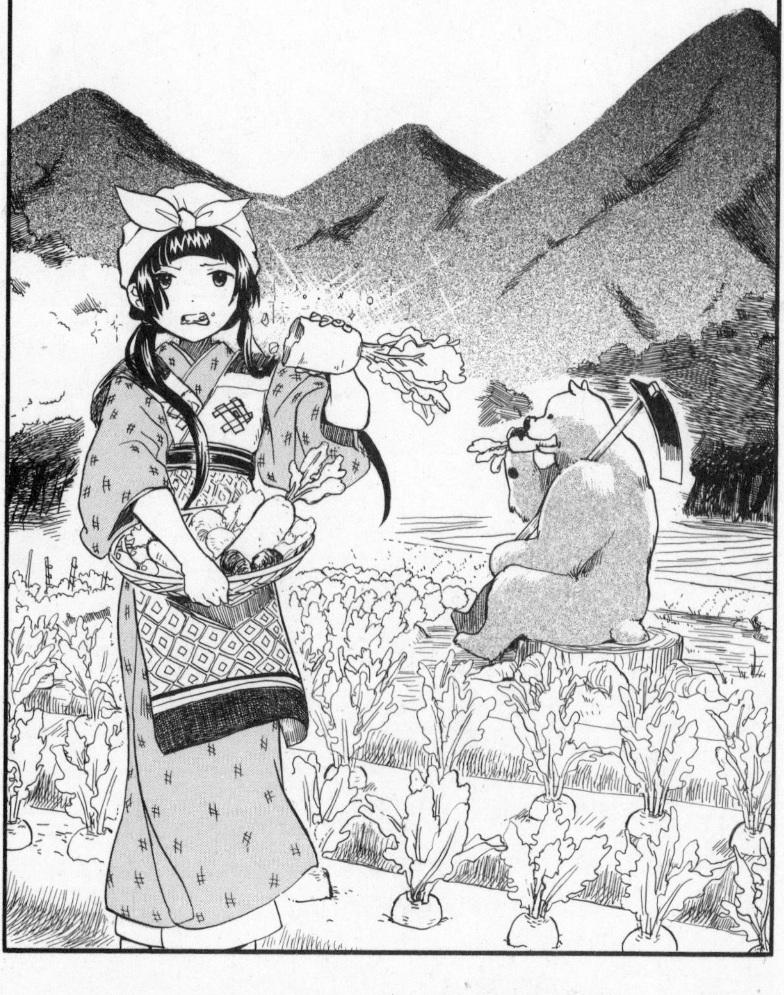

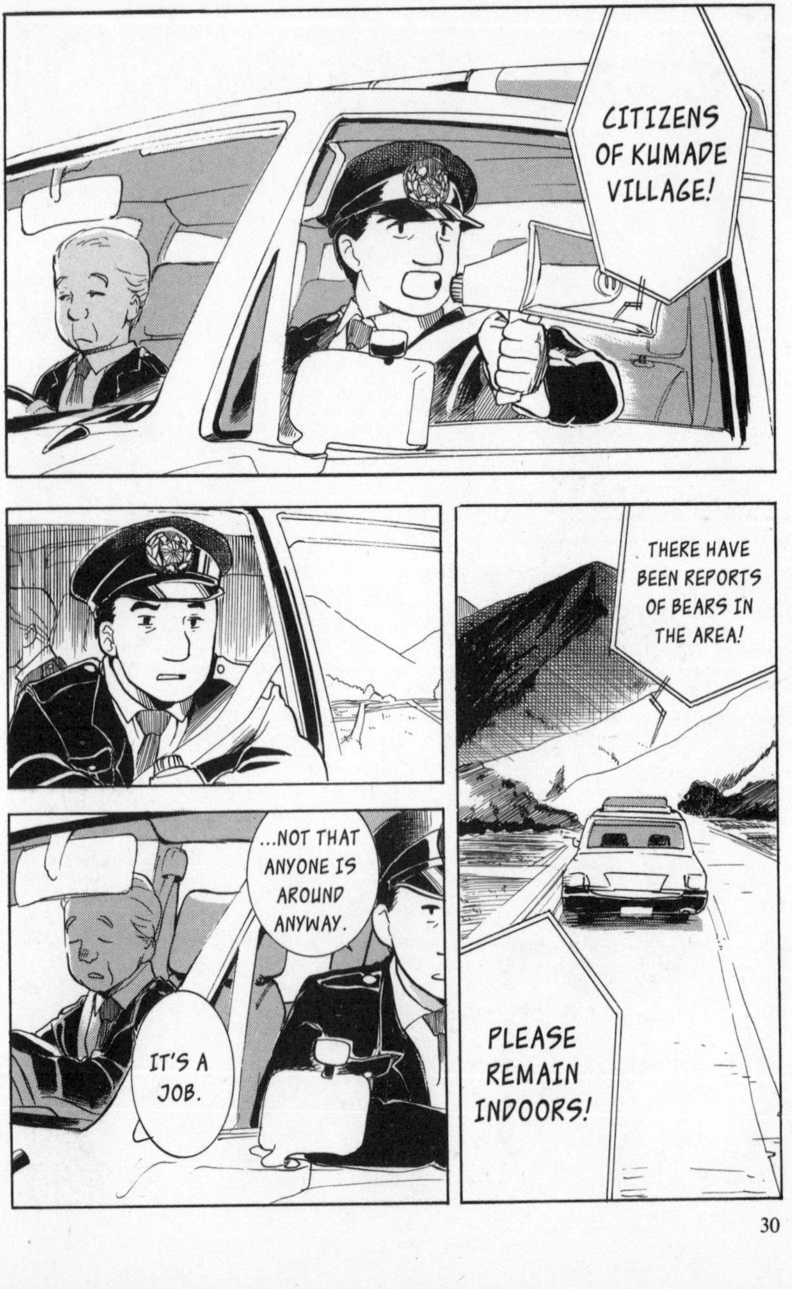
CITIZENS OF KUMADE VILLAGE!
THERE HAVE BEEN REPORTS OF BEARS IN THE AREA!
PLEASE REMAIN INDOORS!
...NOT THAT ANYONE IS AROUND ANYWAY.
IT'S A JOB.

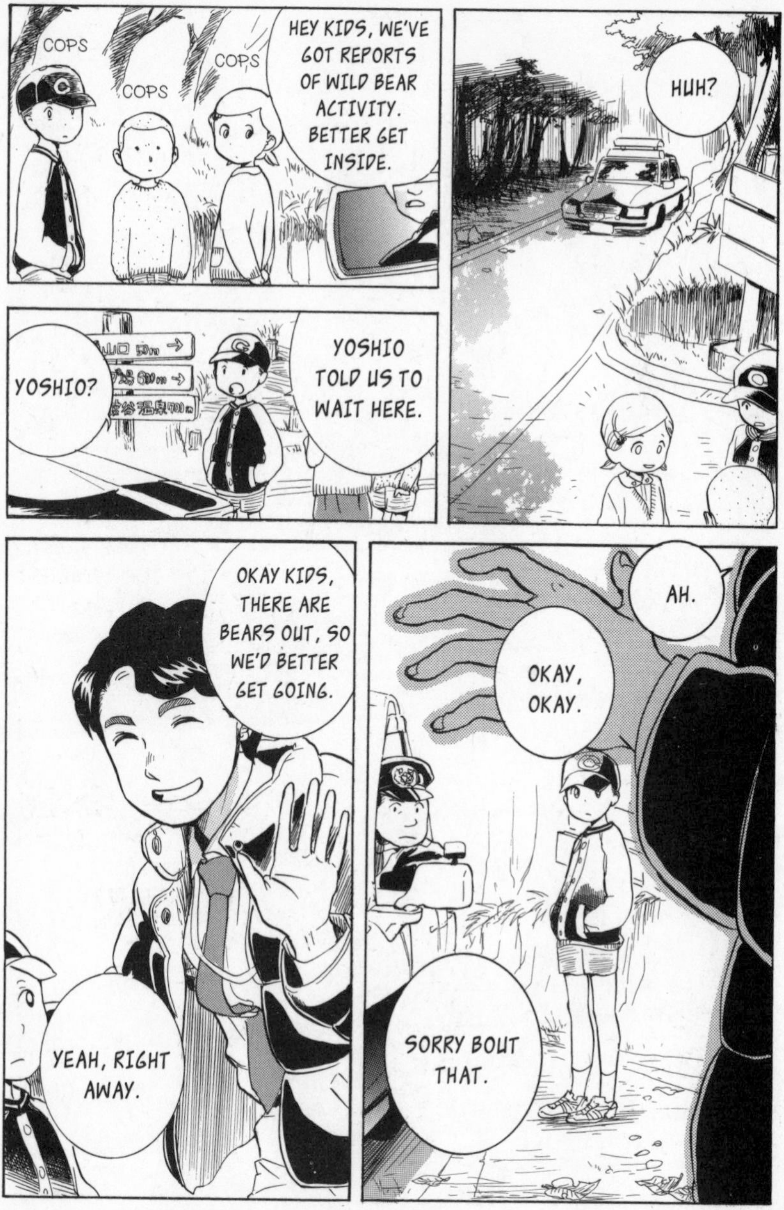
HUH?
HEY KIDS, WE'VE GOT REPORTS OF WILD BEAR ACTIVITY. BETTER GET INSIDE.
COPS
COPS
COPS
YOSHIO TOLD US TO WAIT HERE.
YOSHIO?
AH.
OKAY, OKAY.
SORRY BOUT THAT.
OKAY KIDS, THERE ARE BEARS OUT, SO WE'D BETTER GET GOING.
YEAH, RIGHT AWAY.

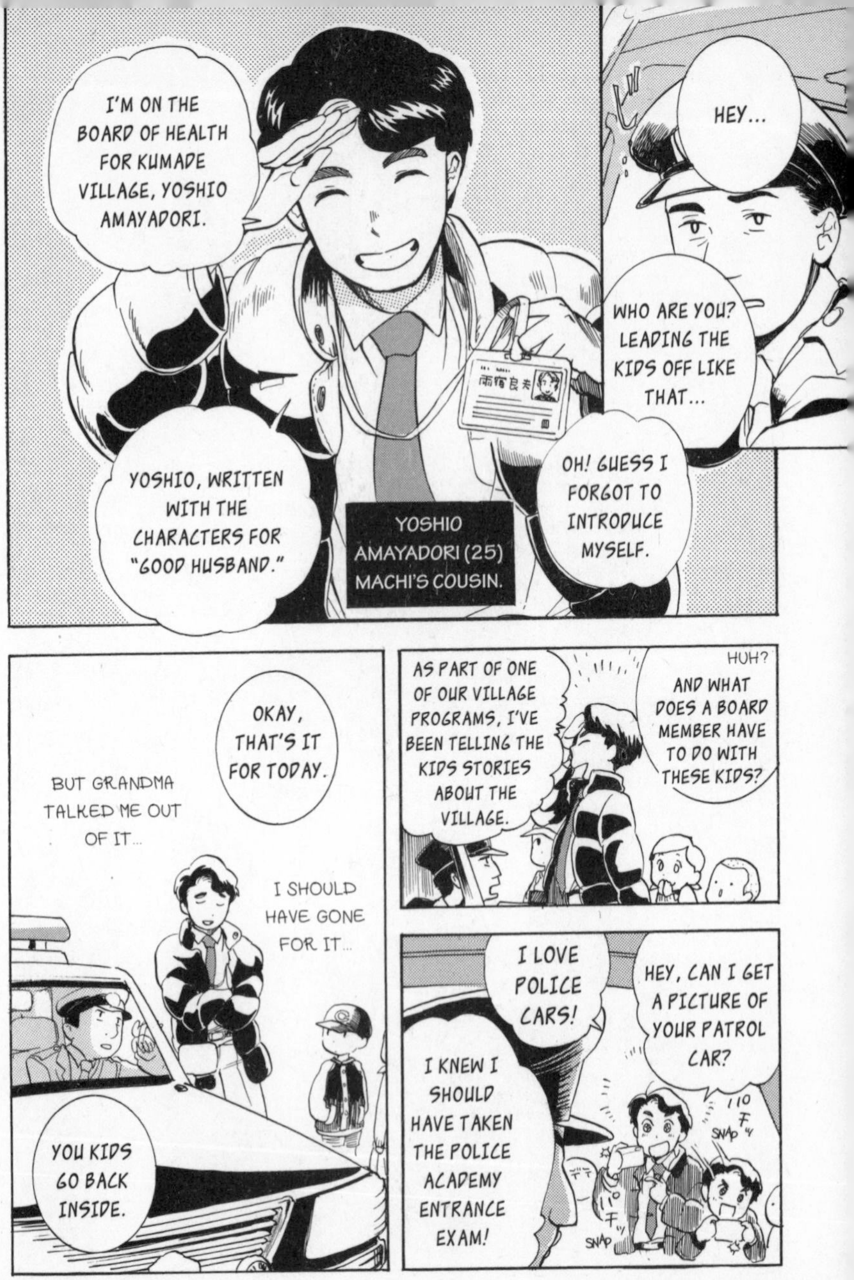
HEY...
WHO ARE YOU? LEADING THE KIDS OFF LIKE THAT...
OH! GUESS I FORGOT TO INTRODUCE MYSELF.
I'M ON THE BOARD OF HEALTH FOR KUMADE VILLAGE, YOSHIO AMAYADORI.
YOSHIO, WRITTEN WITH THE CHARACTERS FOR "GOOD HUSBAND."
YOSHIO AMAYADORI (25) MACHI'S COUSIN.
HUH?
AND WHAT DOES A BOARD MEMBER HAVE TO DO WITH THESE KIDS?
AS PART OF ONE OF OUR VILLAGE PROGRAMS, I'VE BEEN TELLING THE KIDS STORIES ABOUT THE VILLAGE.
HEY, CAN I GET A PICTURE OF YOUR PATROL CAR?
I LOVE POLICE CARS!
I KNEW I SHOULD HAVE TAKEN THE POLICE ACADEMY ENTRANCE EXAM!
SNAP
SNAP
OKAY, THAT'S IT FOR TODAY.
YOU KIDS GO BACK INSIDE.
I SHOULD HAVE GONE FOR IT...
BUT GRANDMA TALKED ME OUT OF IT...

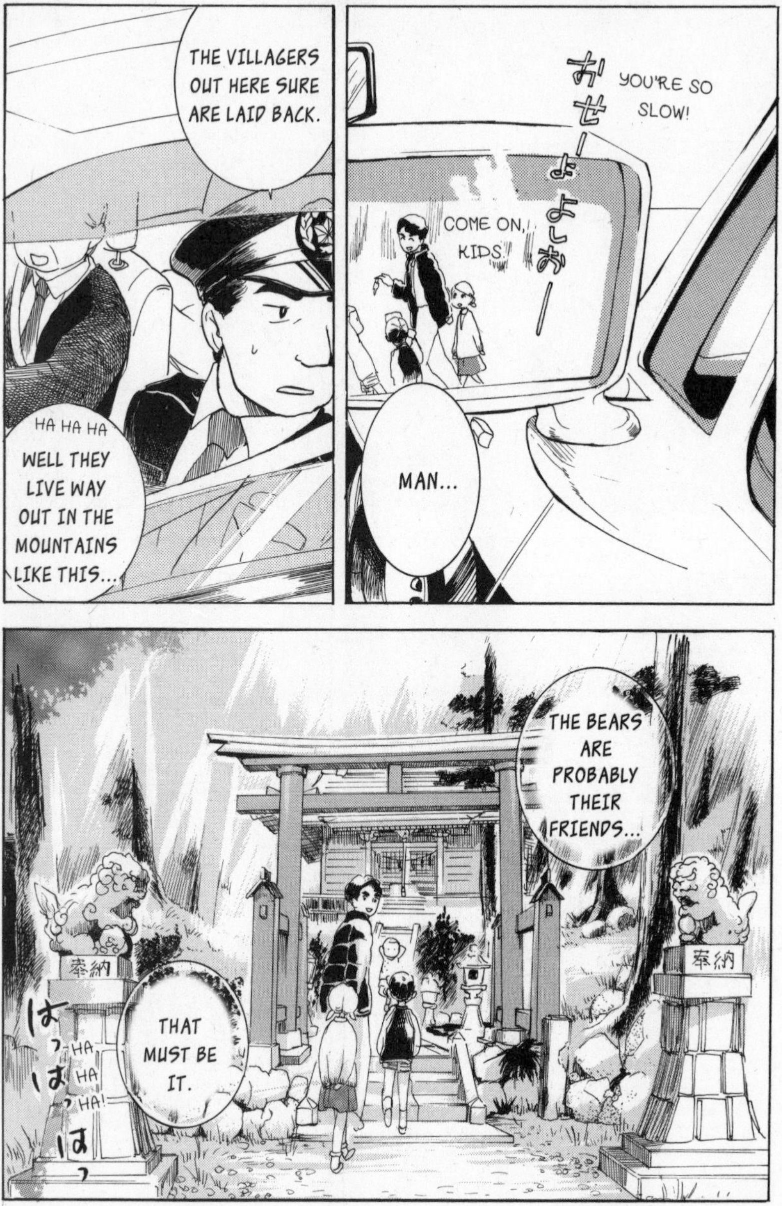
おせーよよしおー
YOU'RE SO SLOW!
COME ON, KIDS!
MAN...
THE VILLAGERS OUT HERE SURE ARE LAID BACK.
HA HA HA
WELL THEY LIVE WAY OUT IN THE MOUNTAINS LIKE THIS...
THE BEARS ARE PROBABLY THEIR FRIENDS...
奉納
THAT MUST BE IT.
奉納
はっはっはっ
HA HA HA!

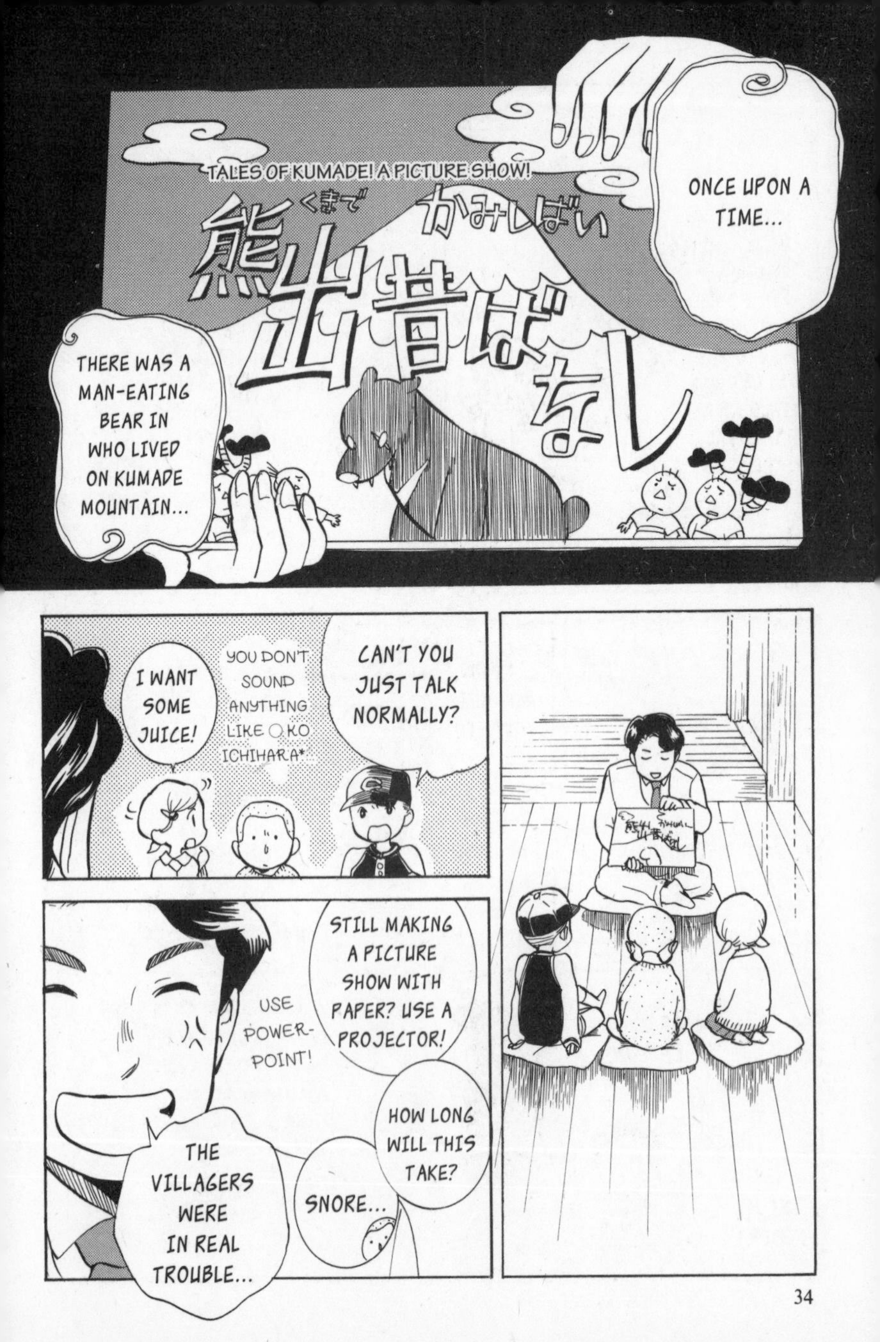

ONCE UPON A TIME...
TALES OF KUMADE! A PICTURE SHOW!
くまで かみしばい
熊出山昔ばなし
THERE WAS A MAN-EATING BEAR IN WHO LIVED ON KUMADE MOUNTAIN...
CAN'T YOU JUST TALK NORMALLY?
YOU DON'T SOUND ANYTHING LIKE ○KO ICHIHARA*...
I WANT SOME JUICE!
STILL MAKING A PICTURE SHOW WITH PAPER? USE A PROJECTOR!
USE POWER-POINT!
HOW LONG WILL THIS TAKE?
SNORE...
THE VILLAGERS WERE IN REAL TROUBLE...

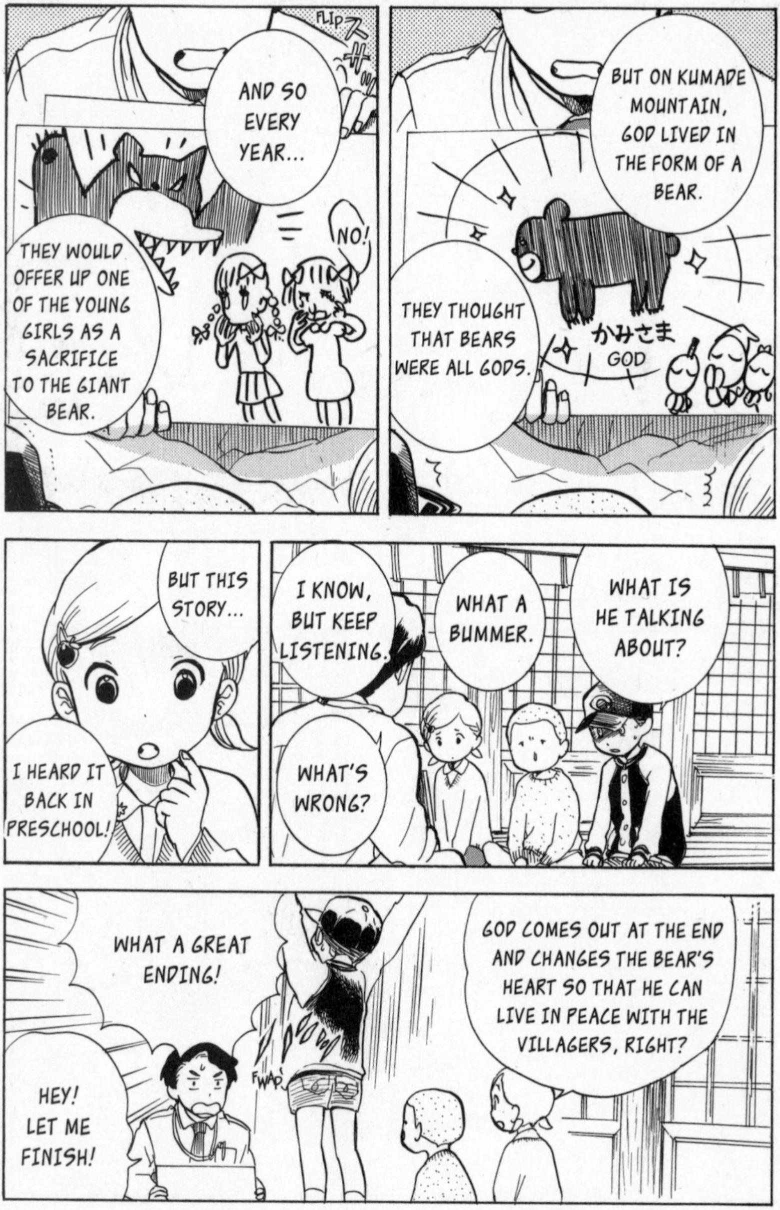
BUT ON KUMADE MOUNTAIN, GOD LIVED IN THE FORM OF A BEAR.
THEY THOUGHT THAT BEARS WERE ALL GODS.
かみさま
GOD
FLIP
AND SO EVERY YEAR...
NO!
THEY WOULD OFFER UP ONE OF THE YOUNG GIRLS AS A SACRIFICE TO THE GIANT BEAR.
WHAT IS HE TALKING ABOUT?
WHAT A BUMMER.
I KNOW, BUT KEEP LISTENING.
WHAT'S WRONG?
BUT THIS STORY...
I HEARD IT BACK IN PRESCHOOL!
GOD COMES OUT AT THE END AND CHANGES THE BEAR'S HEART SO THAT HE CAN LIVE IN PEACE WITH THE VILLAGERS, RIGHT?
FWAP
WHAT A GREAT ENDING!
HEY! LET ME FINISH!

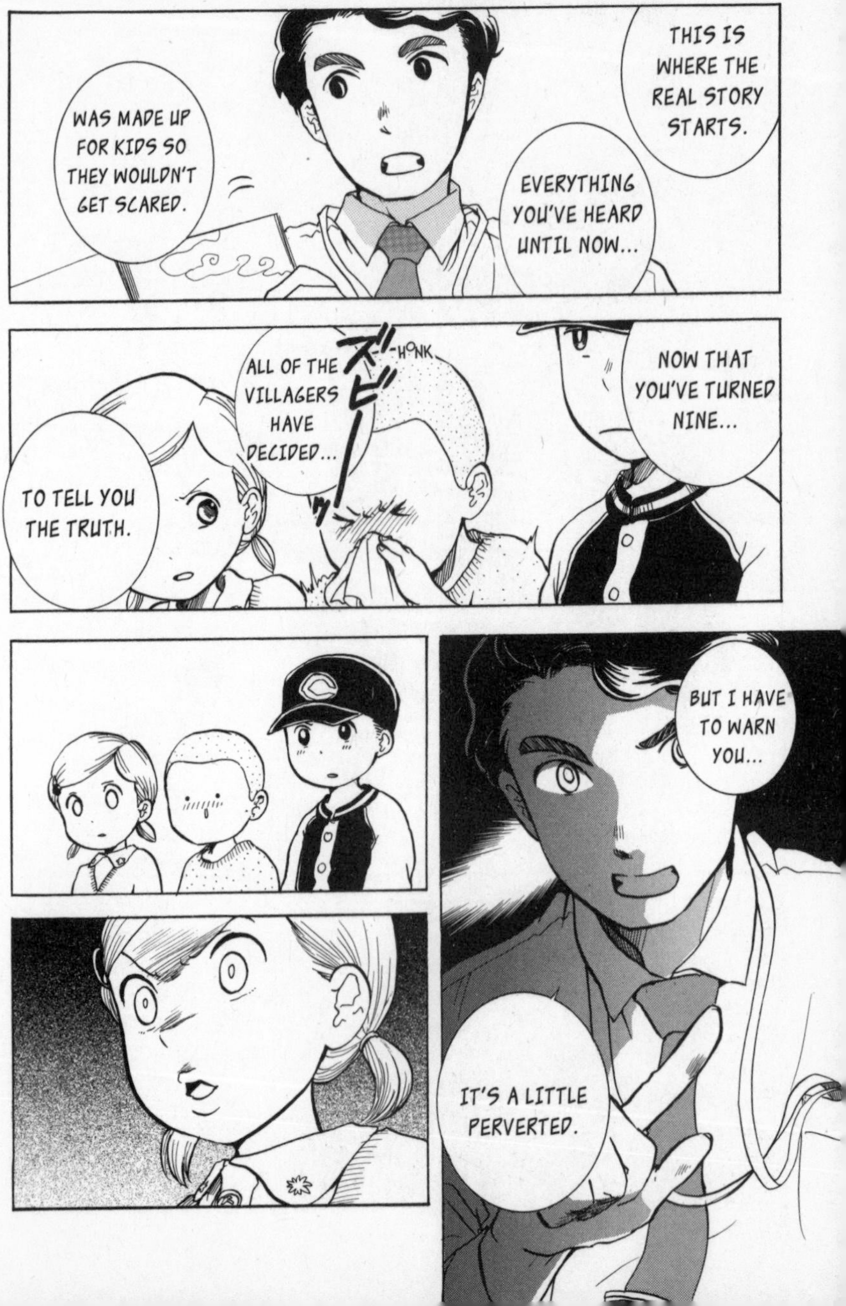
THIS IS WHERE THE REAL STORY STARTS.
EVERYTHING YOU'VE HEARD UNTIL NOW...
WAS MADE UP FOR KIDS SO THEY WOULDN'T GET SCARED.
NOW THAT YOU'VE TURNED NINE...
ズビーッ
HONK
ALL OF THE VILLAGERS HAVE DECIDED...
TO TELL YOU THE TRUTH.
BUT I HAVE TO WARN YOU...
IT'S A LITTLE PERVERTED.

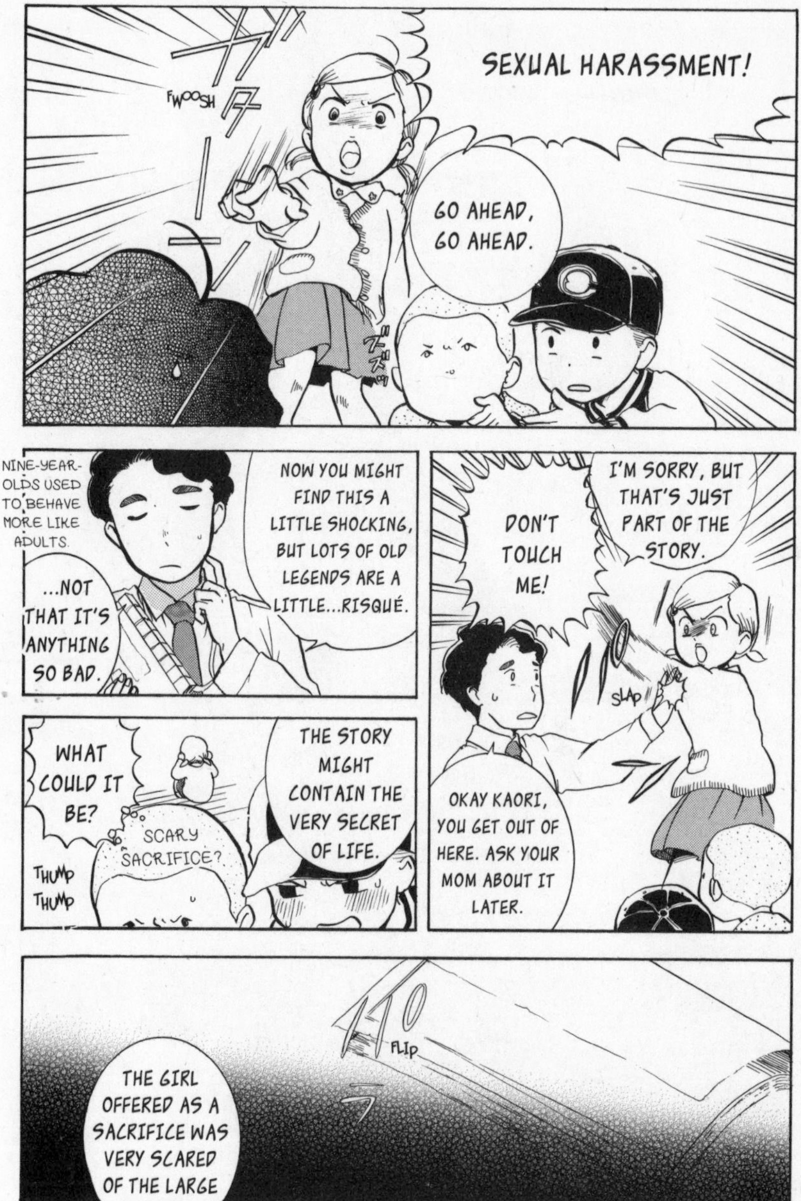
SEXUAL HARASSMENT!
FWOOSH
GO AHEAD, GO AHEAD.
I'M SORRY, BUT THAT'S JUST PART OF THE STORY.
DON'T TOUCH ME!
SLAP
OKAY KAORI, YOU GET OUT OF HERE. ASK YOUR MOM ABOUT IT LATER.
NOW YOU MIGHT FIND THIS A LITTLE SHOCKING, BUT LOTS OF OLD LEGENDS ARE A LITTLE...RISQUÉ.
...NOT THAT IT'S ANYTHING SO BAD.
NINE-YEAR-OLDS USED TO BEHAVE MORE LIKE ADULTS.
THE STORY MIGHT CONTAIN THE VERY SECRET OF LIFE.
WHAT COULD IT BE?
SCARY SACRIFICE?
THUMP THUMP
FLIP
THE GIRL OFFERED AS A SACRIFICE WAS VERY SCARED OF THE LARGE BEAR...

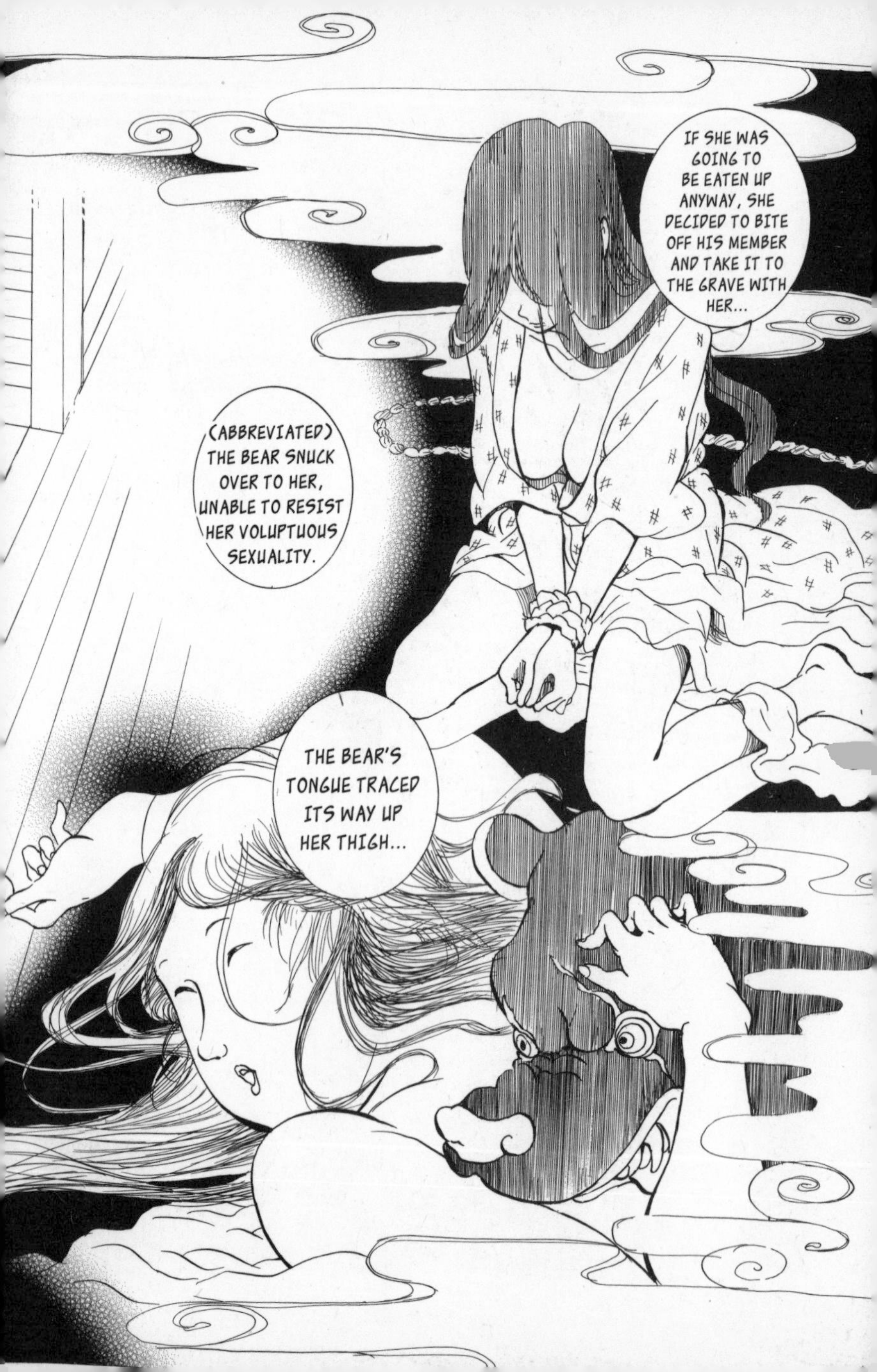
IF SHE WAS GOING TO BE EATEN UP ANYWAY, SHE DECIDED TO BITE OFF HIS MEMBER AND TAKE IT TO THE GRAVE WITH HER...
(ABBREVIATED) THE BEAR SNUCK OVER TO HER, UNABLE TO RESIST HER VOLUPTUOUS SEXUALITY.
THE BEAR'S TONGUE TRACED ITS WAY UP HER THIGH...

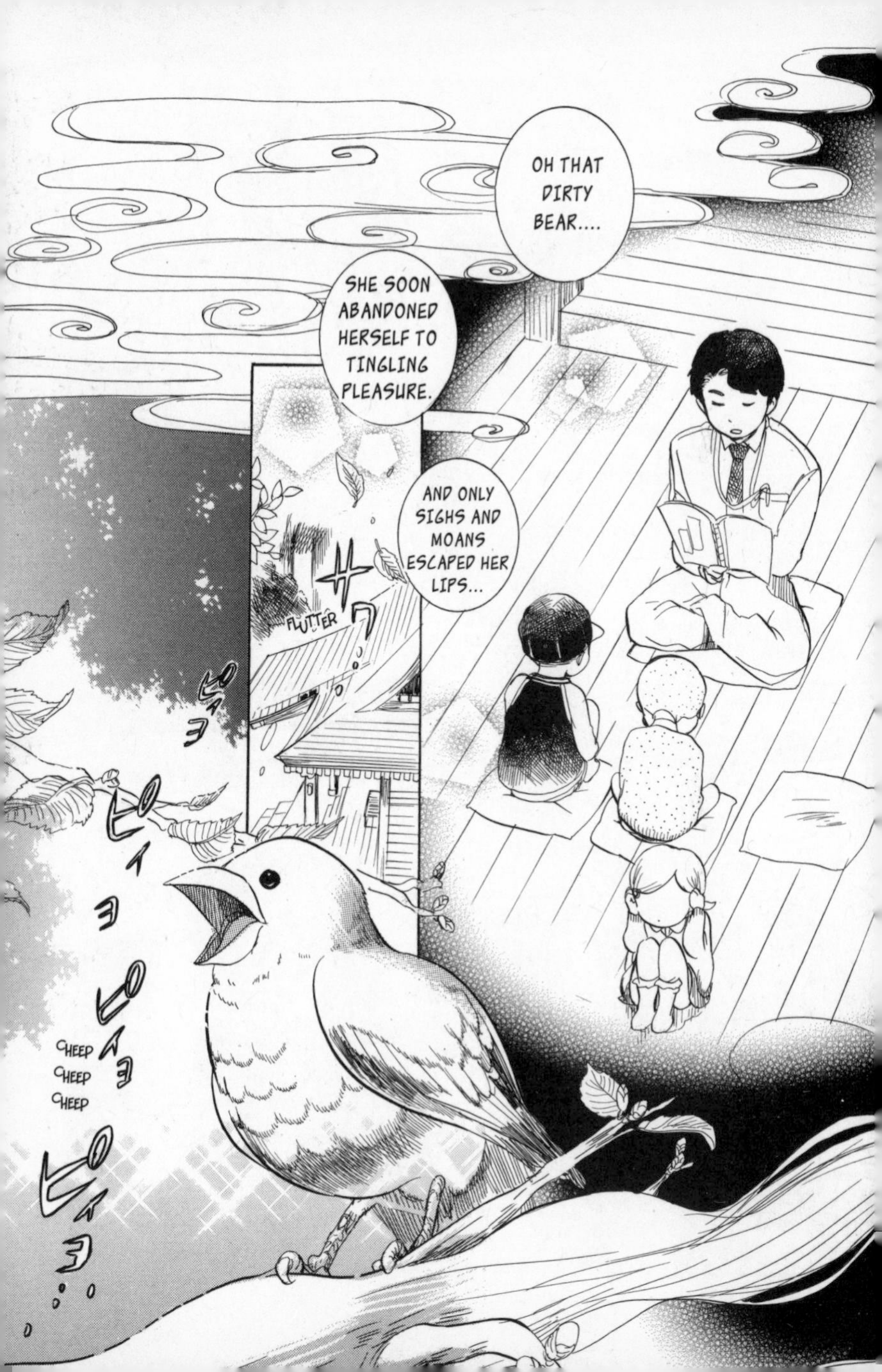
OH THAT DIRTY BEAR....
SHE SOON ABANDONED HERSELF TO TINGLING PLEASURE.
AND ONLY SIGHS AND MOANS ESCAPED HER LIPS...
FLUTTER
CHEEP CHEEP CHEEP

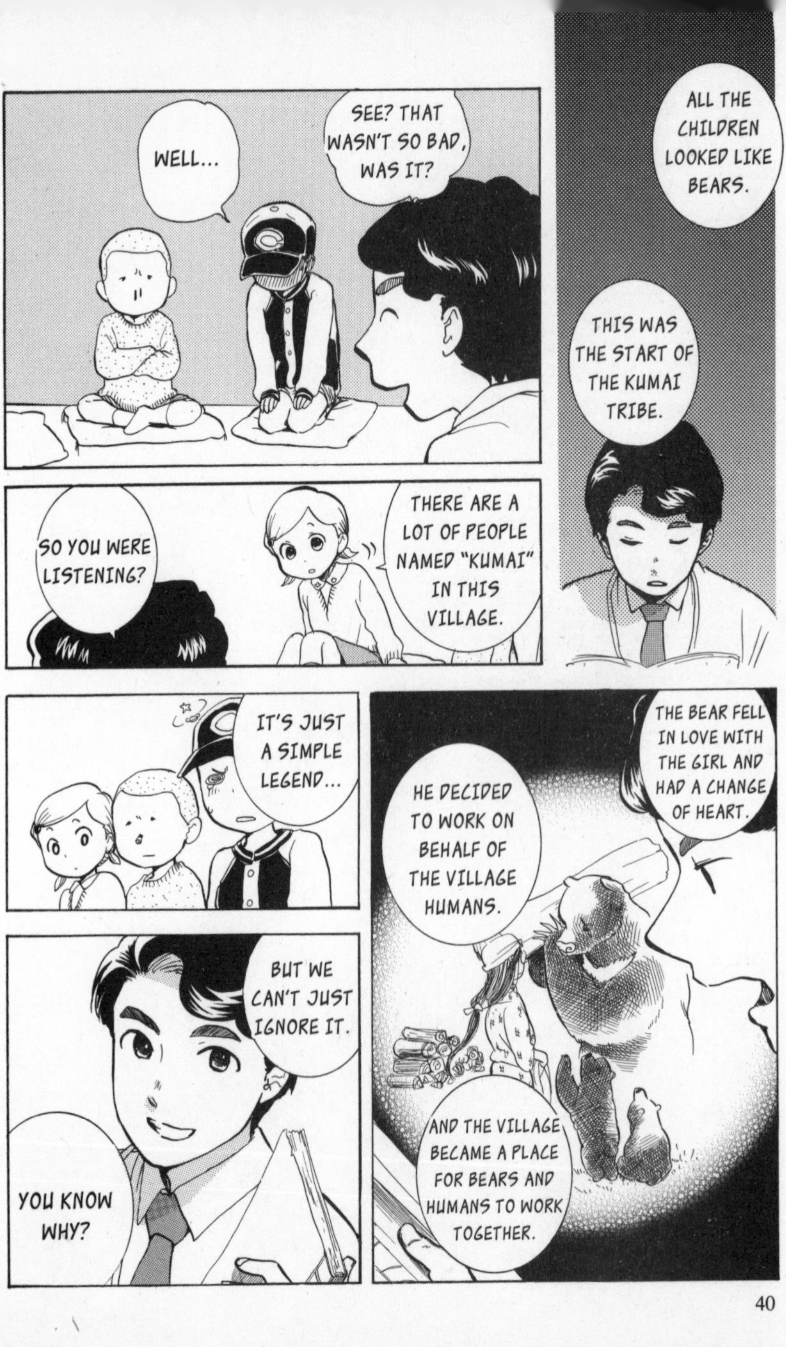
ALL THE CHILDREN LOOKED LIKE BEARS.
THIS WAS THE START OF THE KUMAI TRIBE.
SEE? THAT WASN'T SO BAD, WAS IT?
WELL...
THERE ARE A LOT OF PEOPLE NAMED "KUMAI" IN THIS VILLAGE.
SO YOU WERE LISTENING?
THE BEAR FELL IN LOVE WITH THE GIRL AND HAD A CHANGE OF HEART.
HE DECIDED TO WORK ON BEHALF OF THE VILLAGE HUMANS.
AND THE VILLAGE BECAME A PLACE FOR BEARS AND HUMANS TO WORK TOGETHER.
IT'S JUST A SIMPLE LEGEND...
BUT WE CAN'T JUST IGNORE IT.
YOU KNOW WHY?

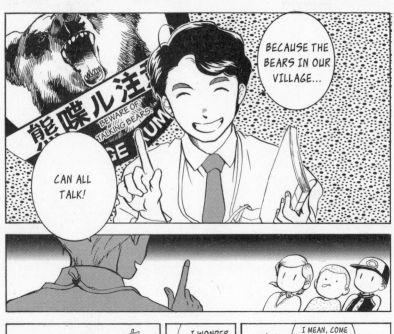

熊喋ル注
BEWARE OF TALKING BEARS.
BECAUSE THE BEARS IN OUR VILLAGE...
CAN ALL TALK!
I MEAN, COME ON! THINK ABOUT IT! IF THEY COULDN'T TALK, HOW COULD WE BE FRIENDS?
EVEN NOW, THE KUMAI AND THE VILLAGERS ARE ON GOOD TERMS.
WHISPER WHISPER
DIDN'T YOUR MOTHER EVER TELL YOU THAT BAD CHILDREN WOULD BE EATEN UP BY BEARS? (THAT'S TRUE!)
I WONDER IF MR. YOSHIO IS FATIGUED...
IT MUST BE HARD TO BE A CIVIL SERVANT.
カラ
RATTLE
JUICE!
THANK YOU!
I REALLY WANTED SOME!

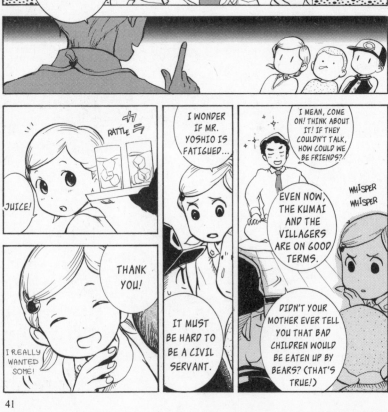

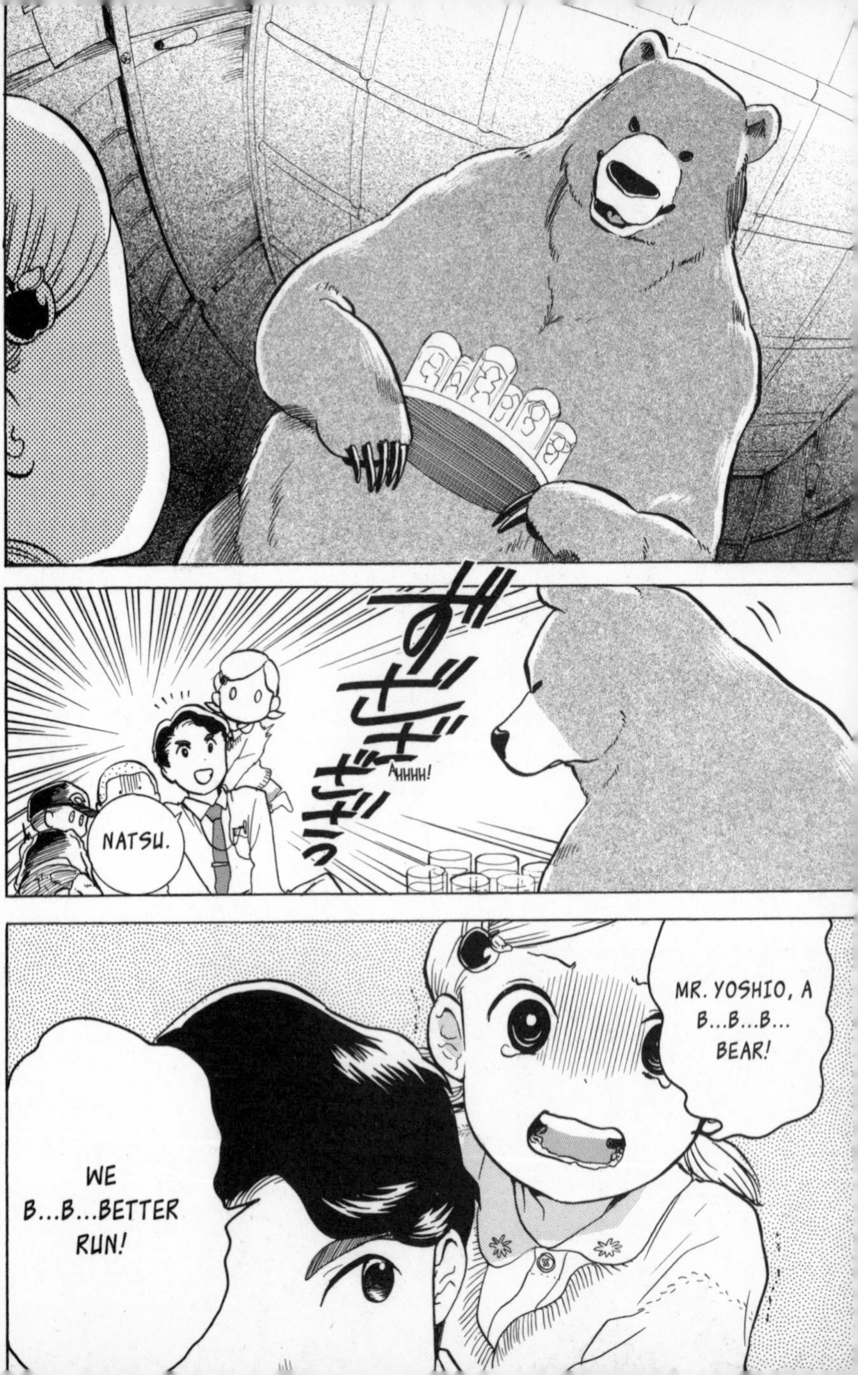
AHHHH!
NATSU.
MR. YOSHIO, A B...B...B... BEAR!
WE B...B...BETTER RUN!

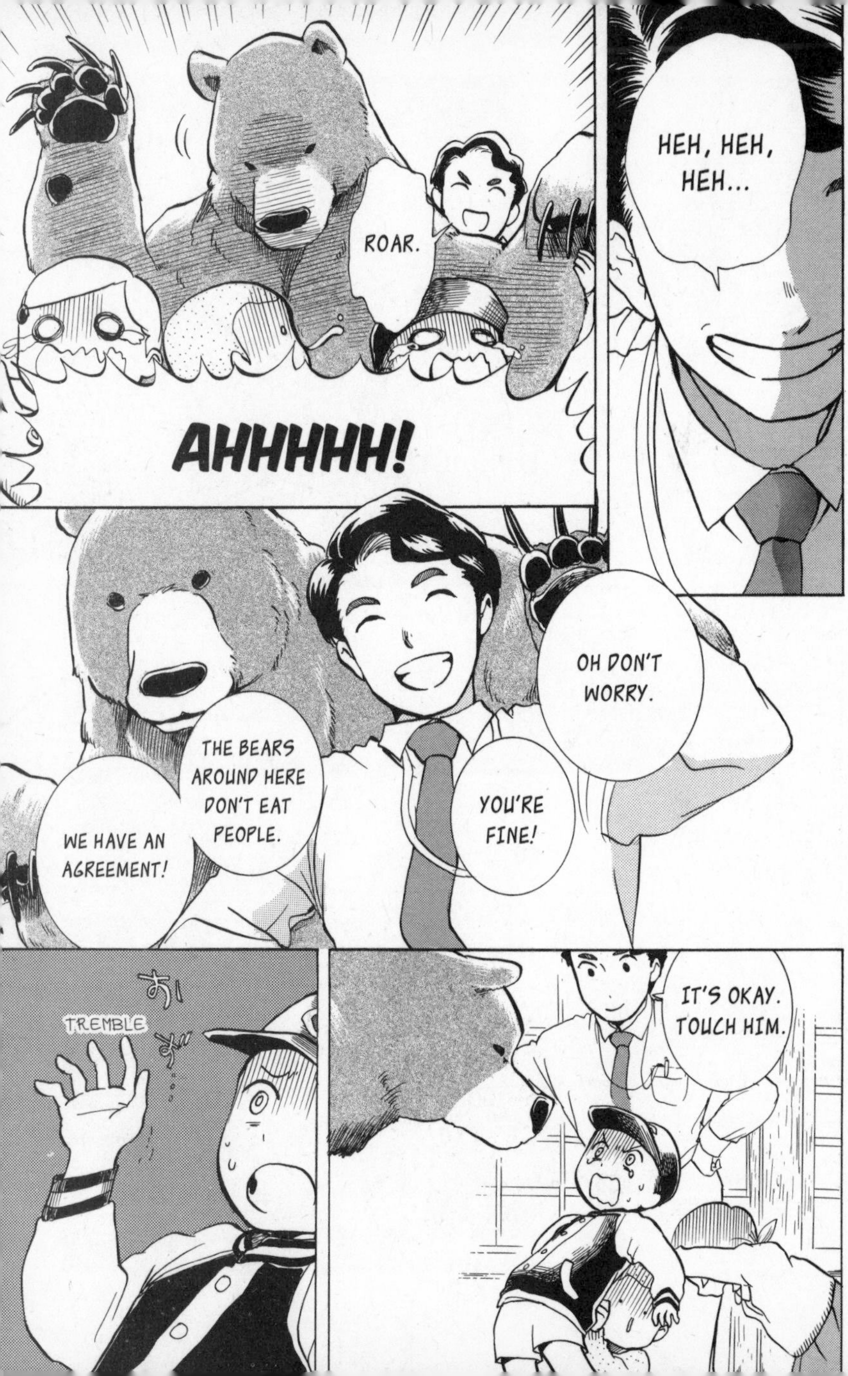
HEH, HEH, HEH...
ROAR.
AHHHHH!
OH DON'T WORRY.
YOU'RE FINE!
THE BEARS AROUND HERE DON'T EAT PEOPLE.
WE HAVE AN AGREEMENT!
IT'S OKAY. TOUCH HIM.
TREMBLE

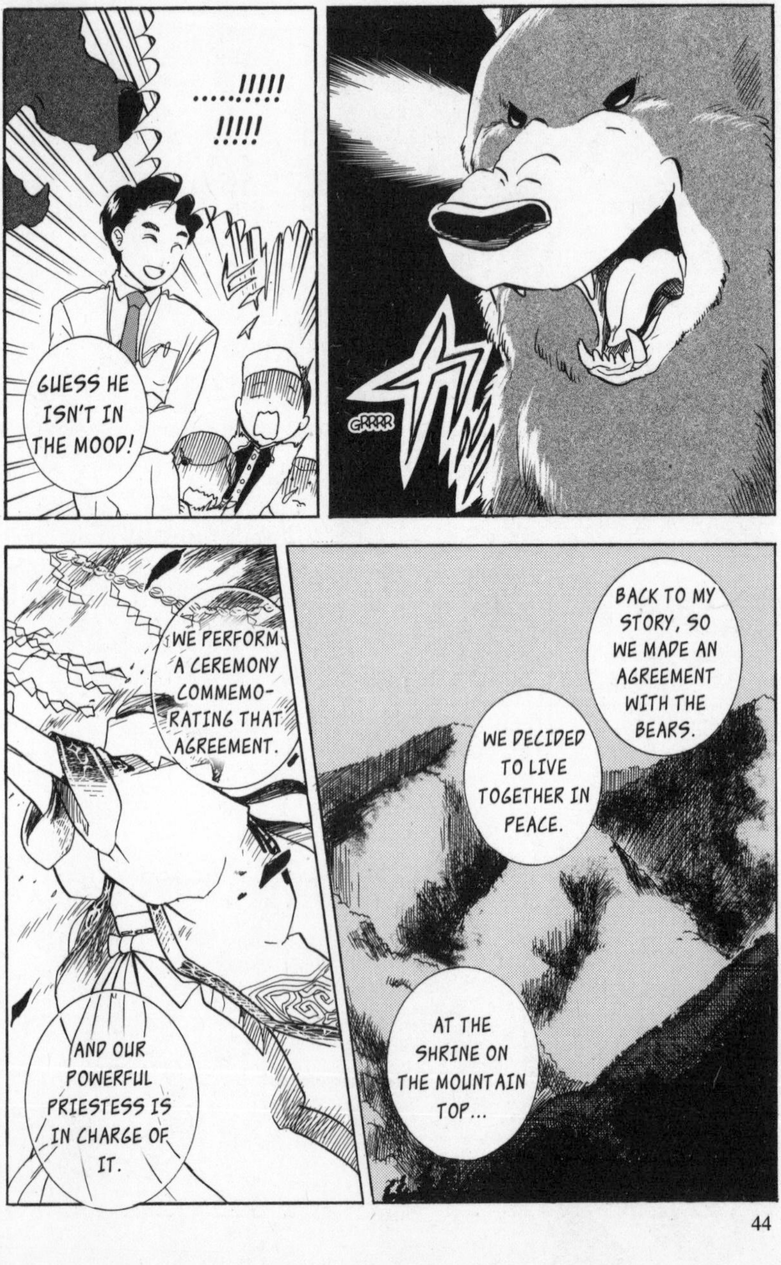
GRRRR
.....!!!!!
!!!!!
GUESS HE ISN'T IN THE MOOD!
BACK TO MY STORY, SO WE MADE AN AGREEMENT WITH THE BEARS.
WE DECIDED TO LIVE TOGETHER IN PEACE.
AT THE SHRINE ON THE MOUNTAIN TOP...
WE PERFORM A CEREMONY COMMEMO-RATING THAT AGREEMENT.
AND OUR POWERFUL PRIESTESS IS IN CHARGE OF IT.

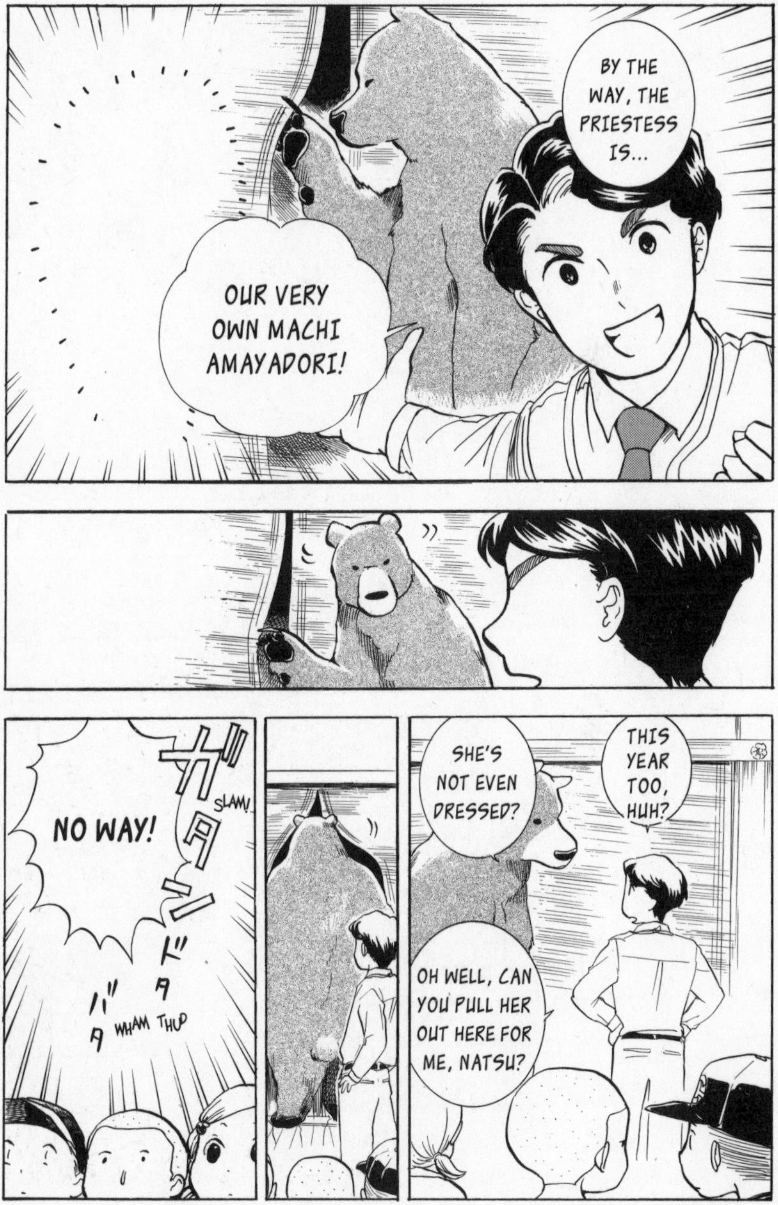
BY THE WAY, THE PRIESTESS IS...
OUR VERY OWN MACHI AMAYADORI!
THIS YEAR TOO, HUH?
SHE'S NOT EVEN DRESSED?
OH WELL, CAN YOU PULL HER OUT HERE FOR ME, NATSU?
SLAM!
NO WAY!
THUD
WHAM

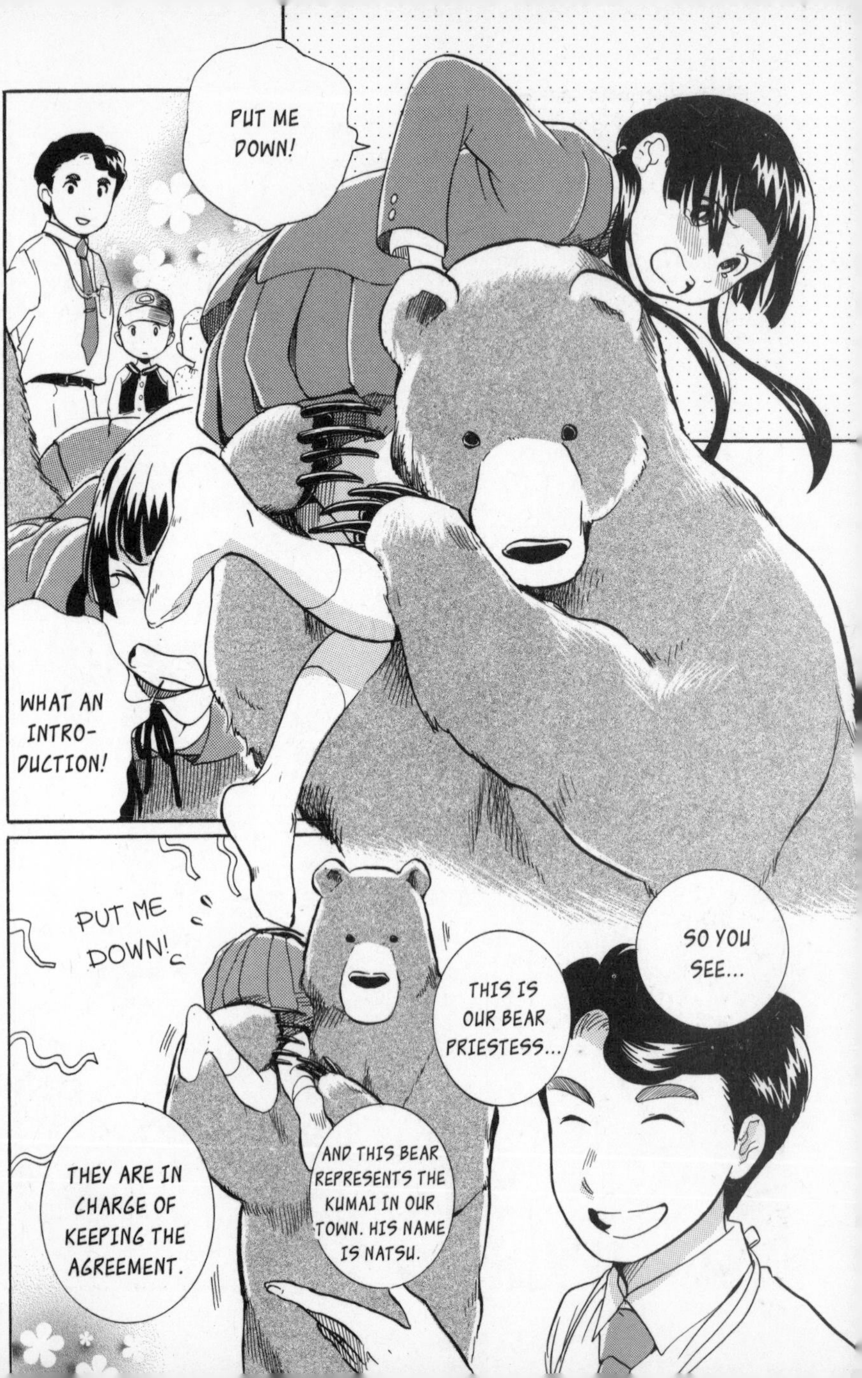
PUT ME DOWN!
WHAT AN INTRO-DUCTION!
SO YOU SEE...
THIS IS OUR BEAR PRIESTESS...
PUT ME DOWN!
AND THIS BEAR REPRESENTS THE KUMAI IN OUR TOWN. HIS NAME IS NATSU.
THEY ARE IN CHARGE OF KEEPING THE AGREEMENT.

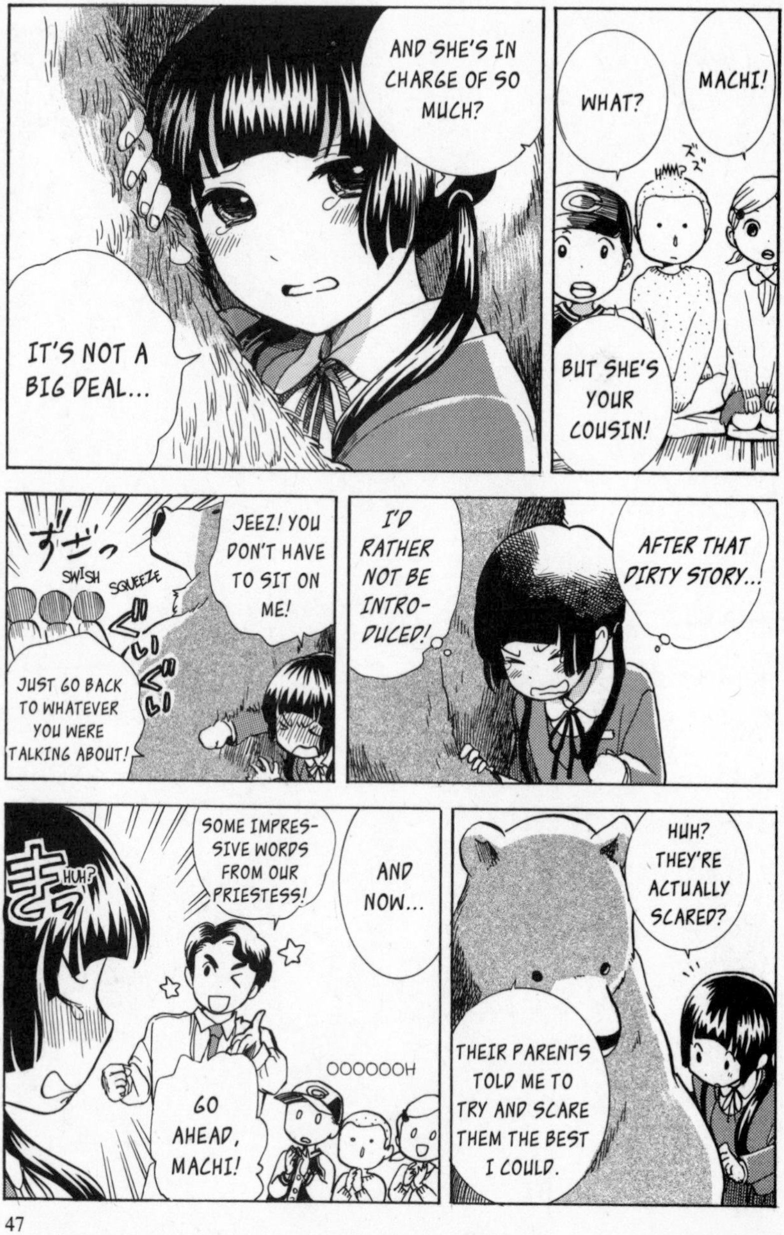
MACHI!
WHAT?
HMM?
ズズ
BUT SHE'S YOUR COUSIN!
AND SHE'S IN CHARGE OF SO MUCH?
IT'S NOT A BIG DEAL...
AFTER THAT DIRTY STORY...
I'D RATHER NOT BE INTRO-DUCED!
JEEZ! YOU DON'T HAVE TO SIT ON ME!
ずざっ
SWISH
SQUEEZE
JUST GO BACK TO WHATEVER YOU WERE TALKING ABOUT!
HUH? THEY'RE ACTUALLY SCARED?
THEIR PARENTS TOLD ME TO TRY AND SCARE THEM THE BEST I COULD.
AND NOW...
SOME IMPRES-SIVE WORDS FROM OUR PRIESTESS!
OOOOOOH
GO AHEAD, MACHI!
きっ
HUH?

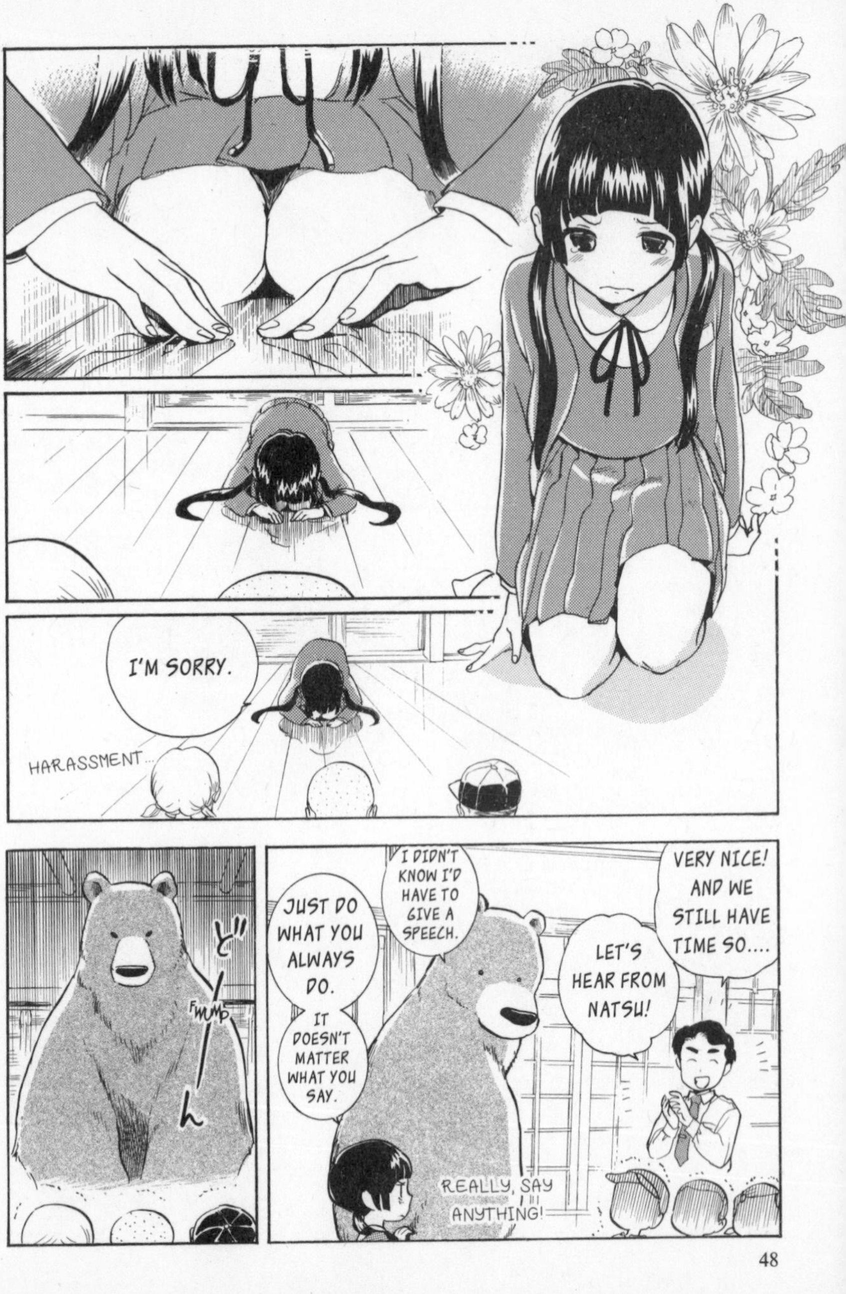
I'M SORRY.
HARASSMENT...
VERY NICE! AND WE STILL HAVE TIME SO....
LET'S HEAR FROM NATSU!
I DIDN'T KNOW I'D HAVE TO GIVE A SPEECH.
JUST DO WHAT YOU ALWAYS DO.
IT DOESN'T MATTER WHAT YOU SAY.
REALLY, SAY ANYTHING!
FWUMP

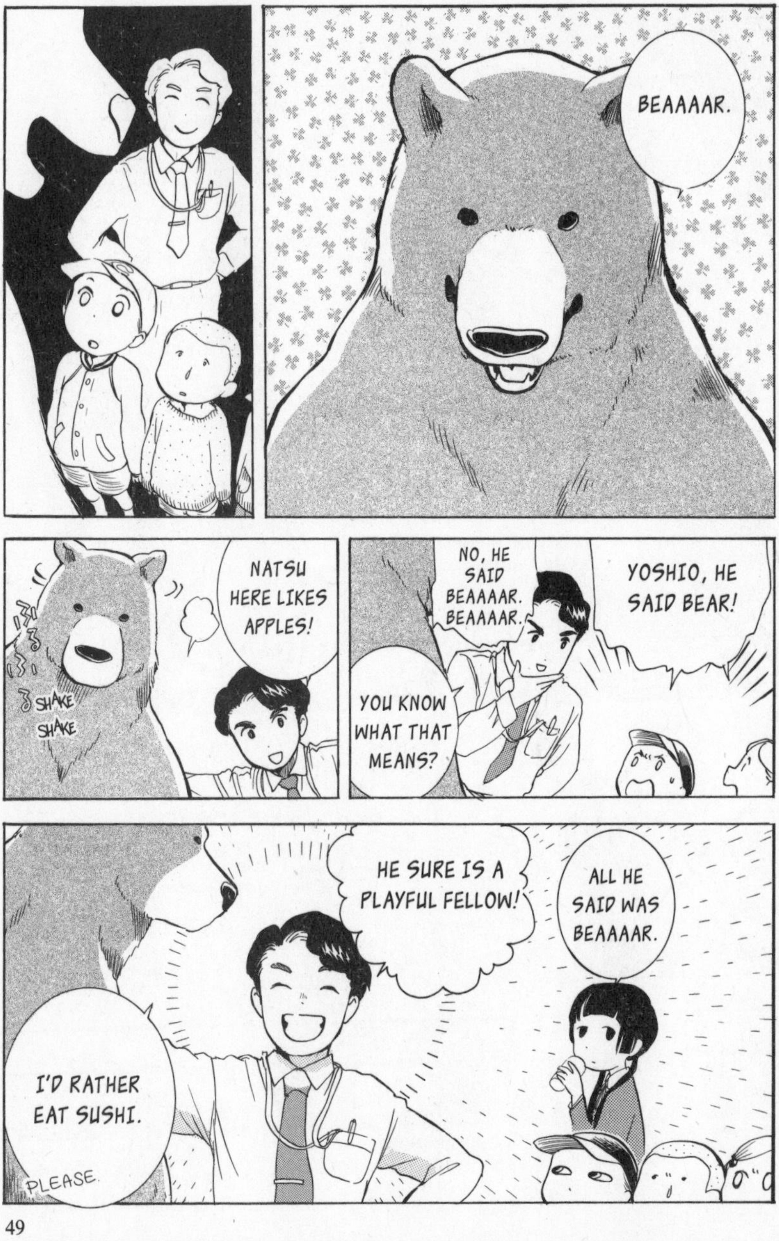
BEAAAAR.
YOSHIO, HE SAID BEAR!
NO, HE SAID BEAAAAR. BEAAAAR.
YOU KNOW WHAT THAT MEANS?
NATSU HERE LIKES APPLES!
SHAKE SHAKE
ALL HE SAID WAS BEAAAAR.
HE SURE IS A PLAYFUL FELLOW!
I'D RATHER EAT SUSHI.
PLEASE.

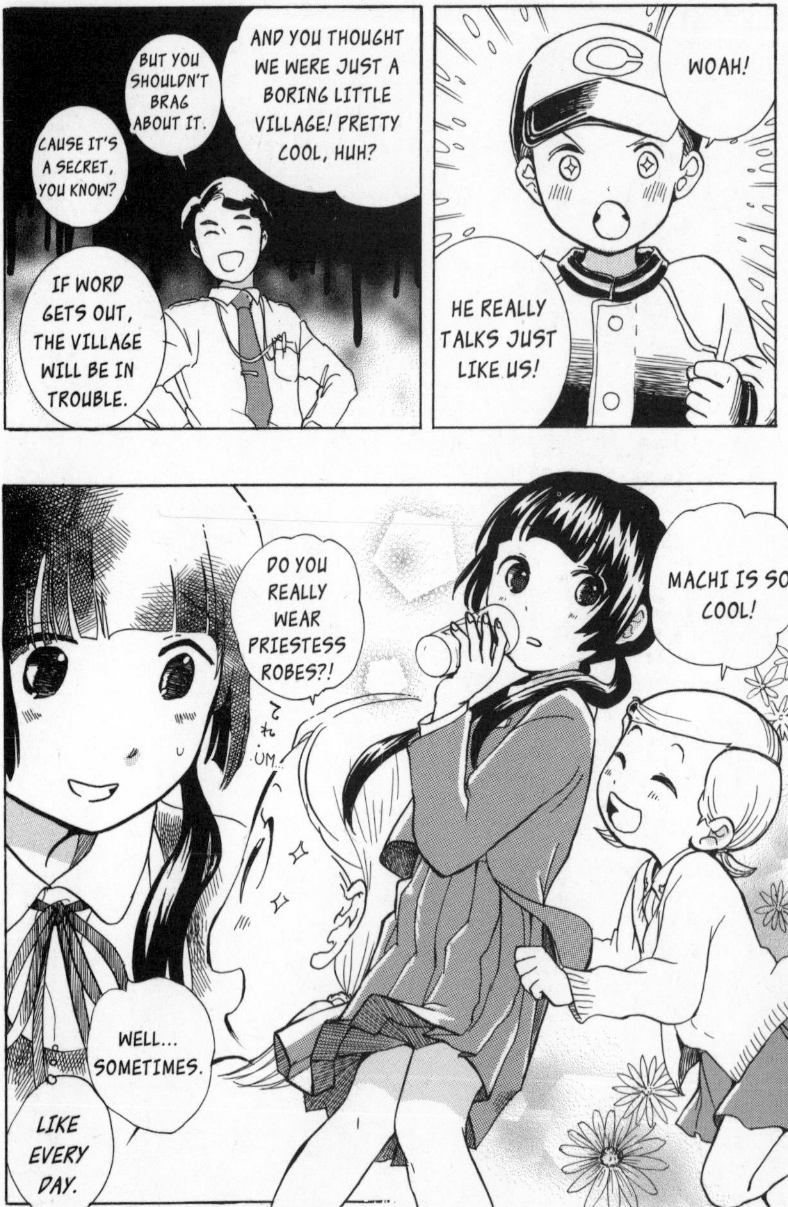
WOAH!
HE REALLY TALKS JUST LIKE US!
AND YOU THOUGHT WE WERE JUST A BORING LITTLE VILLAGE! PRETTY COOL, HUH?
BUT YOU SHOULDN'T BRAG ABOUT IT.
CAUSE IT'S A SECRET, YOU KNOW?
IF WORD GETS OUT, THE VILLAGE WILL BE IN TROUBLE.
MACHI IS SO COOL!
DO YOU REALLY WEAR PRIESTESS ROBES?!
てれ
UM...
WELL... SOMETIMES.
LIKE EVERY DAY.

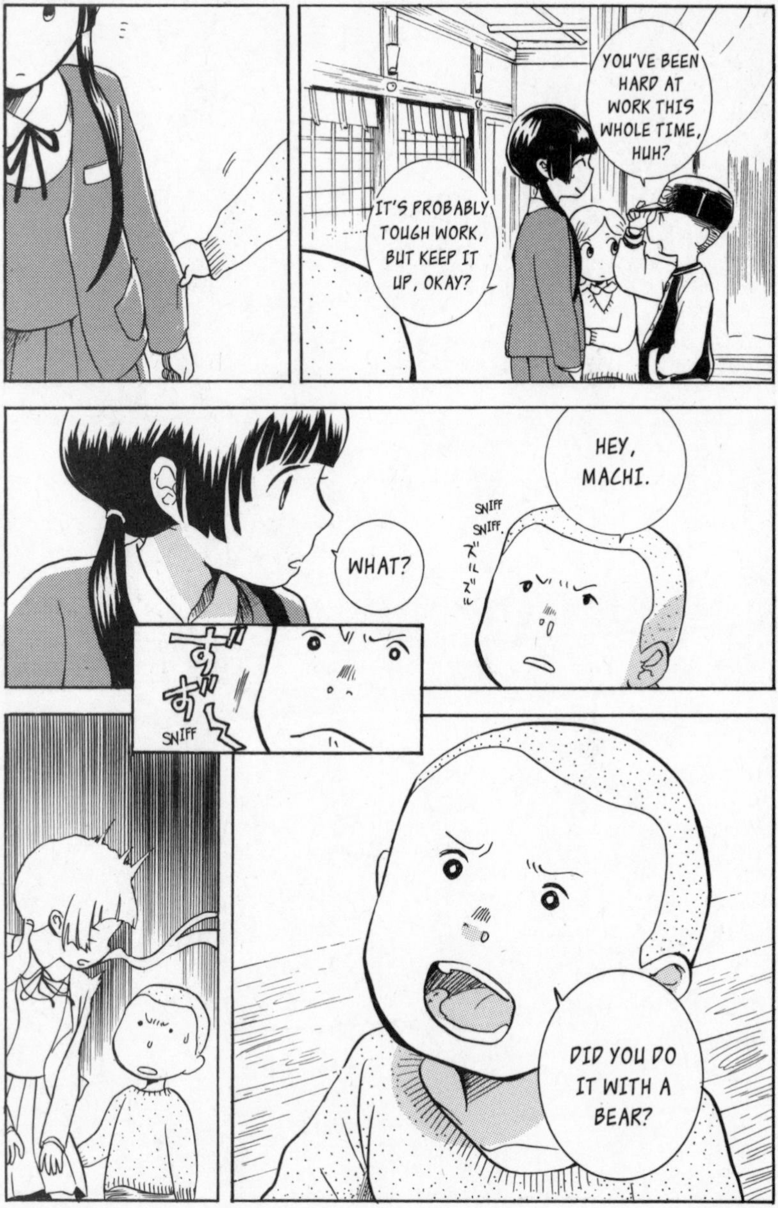
YOU'VE BEEN HARD AT WORK THIS WHOLE TIME, HUH?
IT'S PROBABLY TOUGH WORK, BUT KEEP IT UP, OKAY?
HEY, MACHI.
SNIFF SNIFF.
WHAT?
SNIFF
DID YOU DO IT WITH A BEAR?

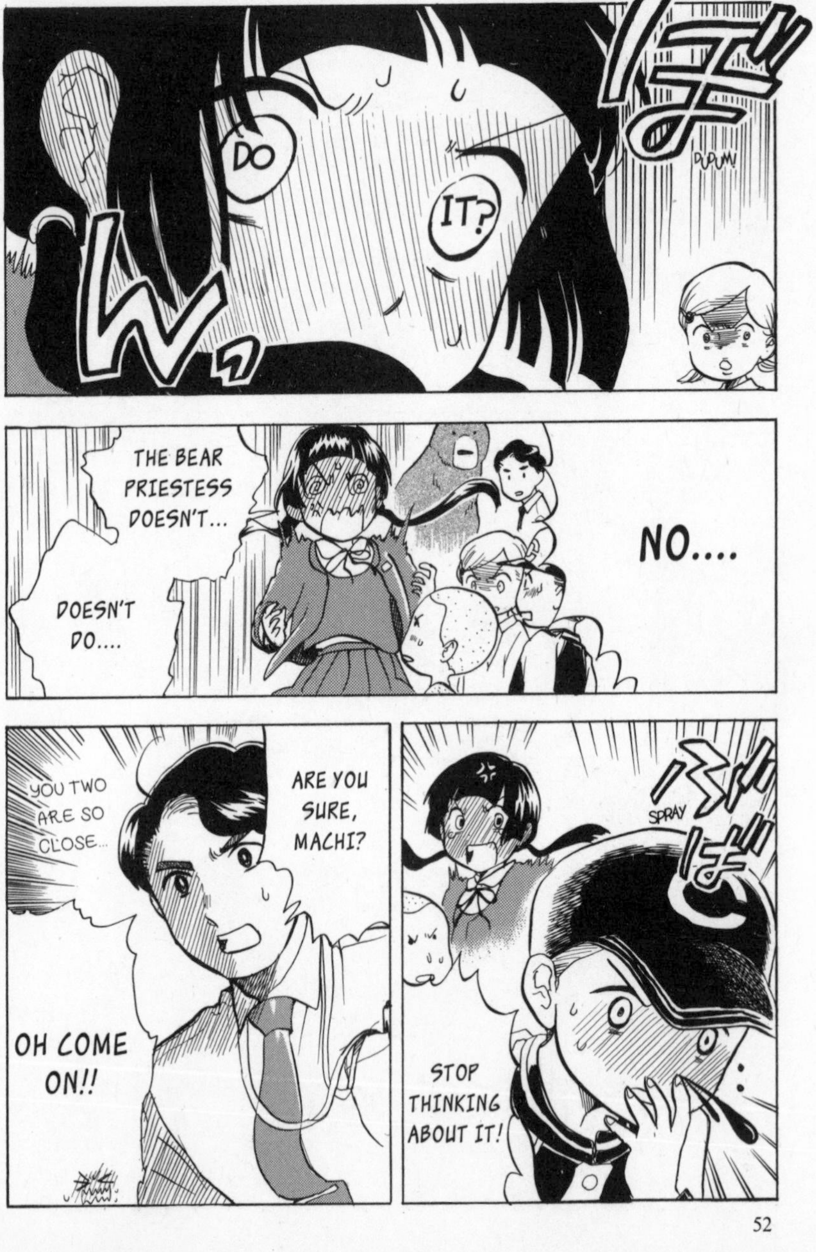
DUPUM!
DO
IT?
NO....
THE BEAR PRIESTESS DOESN'T...
DOESN'T DO....
SPRAY
STOP THINKING ABOUT IT!
ARE YOU SURE, MACHI?
YOU TWO ARE SO CLOSE...
OH COME ON!!

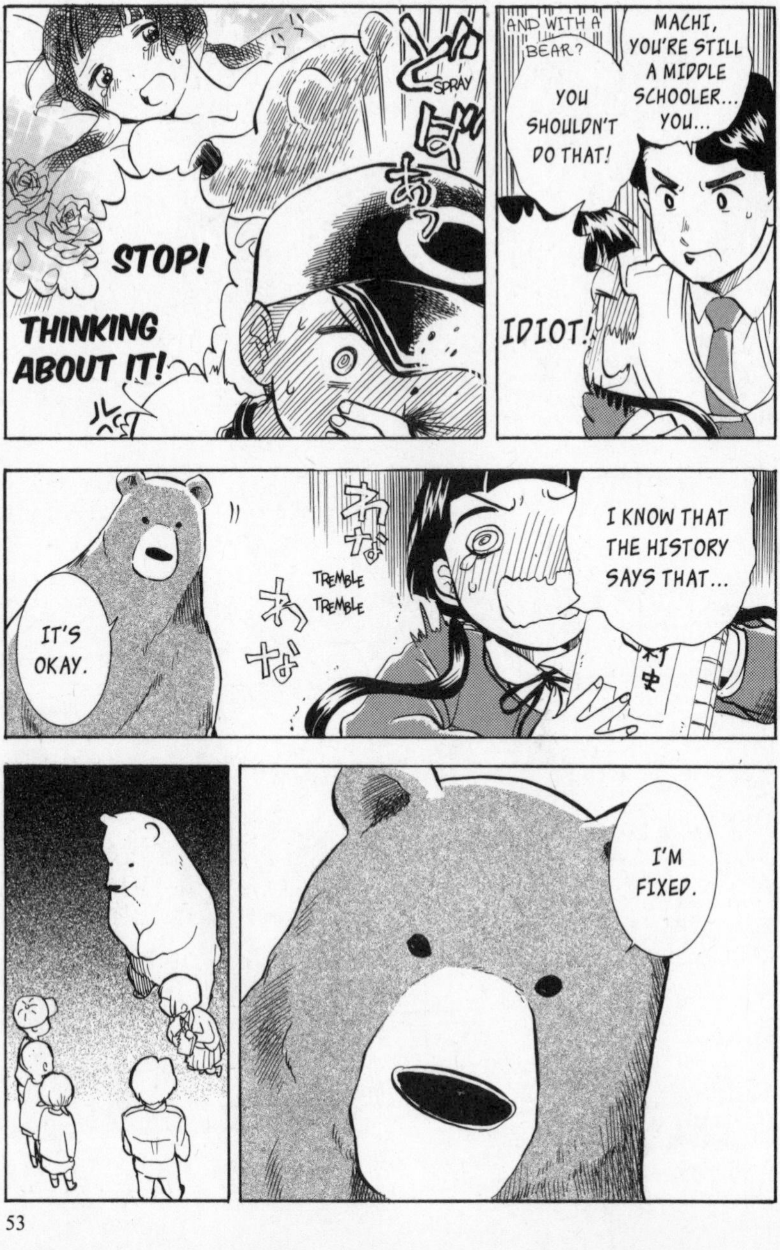
MACHI, YOU'RE STILL A MIDDLE SCHOOLER... YOU...
AND WITH A BEAR?
YOU SHOULDN'T DO THAT!
IDIOT!
どばっ
SPRAY
STOP!
THINKING ABOUT IT!
I KNOW THAT THE HISTORY SAYS THAT...
わなわな
TREMBLE TREMBLE
IT'S OKAY.
I'M FIXED.

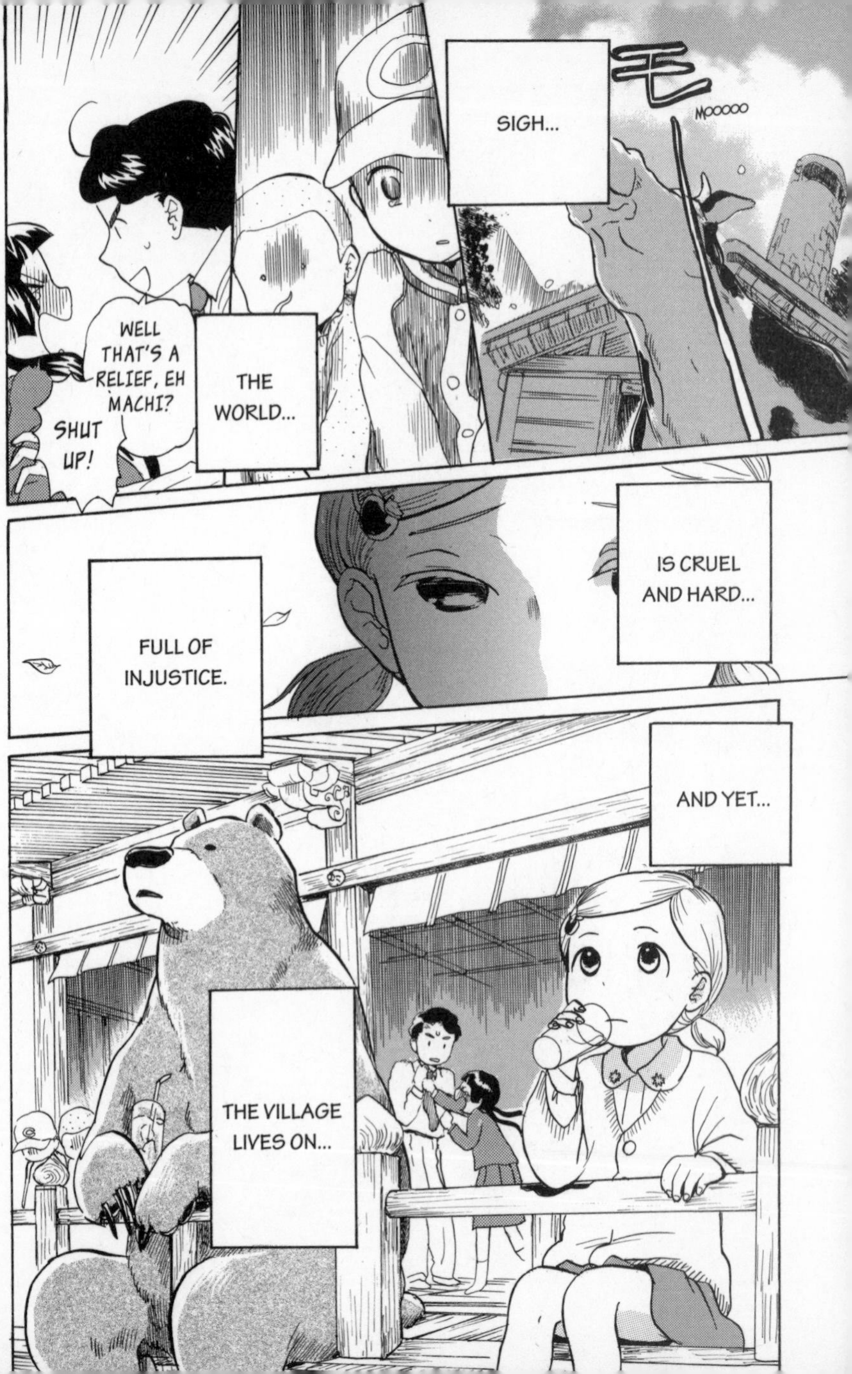
SIGH...
モ
MOOOOO
THE WORLD...
WELL THAT'S A RELIEF, EH MACHI?
SHUT UP!
IS CRUEL AND HARD...
FULL OF INJUSTICE.
AND YET...
THE VILLAGE LIVES ON...

CHILDRENのCです

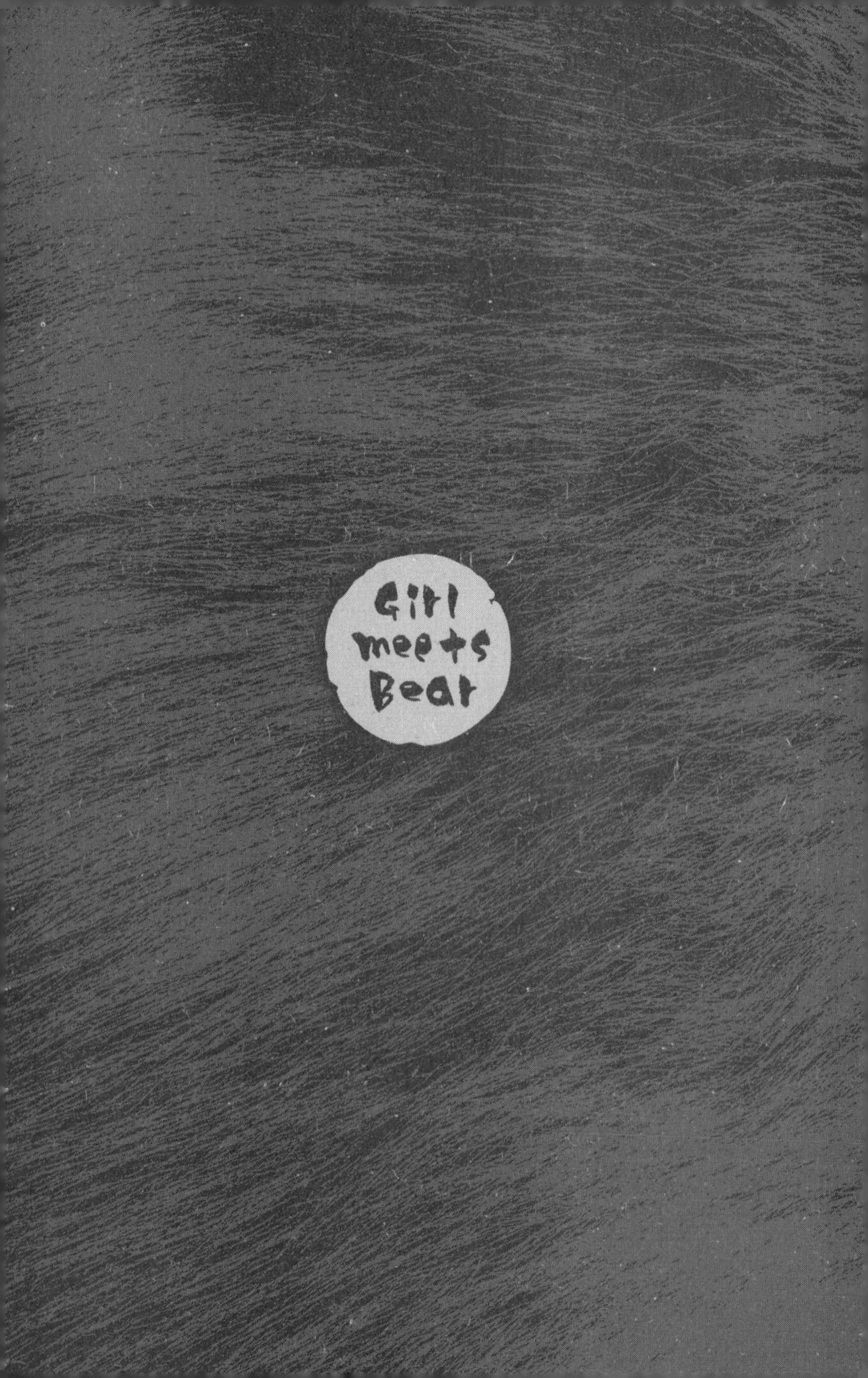
Girl meets Bear

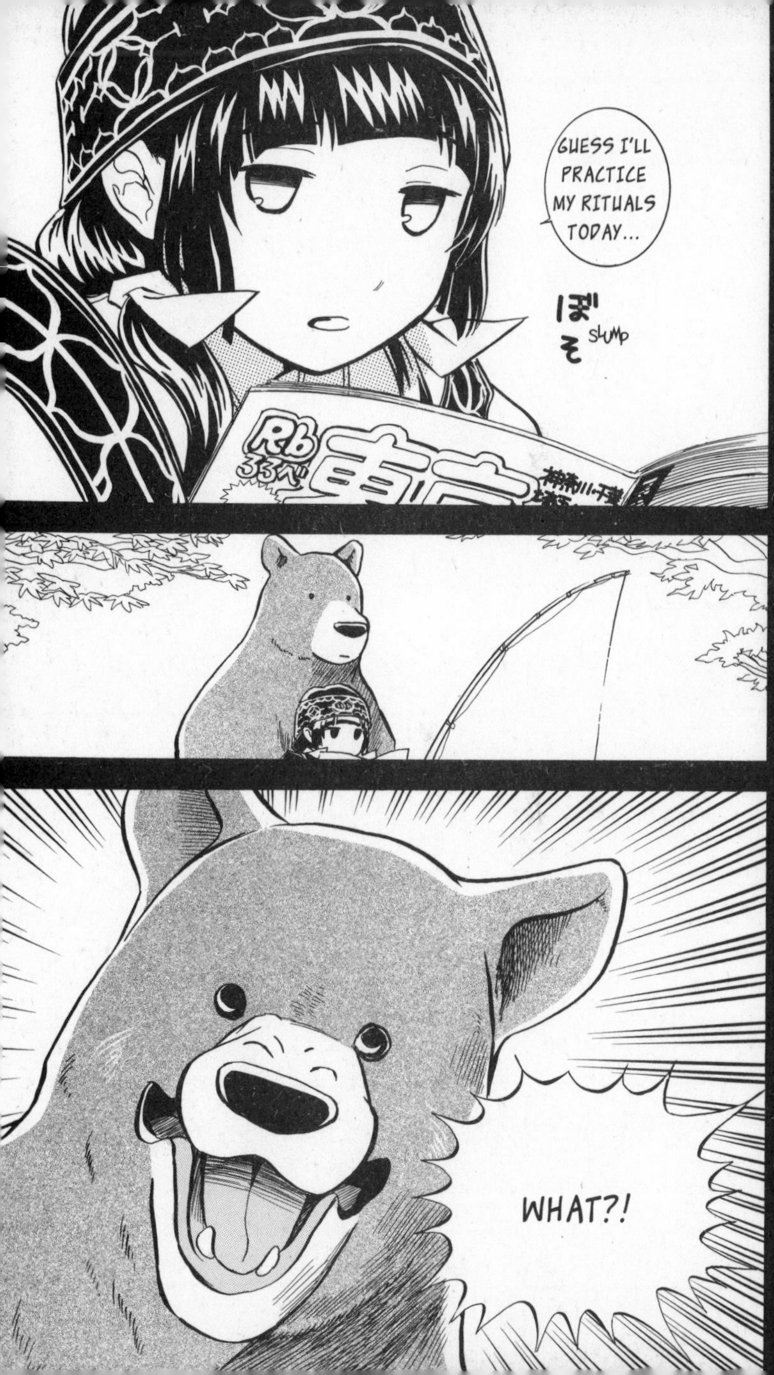
GUESS I'LL PRACTICE MY RITUALS TODAY...
ぼそ
SLUMP
Rb 33ぺ
WHAT?!

CHAPTER 3

A DANCE AT THE MOUNTAIN SHRINE

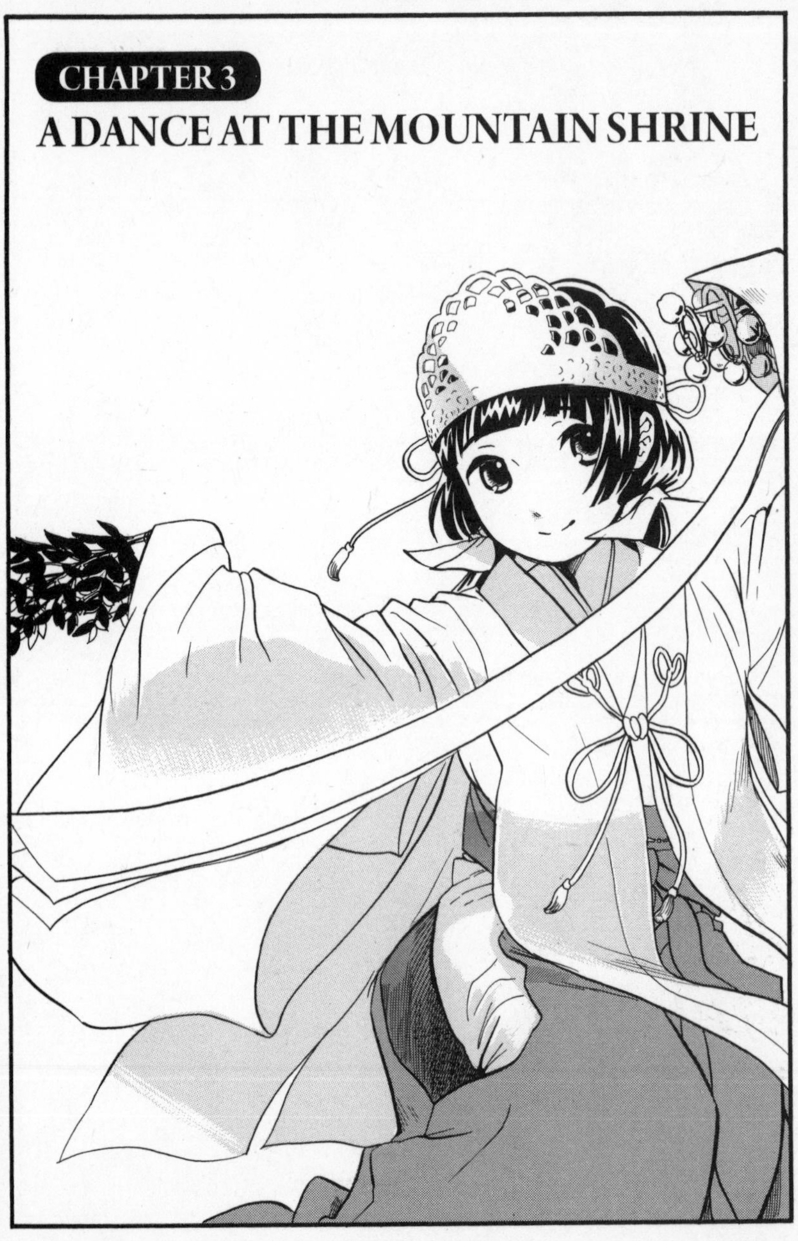

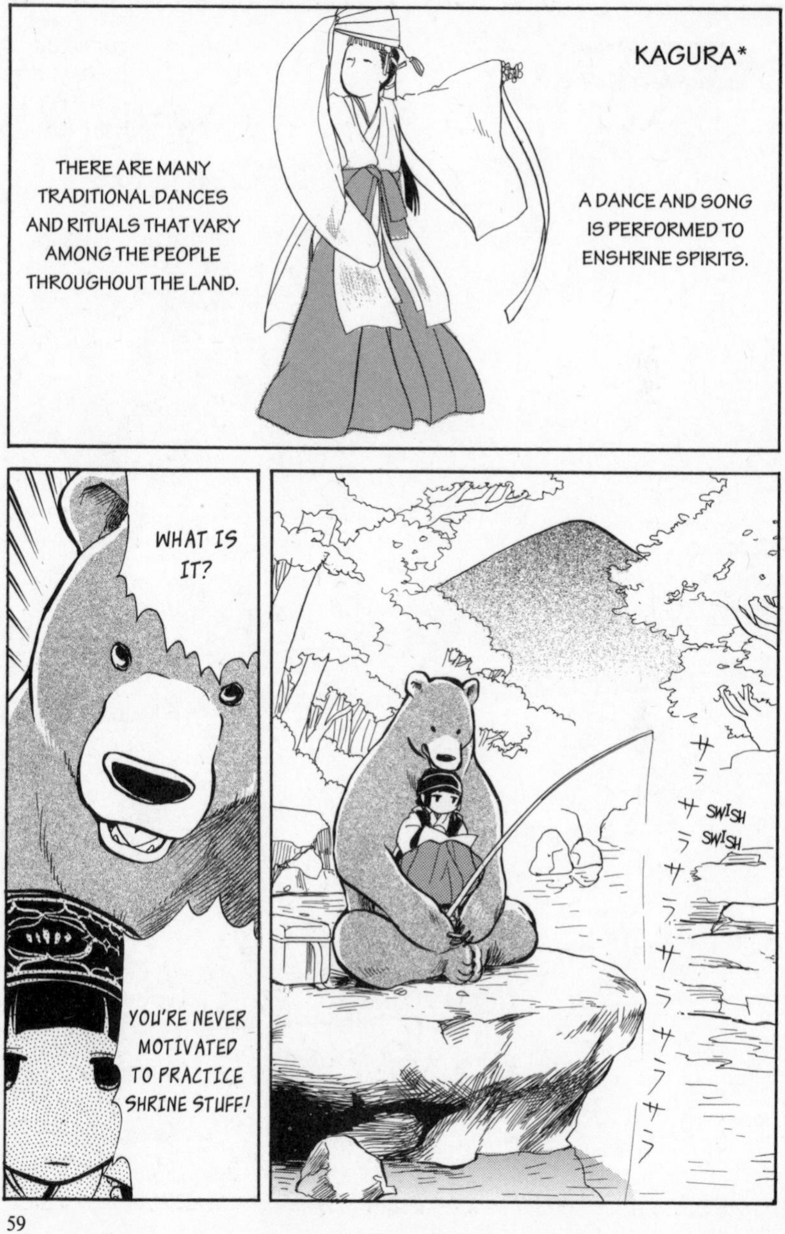
KAGURA*
A DANCE AND SONG IS PERFORMED TO ENSHRINE SPIRITS.
THERE ARE MANY TRADITIONAL DANCES AND RITUALS THAT VARY AMONG THE PEOPLE THROUGHOUT THE LAND.
サラサラサラサラサラサラ
SWISH SWISH
WHAT IS IT?
YOU'RE NEVER MOTIVATED TO PRACTICE SHRINE STUFF!

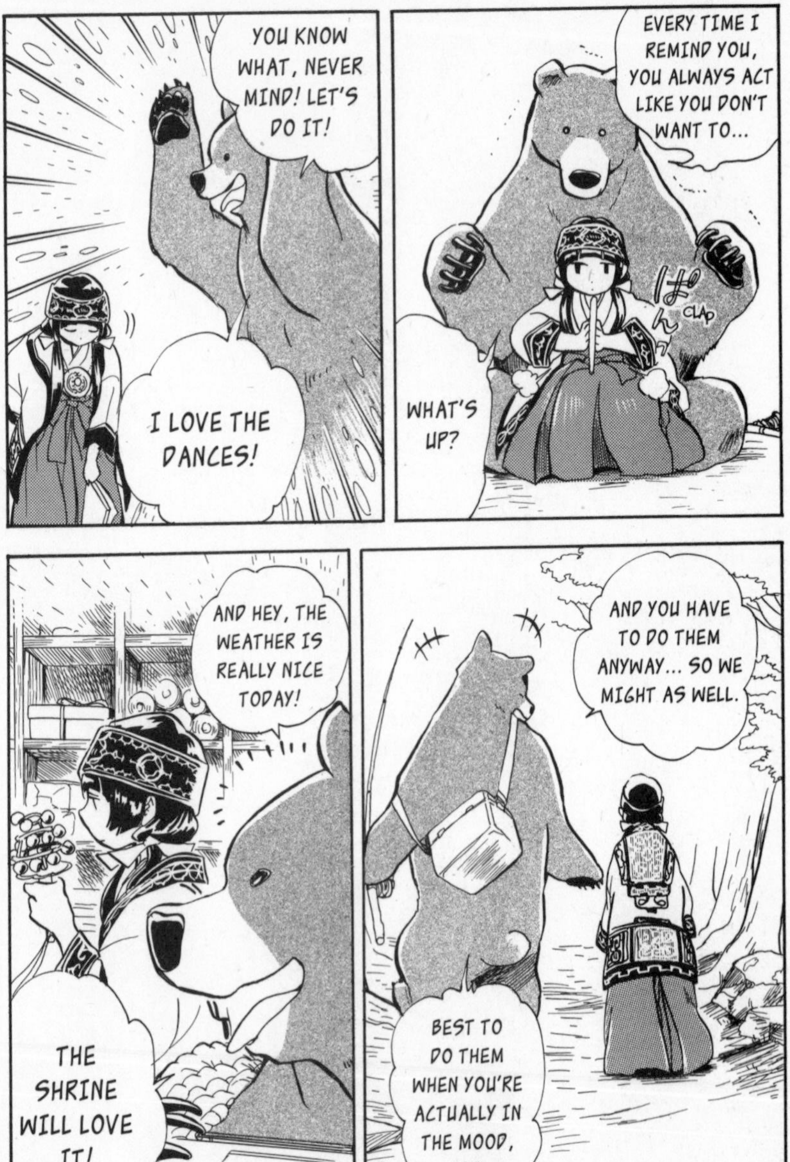
EVERY TIME I REMIND YOU, YOU ALWAYS ACT LIKE YOU DON'T WANT TO...
ぱんっ
CLAP
WHAT'S UP?
YOU KNOW WHAT, NEVER MIND! LET'S DO IT!
I LOVE THE DANCES!
AND YOU HAVE TO DO THEM ANYWAY... SO WE MIGHT AS WELL.
BEST TO DO THEM WHEN YOU'RE ACTUALLY IN THE MOOD, TOO.
AND HEY, THE WEATHER IS REALLY NICE TODAY!
THE SHRINE WILL LOVE IT!

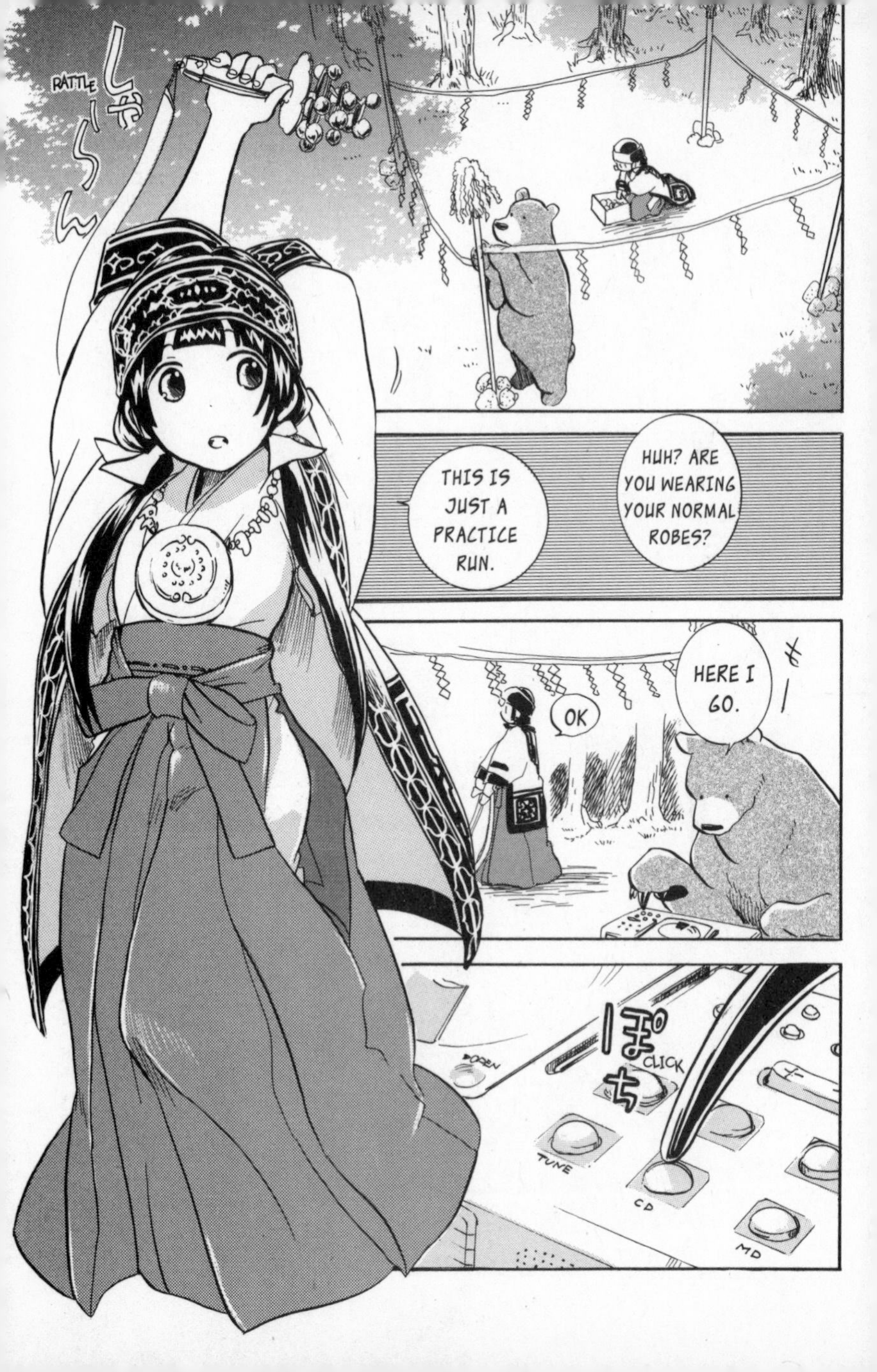
HUH? ARE YOU WEARING YOUR NORMAL ROBES?
THIS IS JUST A PRACTICE RUN.
HERE I GO.
OK
ぽち
CLICK
OPEN
TUNE
CD
MD
しゃらーん
RATTLE

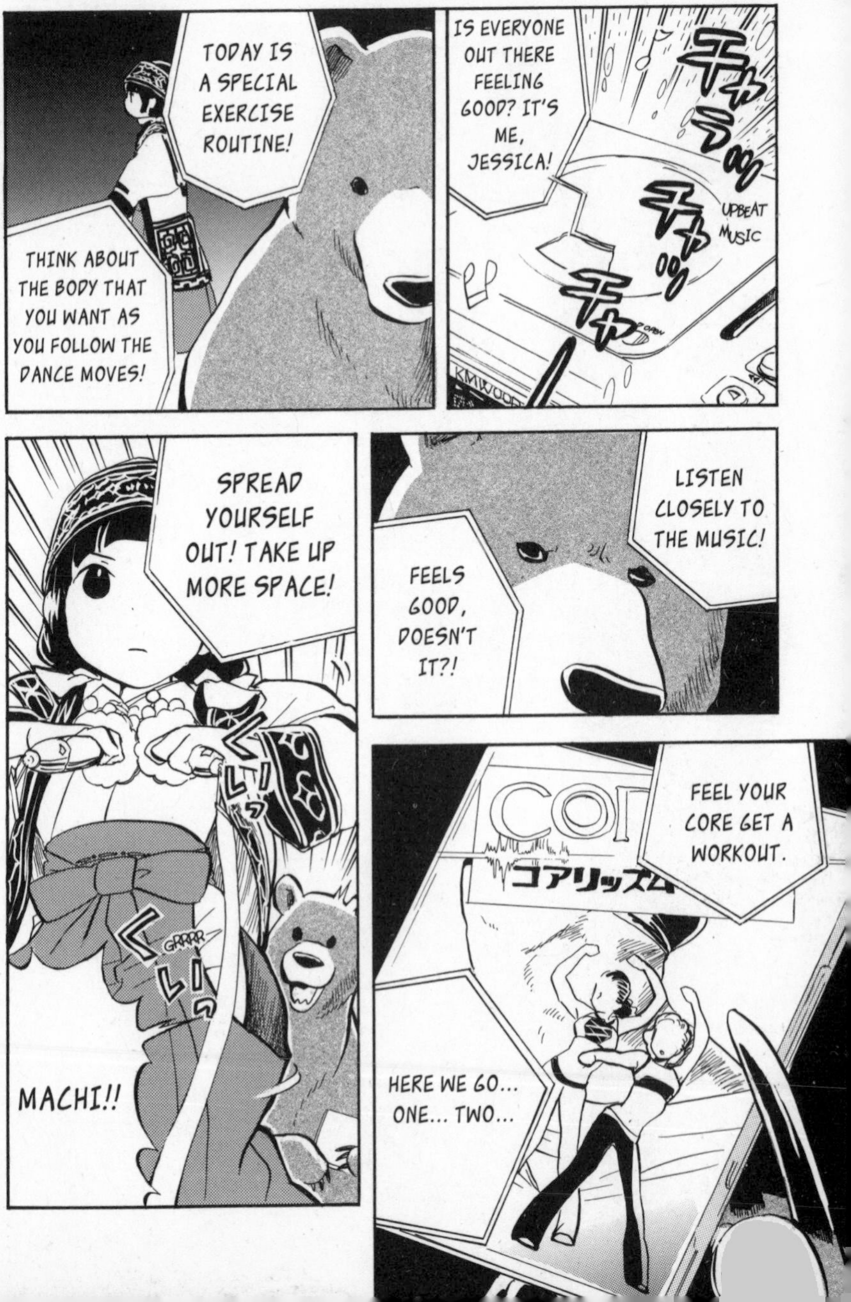
IS EVERYONE OUT THERE FEELING GOOD? IT'S ME, JESSICA!
UPBEAT MUSIC
TODAY IS A SPECIAL EXERCISE ROUTINE!
THINK ABOUT THE BODY THAT YOU WANT AS YOU FOLLOW THE DANCE MOVES!
LISTEN CLOSELY TO THE MUSIC!
FEELS GOOD, DOESN'T IT?!
FEEL YOUR CORE GET A WORKOUT.
コアリッズム
HERE WE GO... ONE... TWO...
SPREAD YOURSELF OUT! TAKE UP MORE SPACE!
GRRRR
MACHI!!

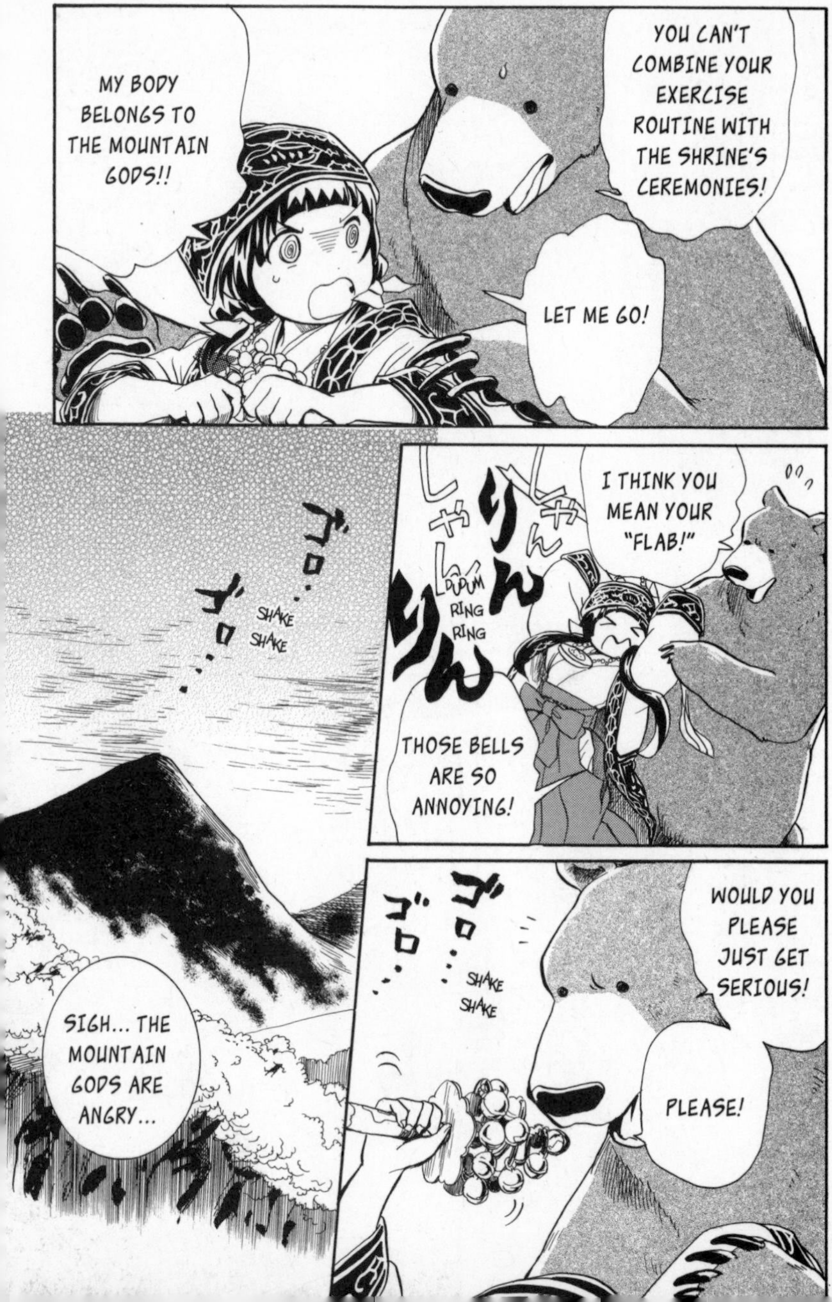
YOU CAN'T COMBINE YOUR EXERCISE ROUTINE WITH THE SHRINE'S CEREMONIES!
MY BODY BELONGS TO THE MOUNTAIN GODS!!
LET ME GO!
I THINK YOU MEAN YOUR "FLAB!"
DUDUM
RING RING
THOSE BELLS ARE SO ANNOYING!
WOULD YOU PLEASE JUST GET SERIOUS!
SHAKE SHAKE
PLEASE!
SHAKE SHAKE
SIGH... THE MOUNTAIN GODS ARE ANGRY...

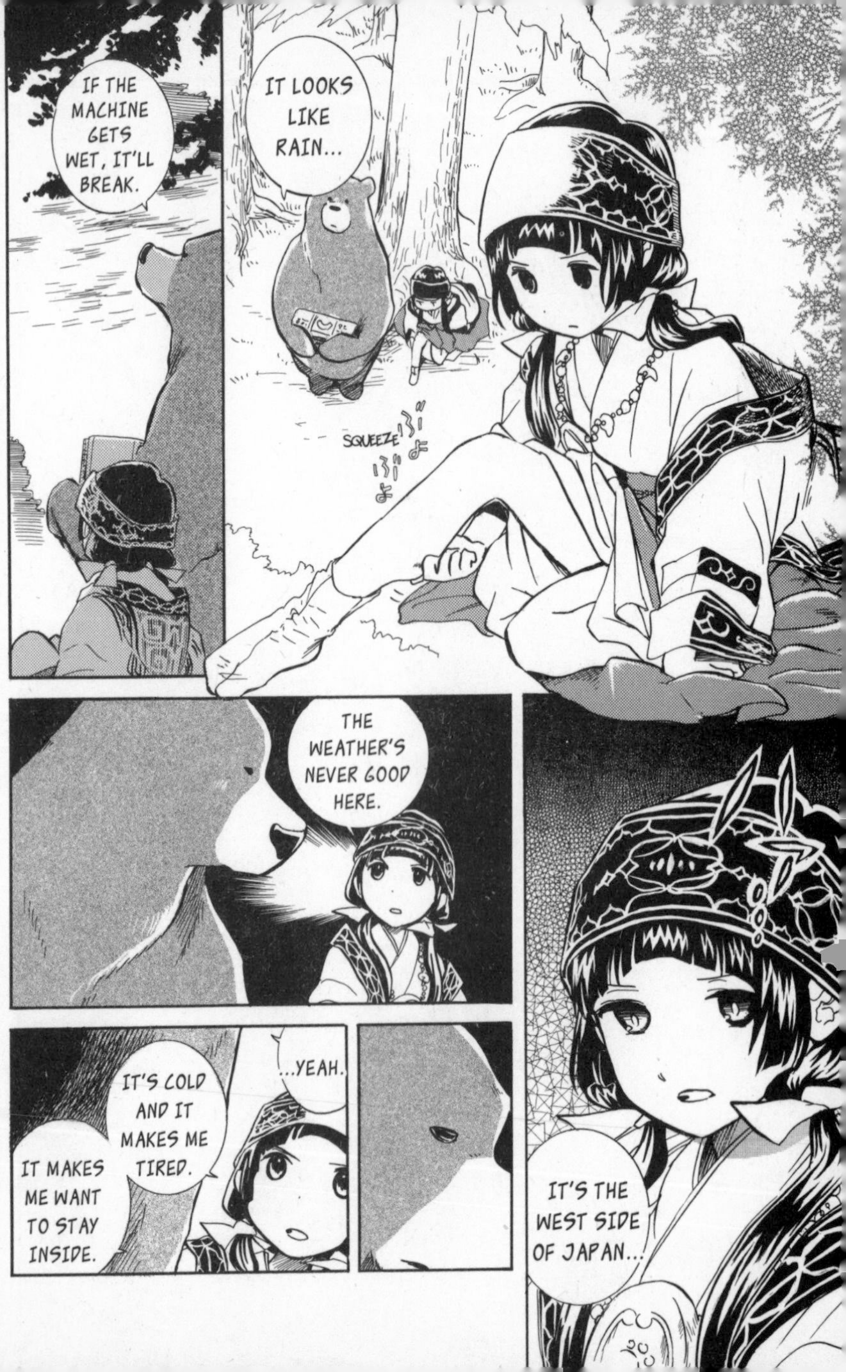
IT LOOKS LIKE RAIN...
SQUEEZE
IF THE MACHINE GETS WET, IT'LL BREAK.
IT'S THE WEST SIDE OF JAPAN...
THE WEATHER'S NEVER GOOD HERE.
...YEAH.
IT'S COLD AND IT MAKES ME TIRED.
IT MAKES ME WANT TO STAY INSIDE.

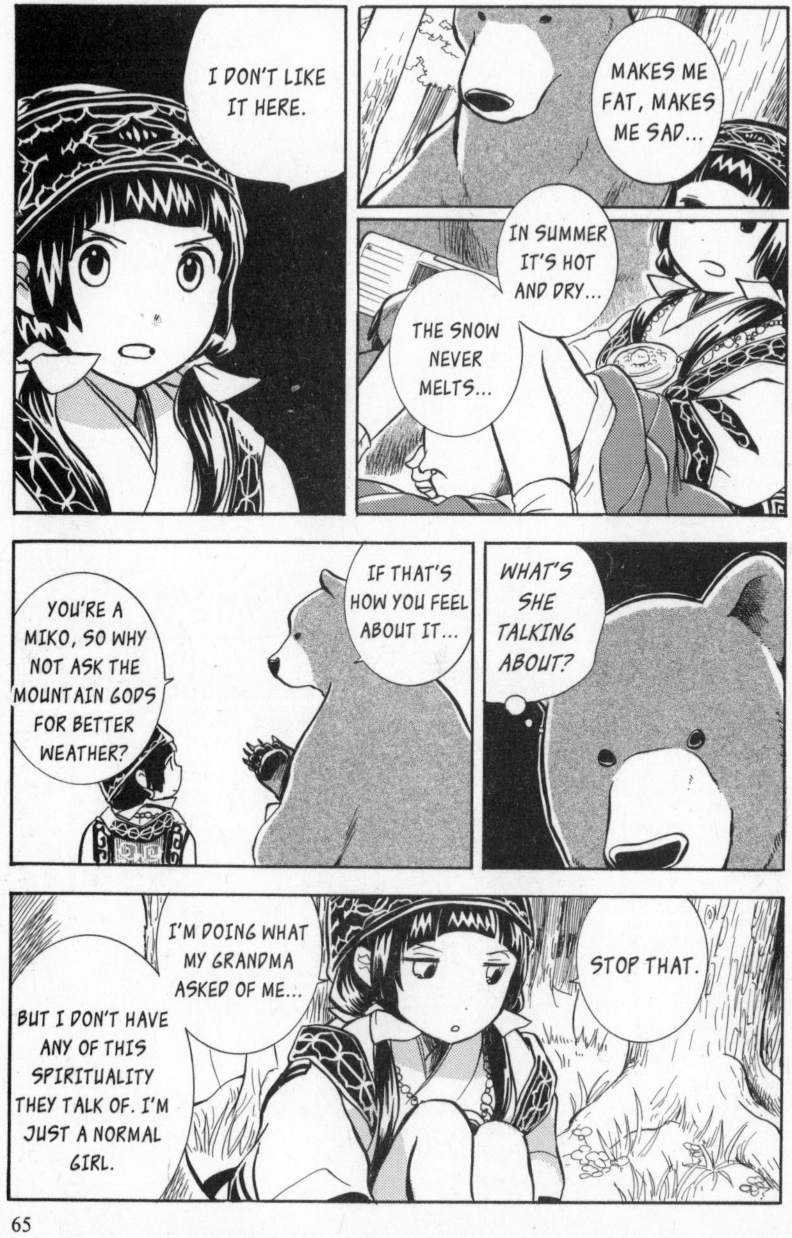
MAKES ME FAT, MAKES ME SAD...
IN SUMMER IT'S HOT AND DRY...
THE SNOW NEVER MELTS...
I DON'T LIKE IT HERE.
WHAT'S SHE TALKING ABOUT?
IF THAT'S HOW YOU FEEL ABOUT IT...
YOU'RE A MIKO, SO WHY NOT ASK THE MOUNTAIN GODS FOR BETTER WEATHER?
STOP THAT.
I'M DOING WHAT MY GRANDMA ASKED OF ME...
BUT I DON'T HAVE ANY OF THIS SPIRITUALITY THEY TALK OF. I'M JUST A NORMAL GIRL.

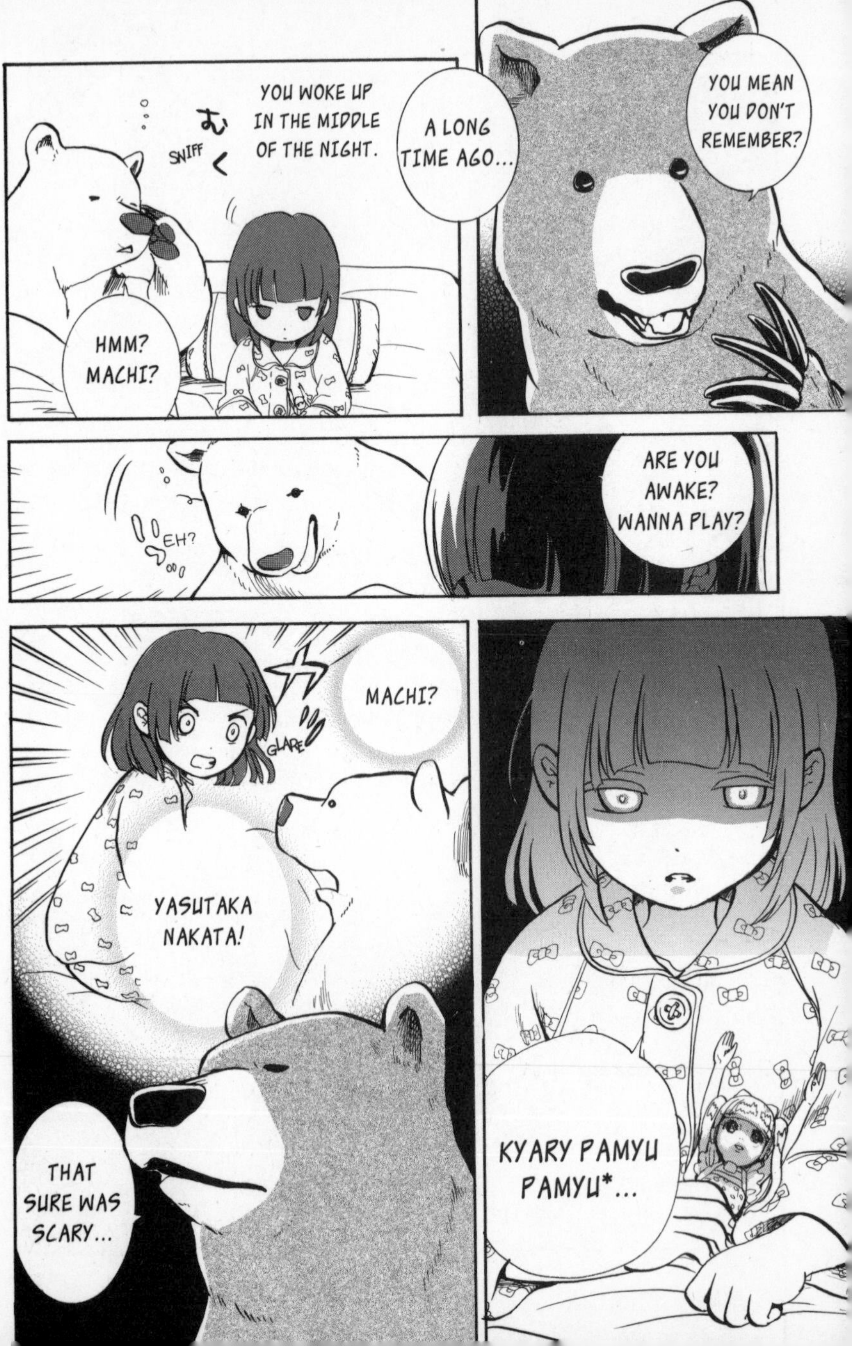
YOU MEAN YOU DON'T REMEMBER?
A LONG TIME AGO...
YOU WOKE UP IN THE MIDDLE OF THE NIGHT.
SNIFF
HMM? MACHI?
ARE YOU AWAKE? WANNA PLAY?
EH?
KYARY PAMYU PAMYU*...
MACHI?
GLARE
YASUTAKA NAKATA!
THAT SURE WAS SCARY...

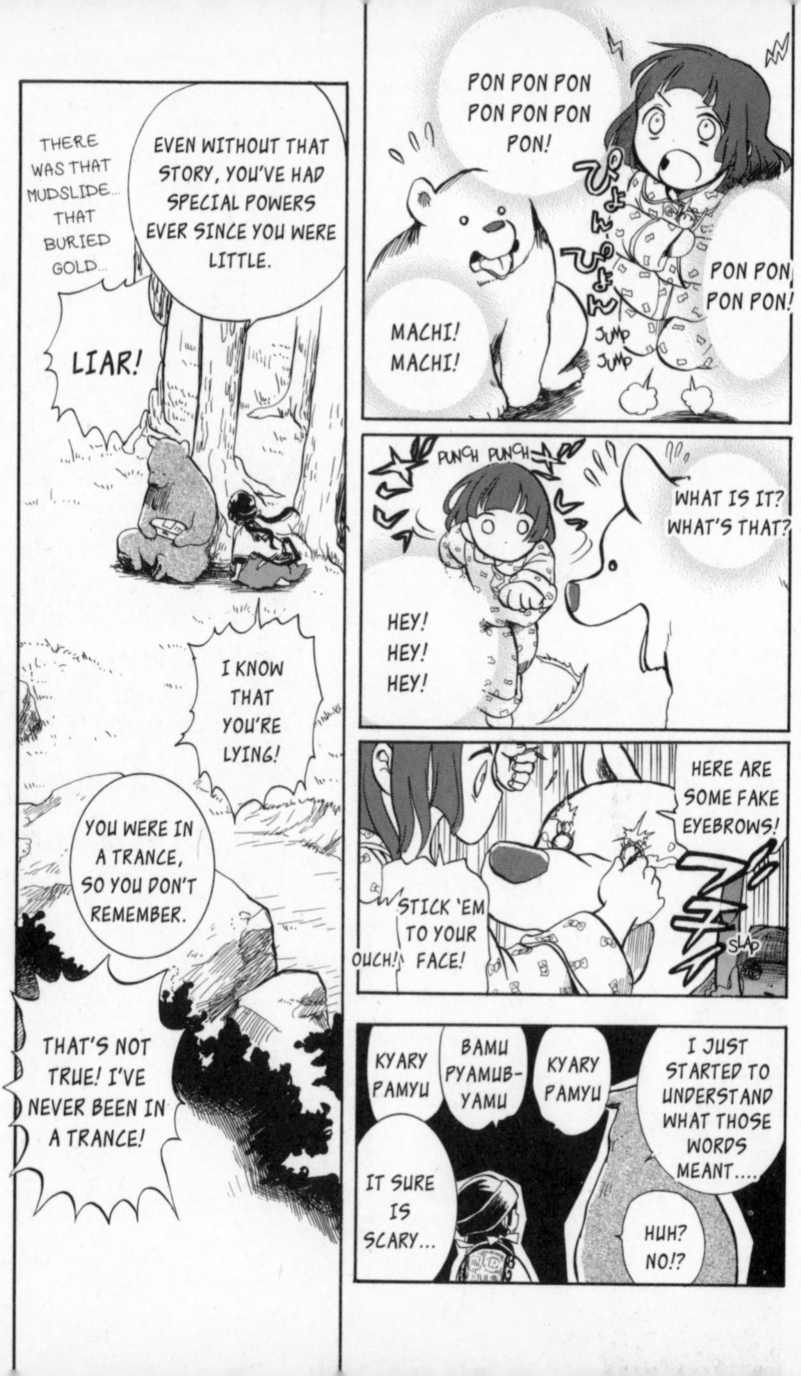
PON PON PON PON PON PON PON!
ぴょんぴょん
PON PON, PON PON!
JUMP JUMP
MACHI! MACHI!
WHAT IS IT? WHAT'S THAT?
PUNCH PUNCH
HEY! HEY! HEY!
HERE ARE SOME FAKE EYEBROWS!
SLAP
STICK 'EM TO YOUR FACE!
OUCH!
I JUST STARTED TO UNDERSTAND WHAT THOSE WORDS MEANT....
KYARY PAMYU
BAMU PYAMUB-YAMU
KYARY PAMYU
HUH? NO!?
IT SURE IS SCARY...
EVEN WITHOUT THAT STORY, YOU'VE HAD SPECIAL POWERS EVER SINCE YOU WERE LITTLE.
THERE WAS THAT MUDSLIDE... THAT BURIED GOLD...
LIAR!
I KNOW THAT YOU'RE LYING!
YOU WERE IN A TRANCE, SO YOU DON'T REMEMBER.
THAT'S NOT TRUE! I'VE NEVER BEEN IN A TRANCE!

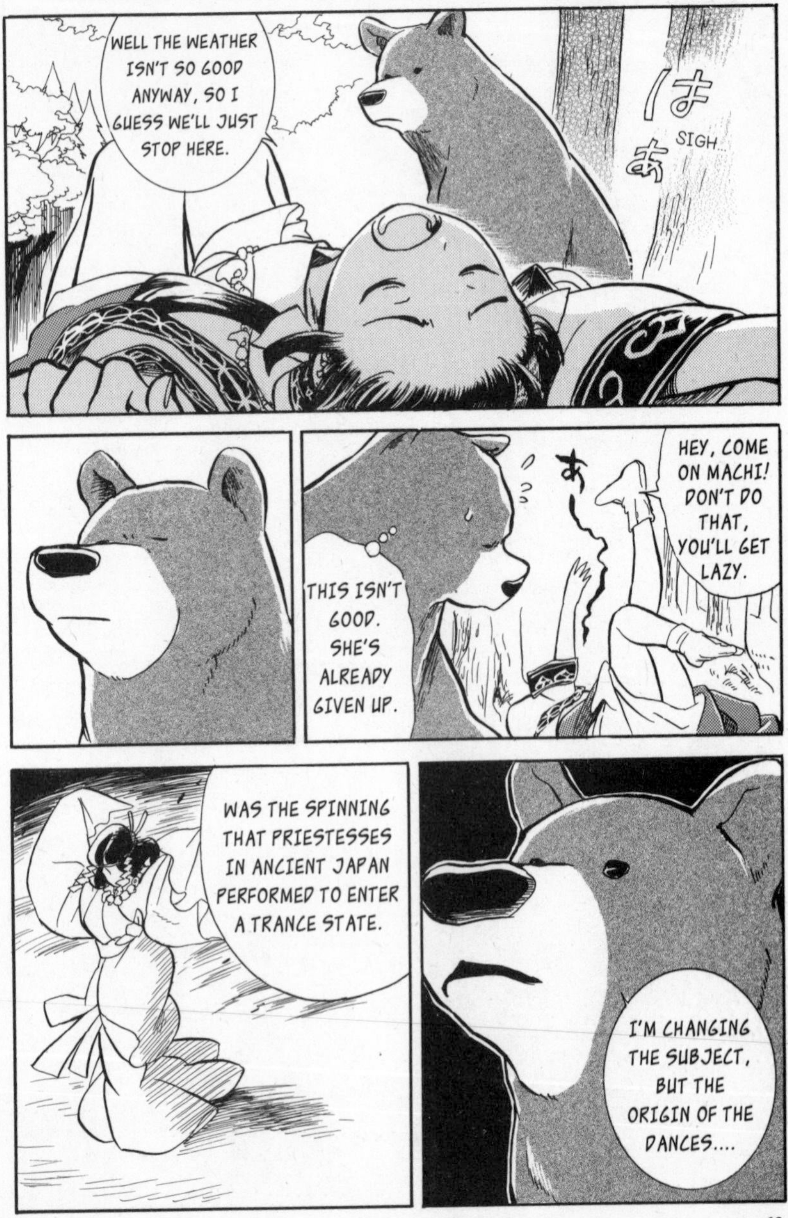
はあ
SIGH...
WELL THE WEATHER ISN'T SO GOOD ANYWAY, SO I GUESS WE'LL JUST STOP HERE.
HEY, COME ON MACHI! DON'T DO THAT, YOU'LL GET LAZY.
あ
THIS ISN'T GOOD. SHE'S ALREADY GIVEN UP.
I'M CHANGING THE SUBJECT, BUT THE ORIGIN OF THE DANCES....
WAS THE SPINNING THAT PRIESTESSES IN ANCIENT JAPAN PERFORMED TO ENTER A TRANCE STATE.

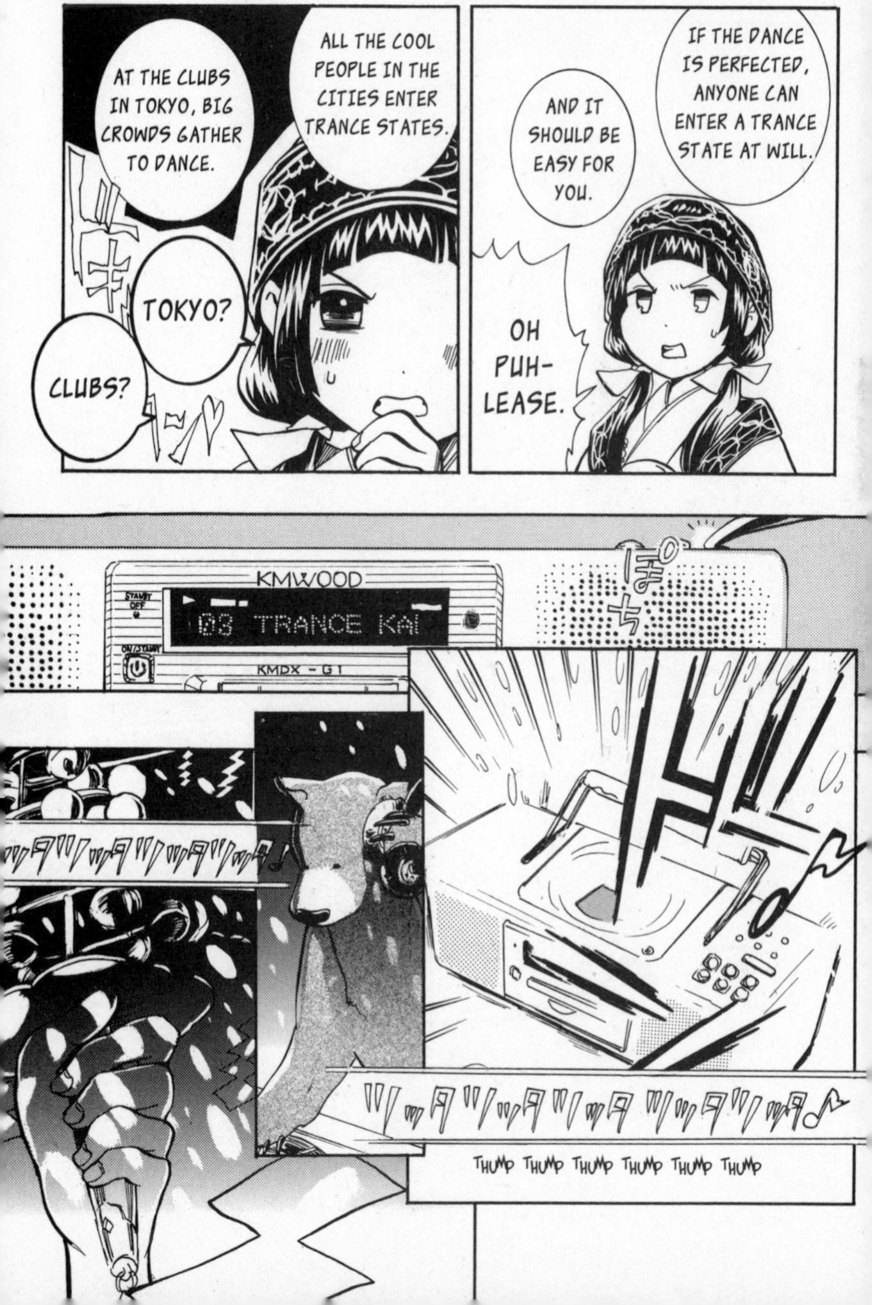
IF THE DANCE IS PERFECTED, ANYONE CAN ENTER A TRANCE STATE AT WILL.
AND IT SHOULD BE EASY FOR YOU.
OH PUH-LEASE.
ALL THE COOL PEOPLE IN THE CITIES ENTER TRANCE STATES.
AT THE CLUBS IN TOKYO, BIG CROWDS GATHER TO DANCE.
TOKYO?
CLUBS?
ぽち
KMWOOD
03 TRANCE KAI
KMDX - G1
THUMP THUMP THUMP THUMP THUMP THUMP

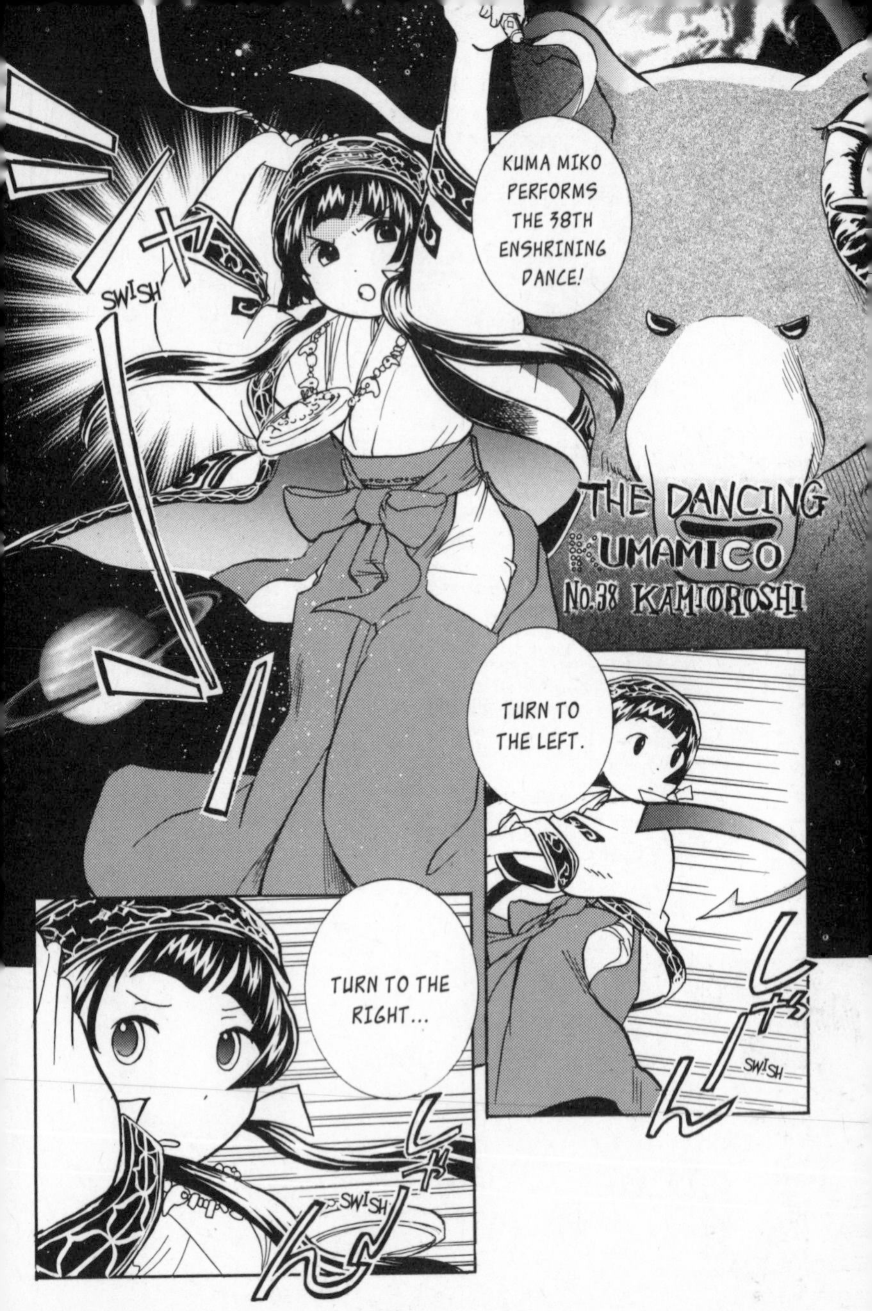
KUMA MIKO PERFORMS THE 38TH ENSHRINING DANCE!
SWISH
THE DANCING KUMAMICO
No.38 KAMIOROSHI
TURN TO THE LEFT.
SWISH
TURN TO THE RIGHT...
SWISH

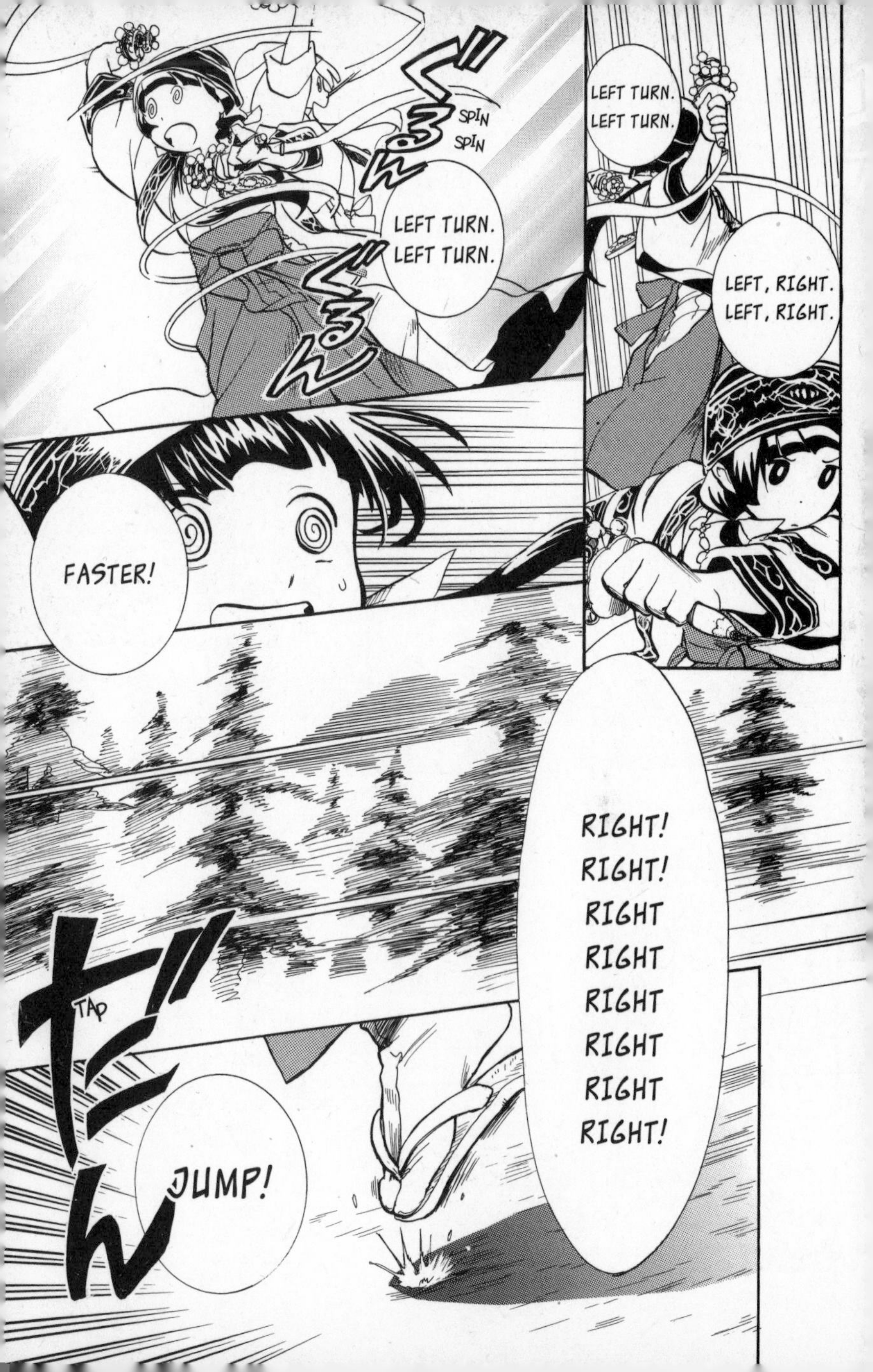
LEFT TURN. LEFT TURN.
LEFT, RIGHT. LEFT, RIGHT.
ぐるん
SPIN SPIN
LEFT TURN. LEFT TURN.
ぐるん
FASTER!
RIGHT! RIGHT! RIGHT RIGHT RIGHT RIGHT RIGHT RIGHT!
TAP
JUMP!

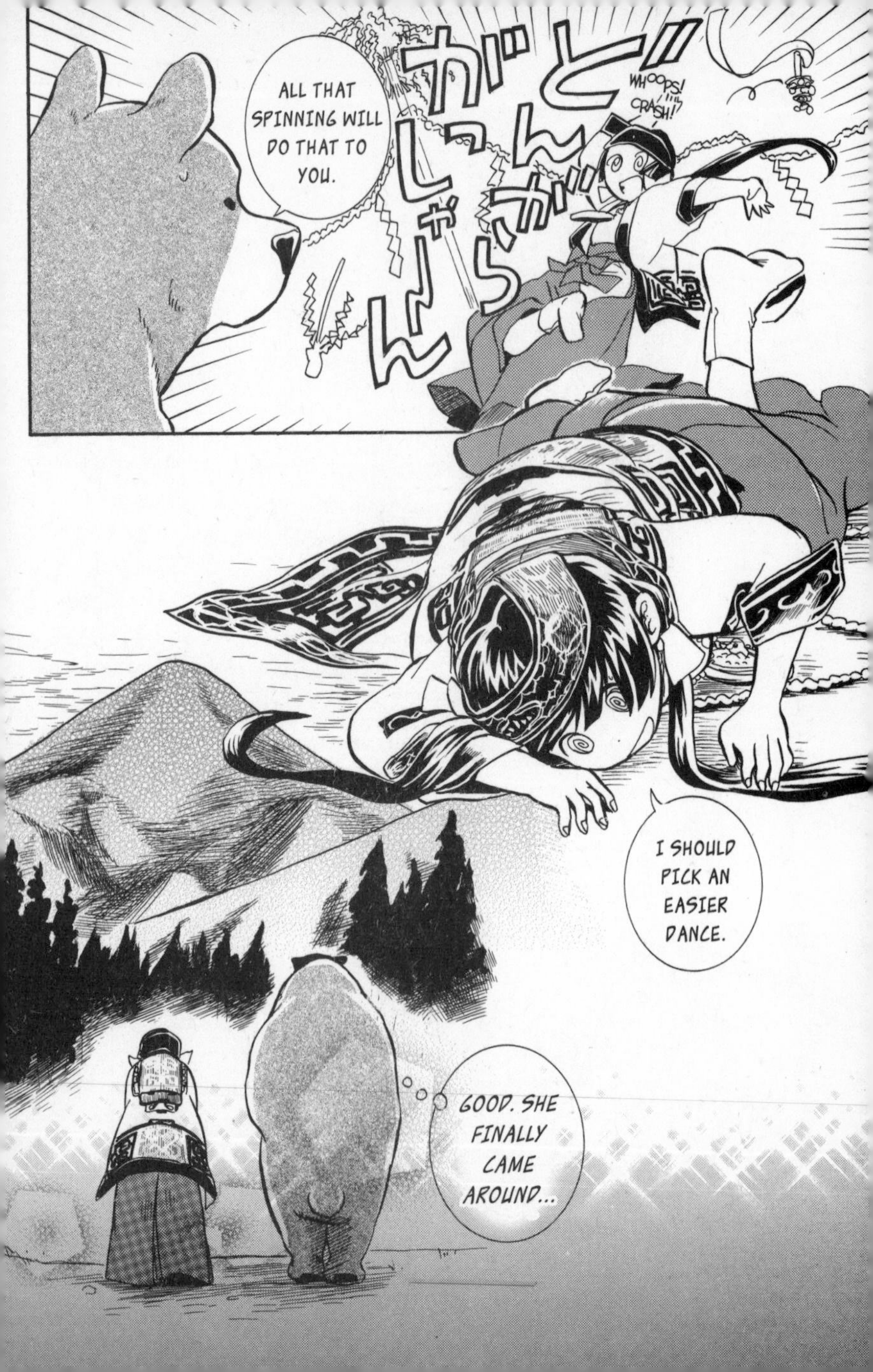
WHOOPS!
CRASH!
どんがら
がっしゃん
ALL THAT SPINNING WILL DO THAT TO YOU.
I SHOULD PICK AN EASIER DANCE.
GOOD. SHE FINALLY CAME AROUND...

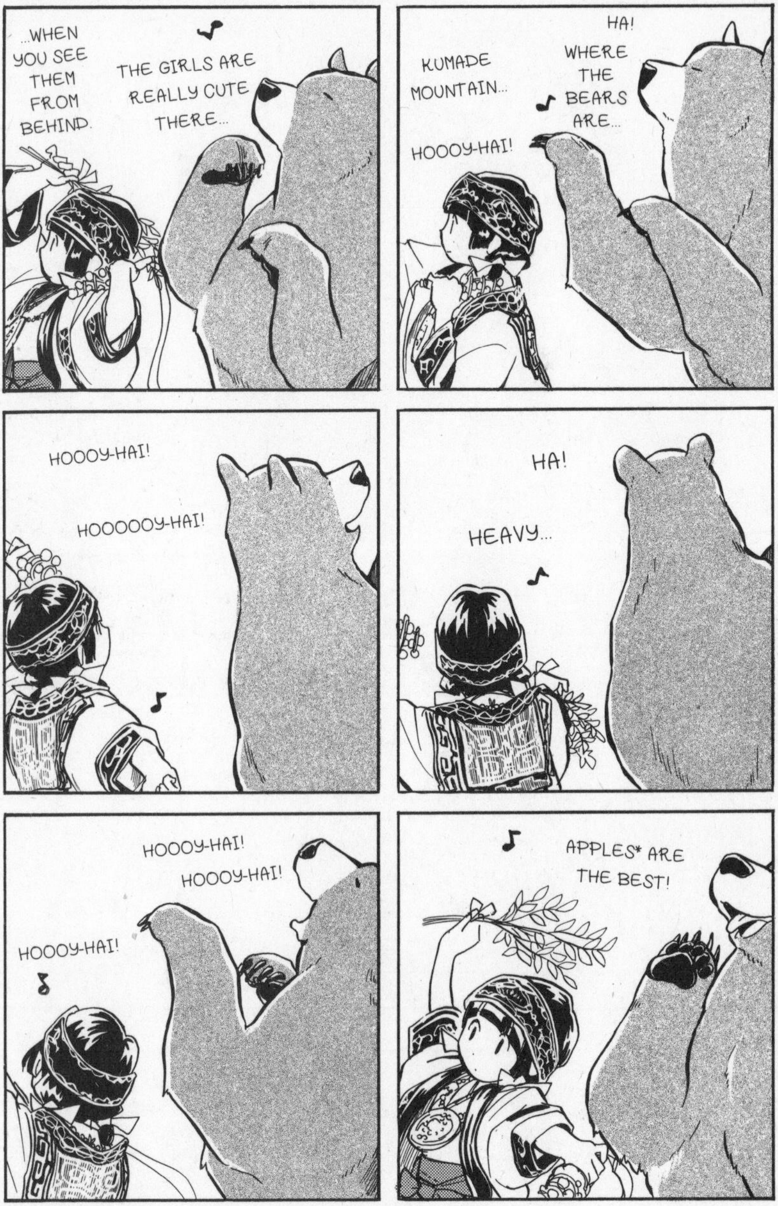
HA!
WHERE THE BEARS ARE...
KUMADE MOUNTAIN...
HOOOY-HAI!
THE GIRLS ARE REALLY CUTE THERE...
...WHEN YOU SEE THEM FROM BEHIND.
HA!
HEAVY...
HOOOY-HAI!
HOOOOOY-HAI!
APPLES* ARE THE BEST!
HOOOY-HAI!
HOOOY-HAI!
HOOOY-HAI!

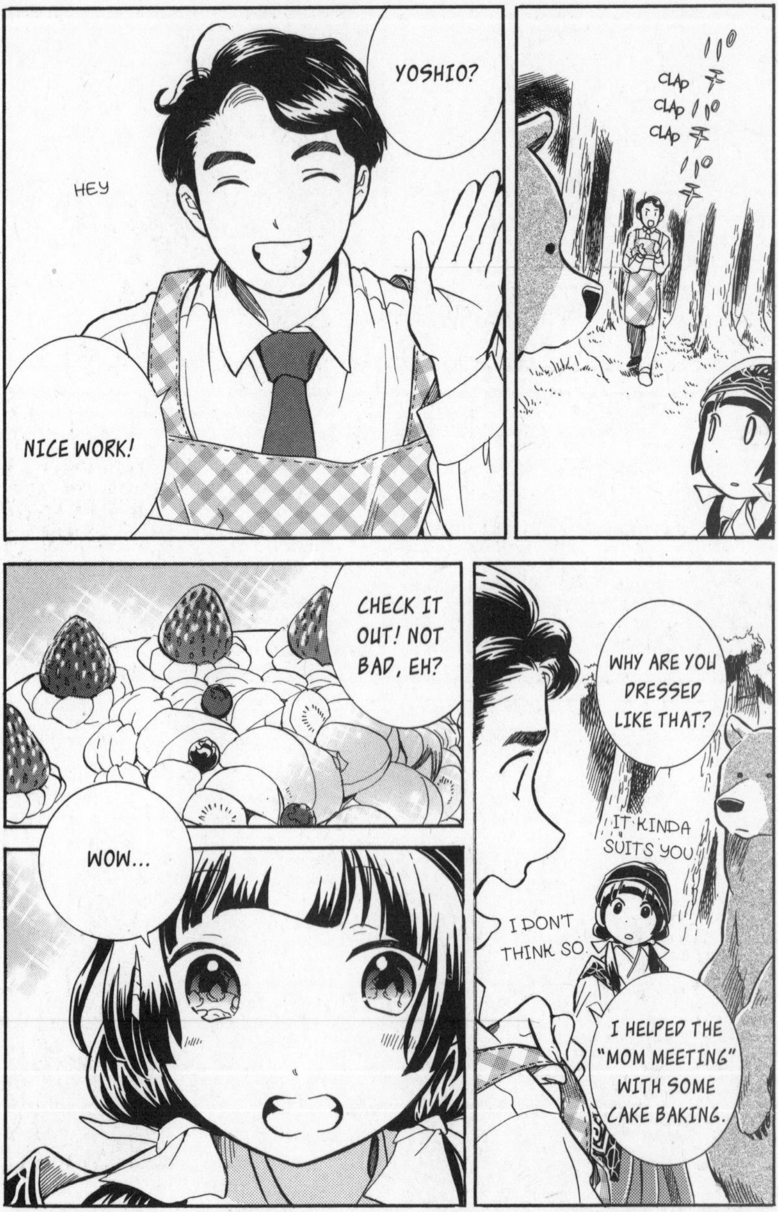
CLAP
CLAP
CLAP
YOSHIO?
HEY
NICE WORK!
WHY ARE YOU DRESSED LIKE THAT?
IT KINDA SUITS YOU
I DON'T THINK SO.
I HELPED THE "MOM MEETING" WITH SOME CAKE BAKING.
CHECK IT OUT! NOT BAD, EH?
WOW...

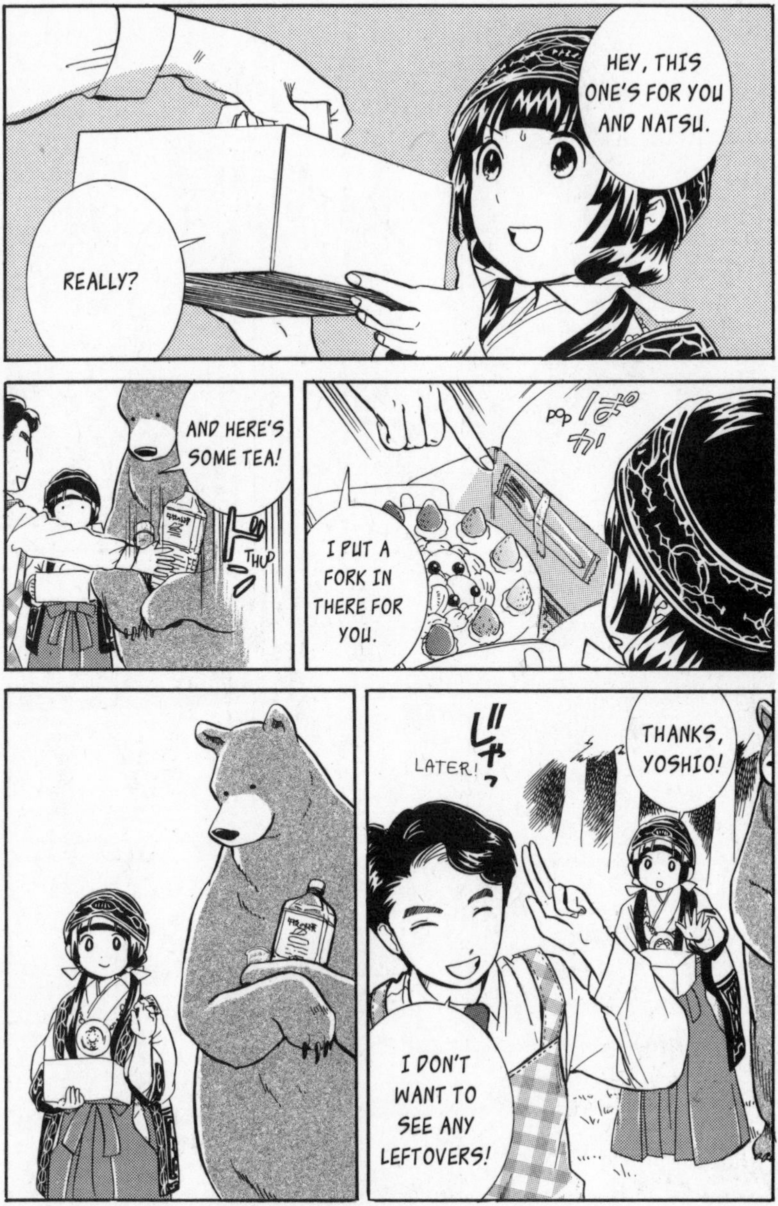
HEY, THIS ONE'S FOR YOU AND NATSU.
REALLY?
POP
ぱか
I PUT A FORK IN THERE FOR YOU.
AND HERE'S SOME TEA!
THUD
THANKS, YOSHIO!
じゃっ
LATER!
I DON'T WANT TO SEE ANY LEFTOVERS!

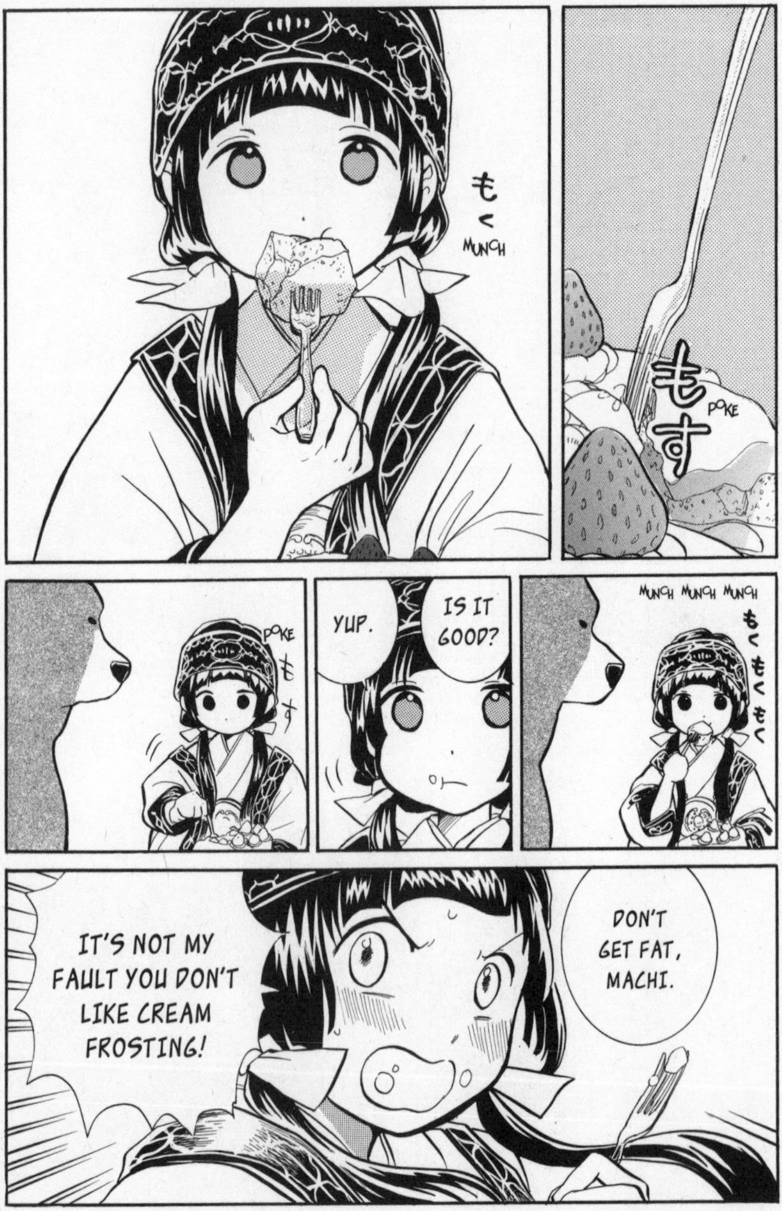
もす
POKE
もく
MUNCH
MUNCH MUNCH MUNCH
もくもくもく
IS IT GOOD?
YUP.
POKE
もす
DON'T GET FAT, MACHI.
IT'S NOT MY FAULT YOU DON'T LIKE CREAM FROSTING!

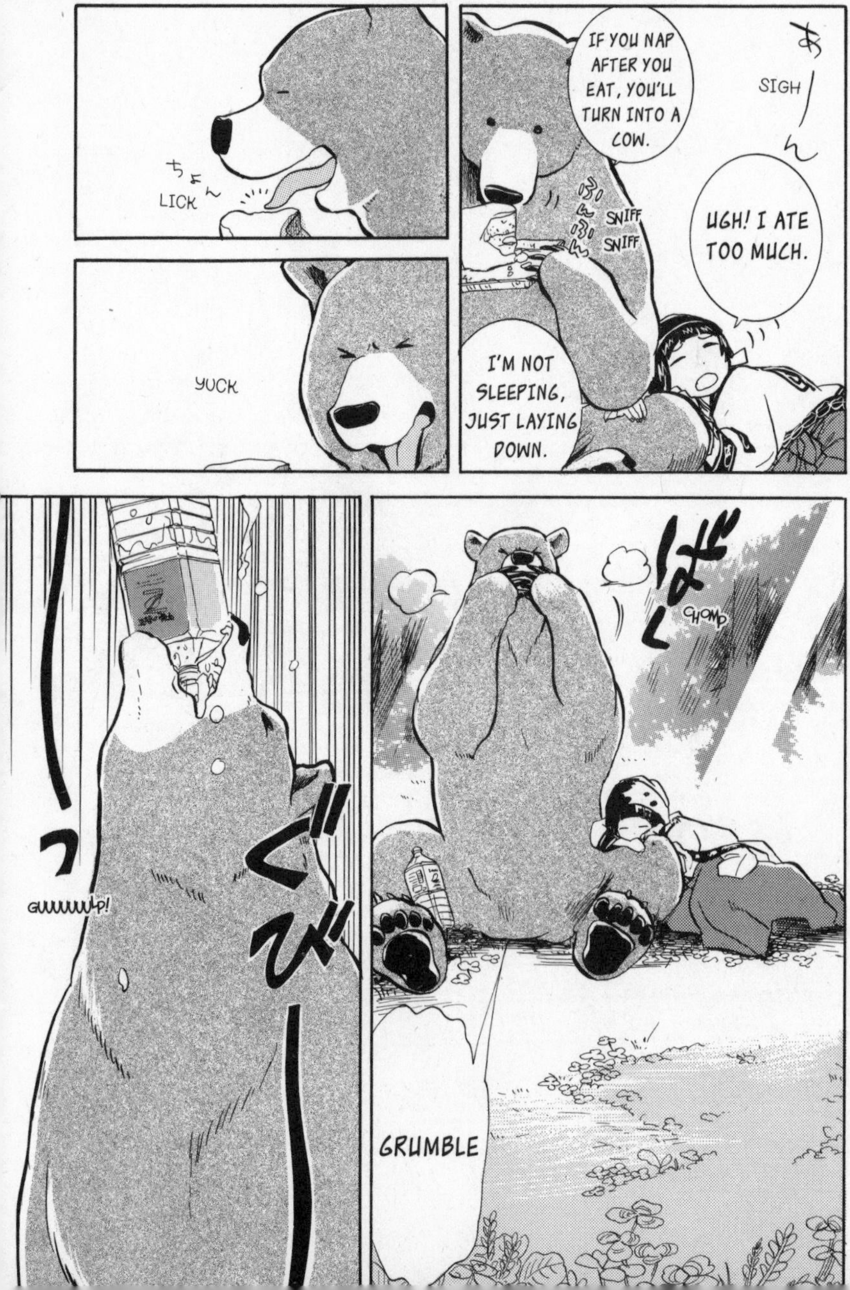

あーん
SIGH
UGH! I ATE TOO MUCH.
IF YOU NAP AFTER YOU EAT, YOU'LL TURN INTO A COW.
ふんふん
SNIFF SNIFF
I'M NOT SLEEPING, JUST LAYING DOWN.
ちょん
LICK
YUCK
ぱく
CHOMP
GRUMBLE
ぐびっ
GUUUUULP!

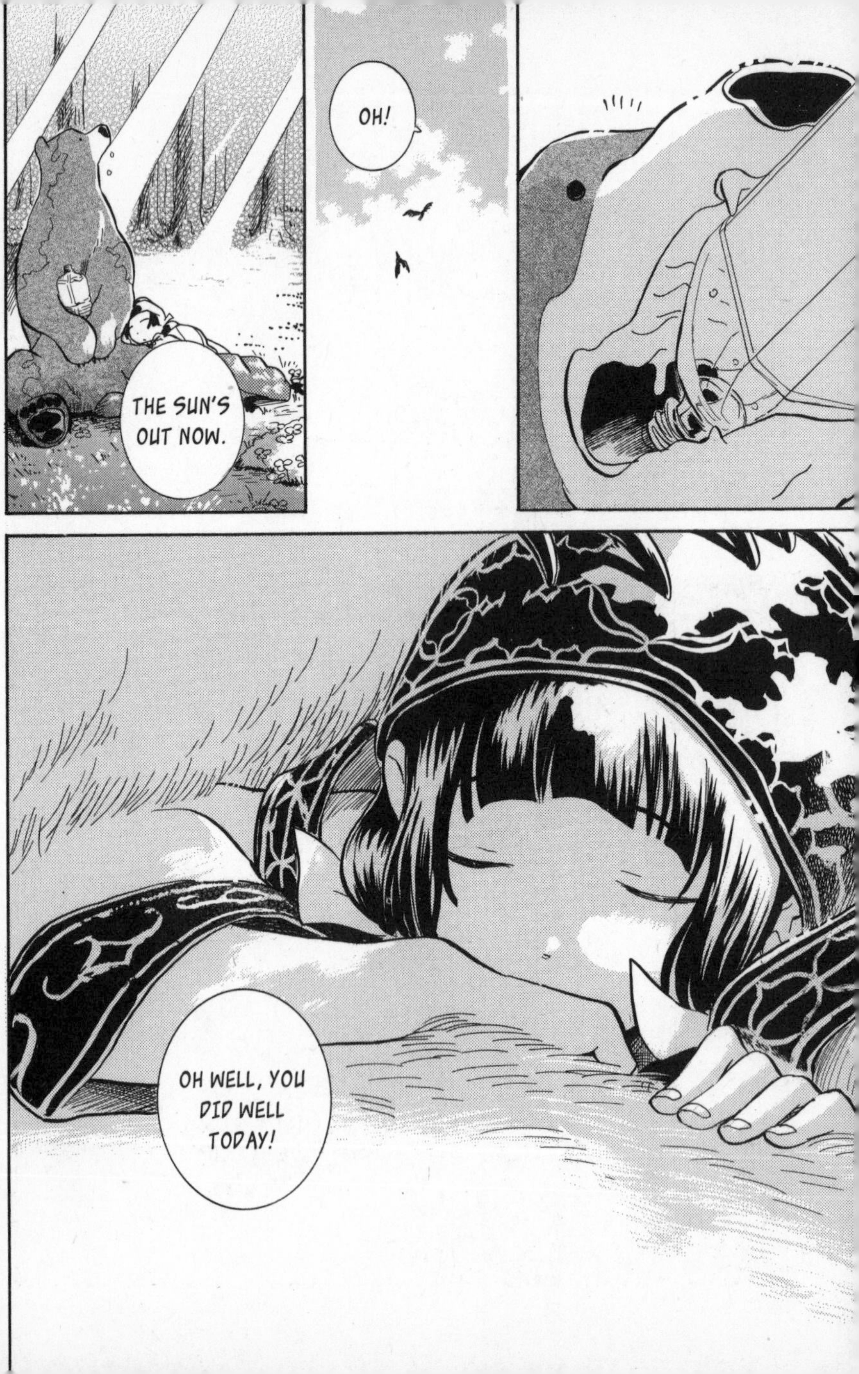
OH!
THE SUN'S OUT NOW.
OH WELL, YOU DID WELL TODAY!

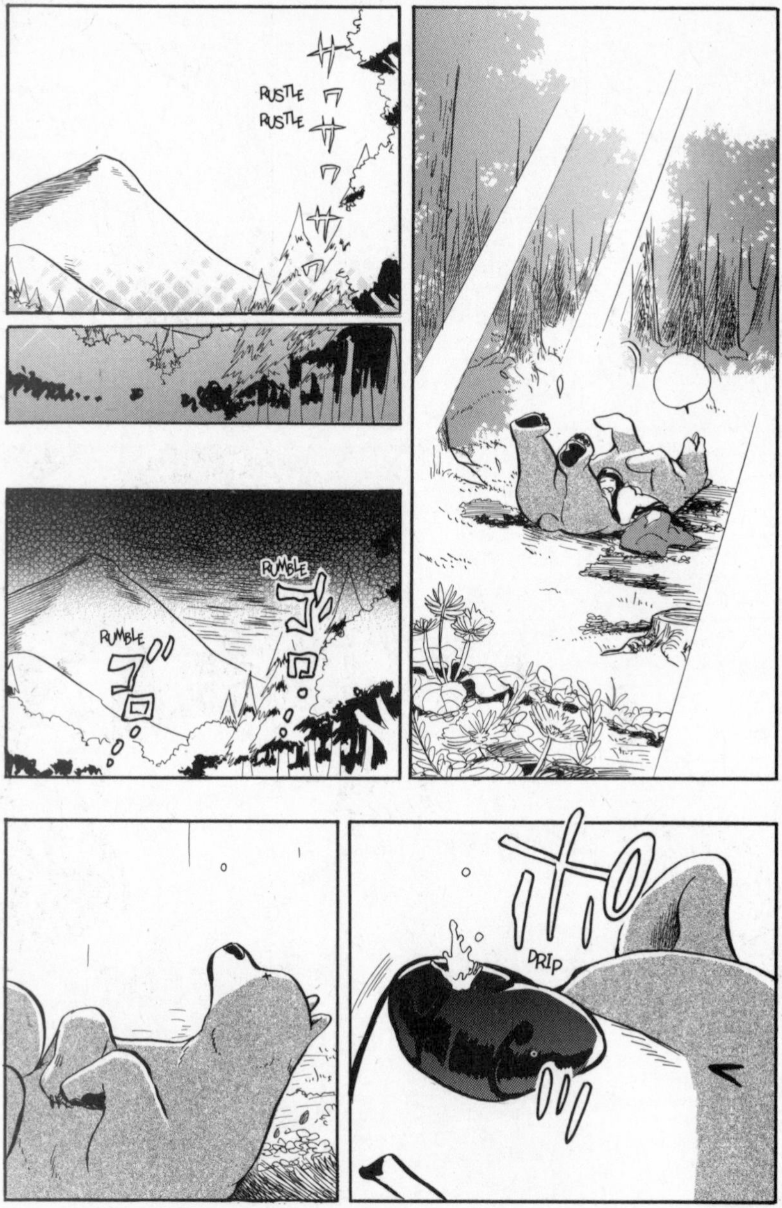
RUSTLE
RUSTLE
ザワザワザワ
RUMBLE
ゴロ
RUMBLE
ゴロ
DRIP

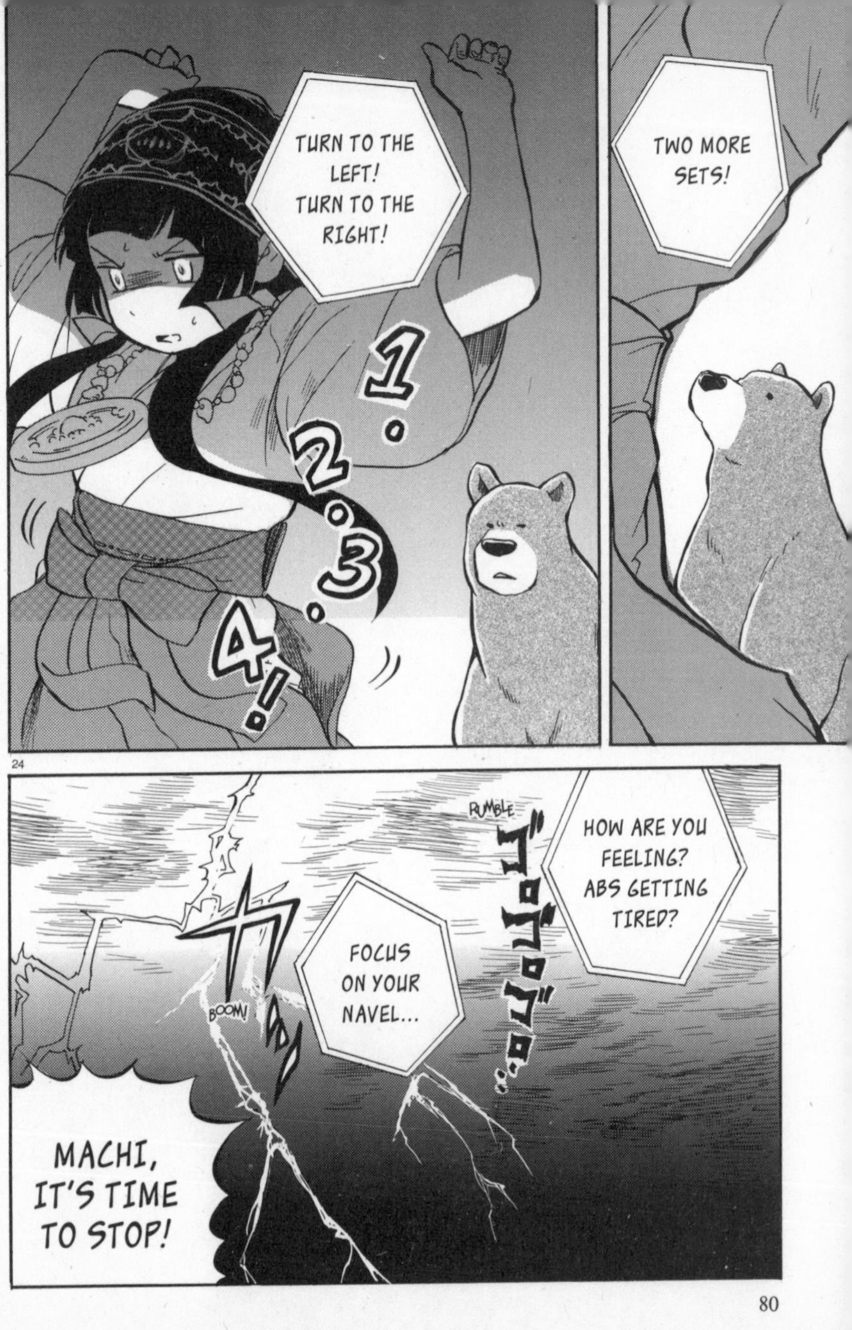
TWO MORE SETS!
TURN TO THE LEFT! TURN TO THE RIGHT!
1. 2. 3. 4!
24
RUMBLE
HOW ARE YOU FEELING? ABS GETTING TIRED?
FOCUS ON YOUR NAVEL...
BOOM!
MACHI, IT'S TIME TO STOP!

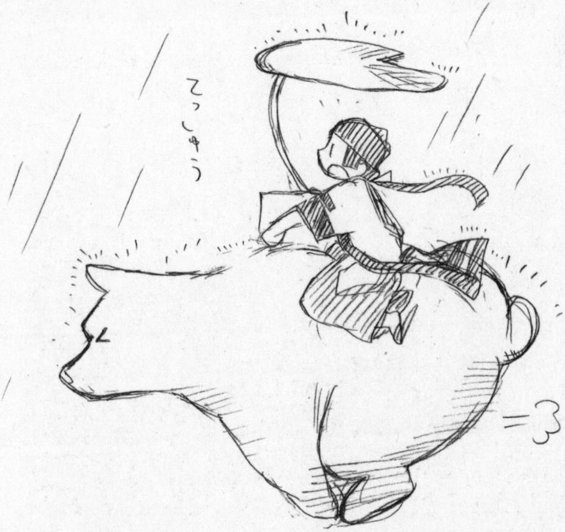
てっしゅう

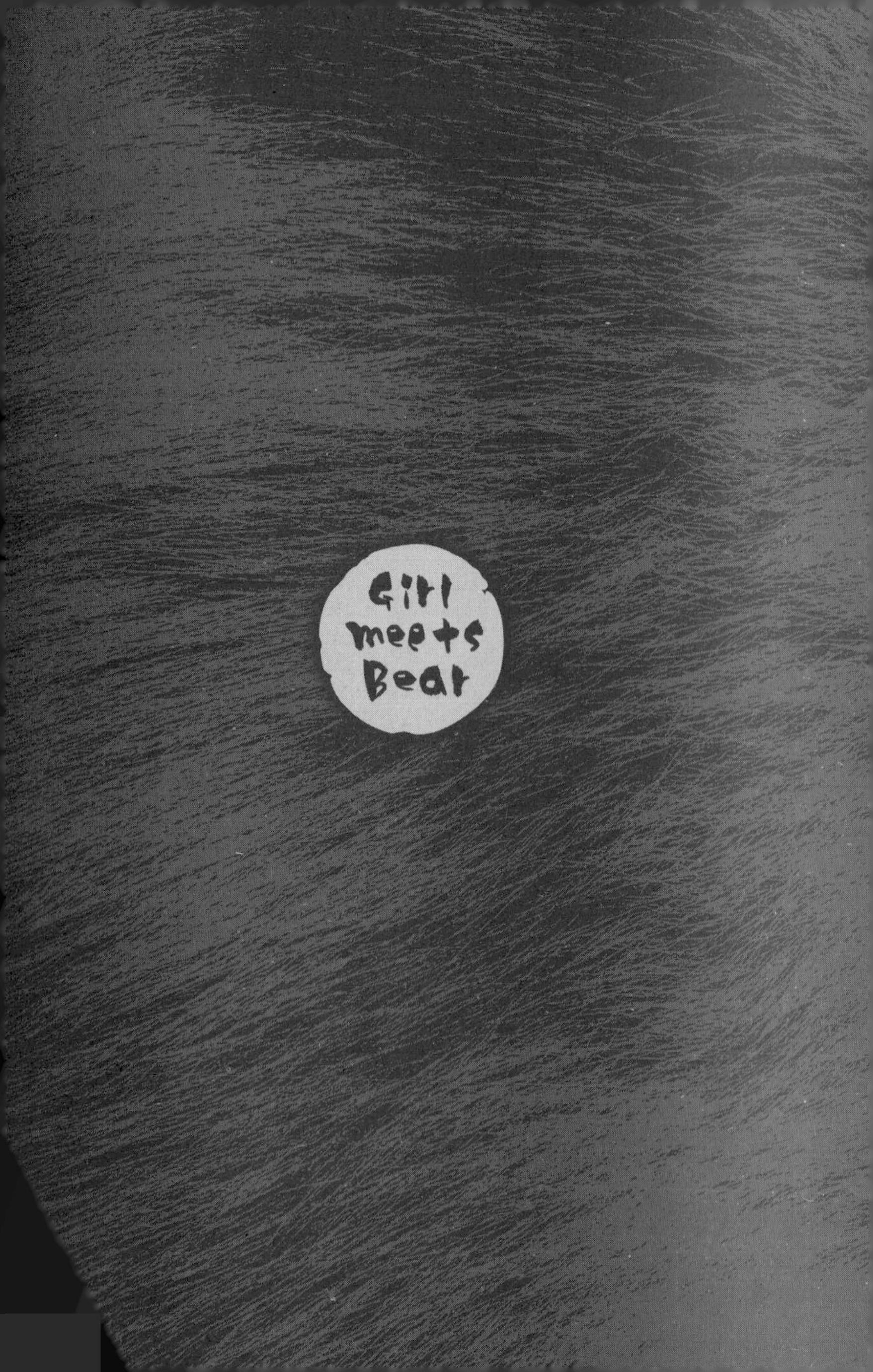
Girl meets Bear

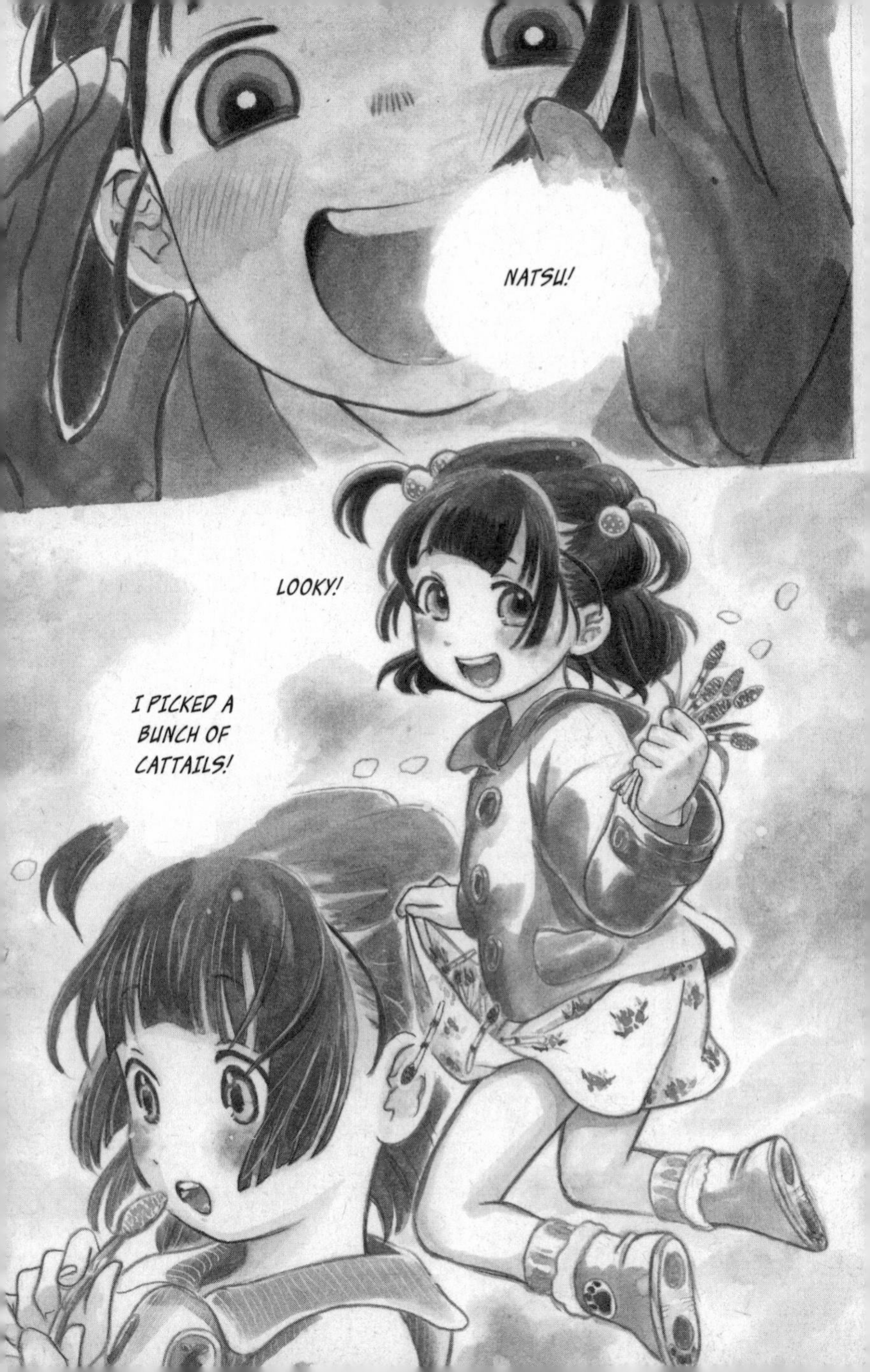
NATSU!
LOOKY!
I PICKED A BUNCH OF CATTAILS!

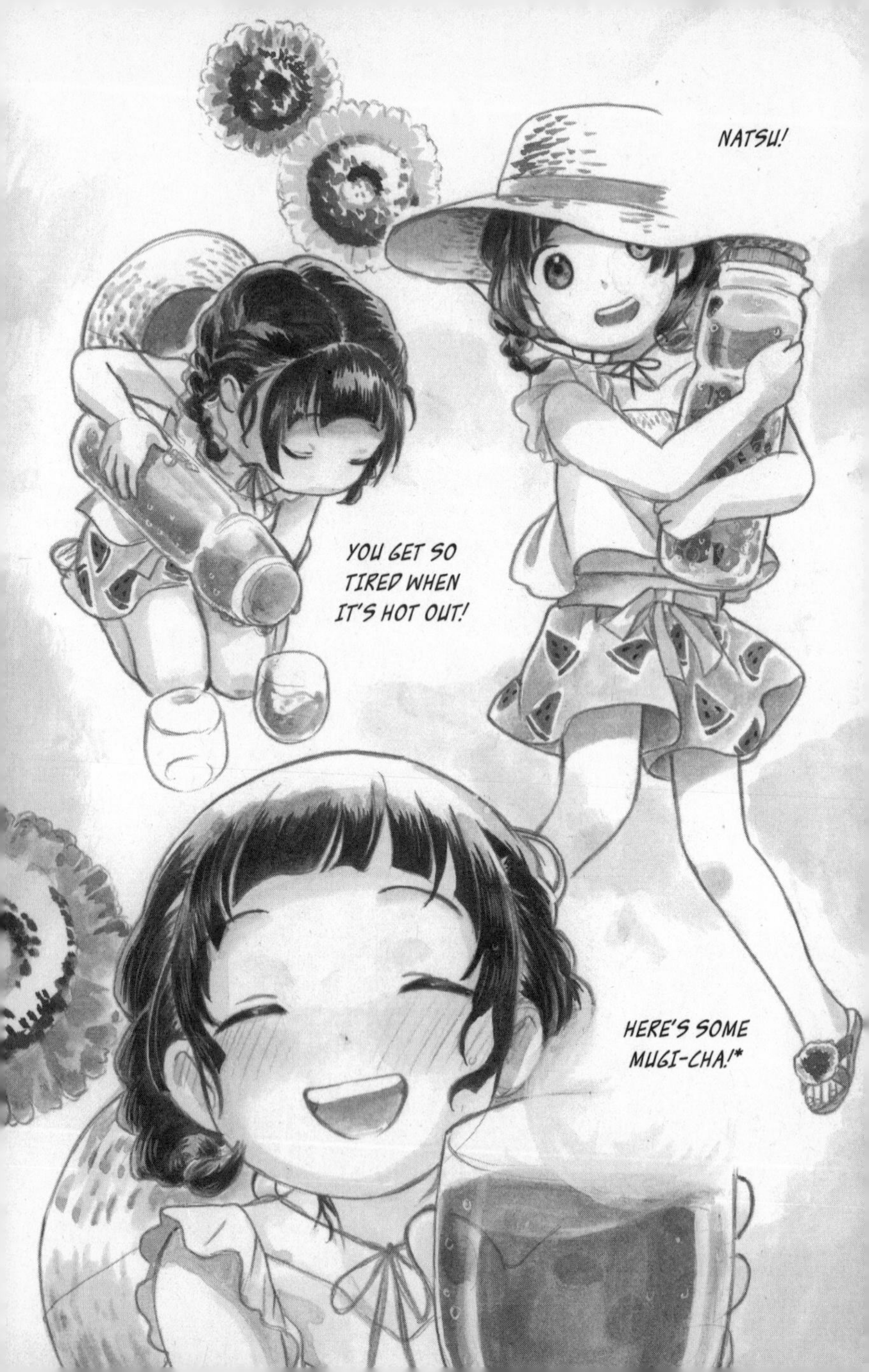
NATSU!
YOU GET SO TIRED WHEN IT'S HOT OUT!
HERE'S SOME MUGI-CHA!*

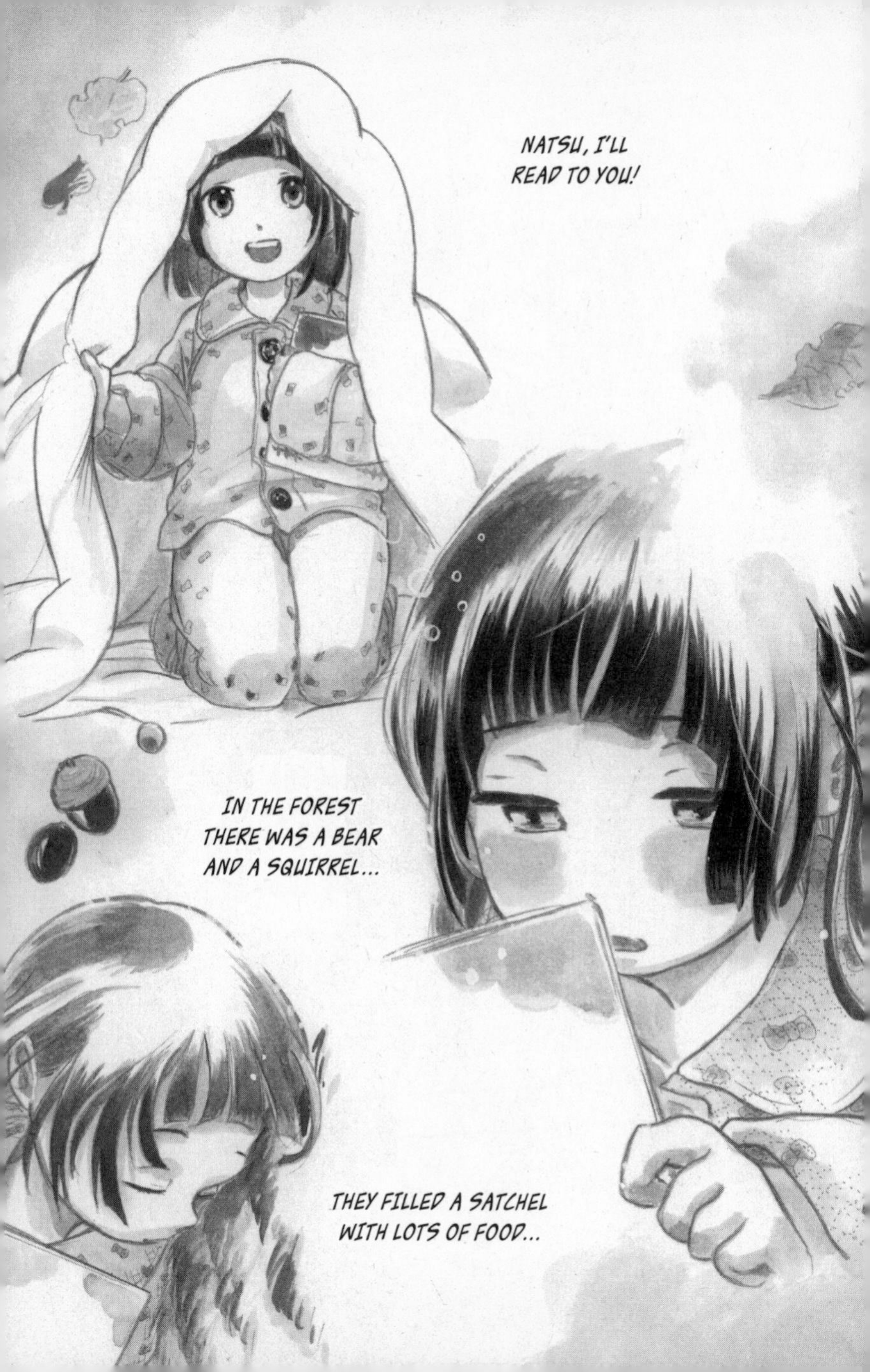
NATSU, I'LL READ TO YOU!
IN THE FOREST THERE WAS A BEAR AND A SQUIRREL...
THEY FILLED A SATCHEL WITH LOTS OF FOOD...

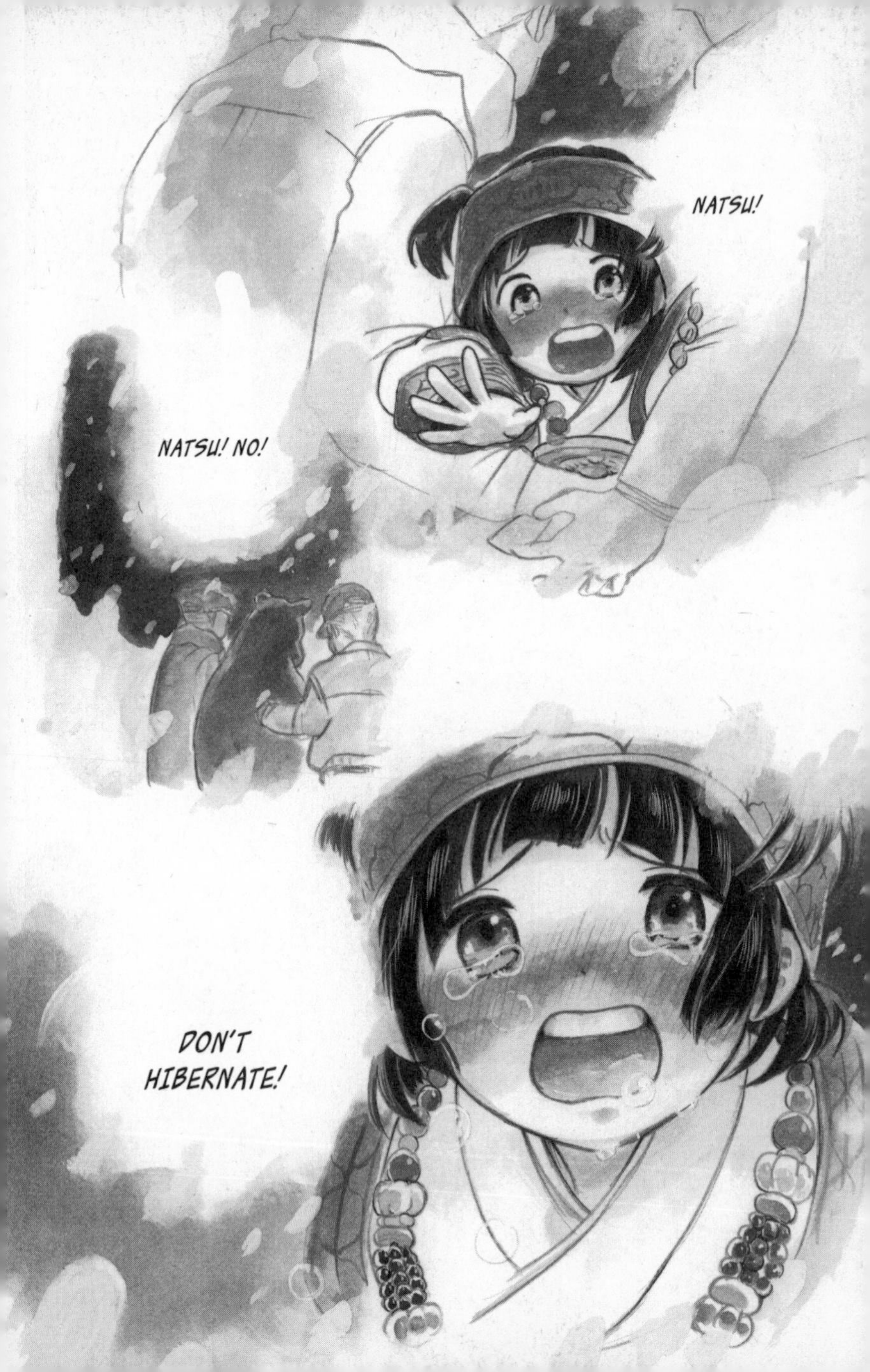
NATSU!
NATSU! NO!
DON'T HIBERNATE!

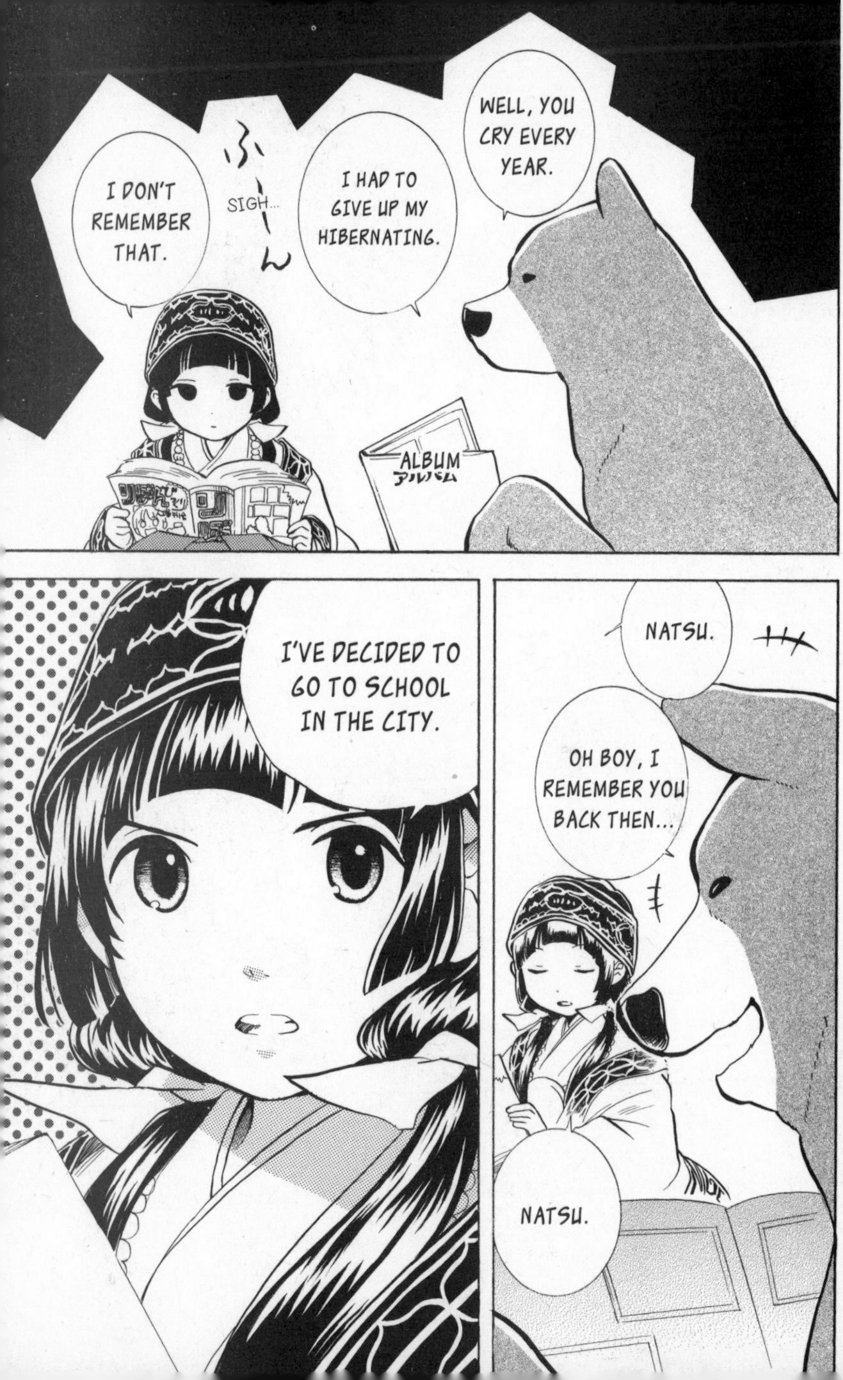
WELL, YOU CRY EVERY YEAR.
I HAD TO GIVE UP MY HIBERNATING.
ふ～ん
SIGH...
I DON'T REMEMBER THAT.
ALBUM
アルバム
NATSU.
OH BOY, I REMEMBER YOU BACK THEN...
NATSU.
I'VE DECIDED TO GO TO SCHOOL IN THE CITY.

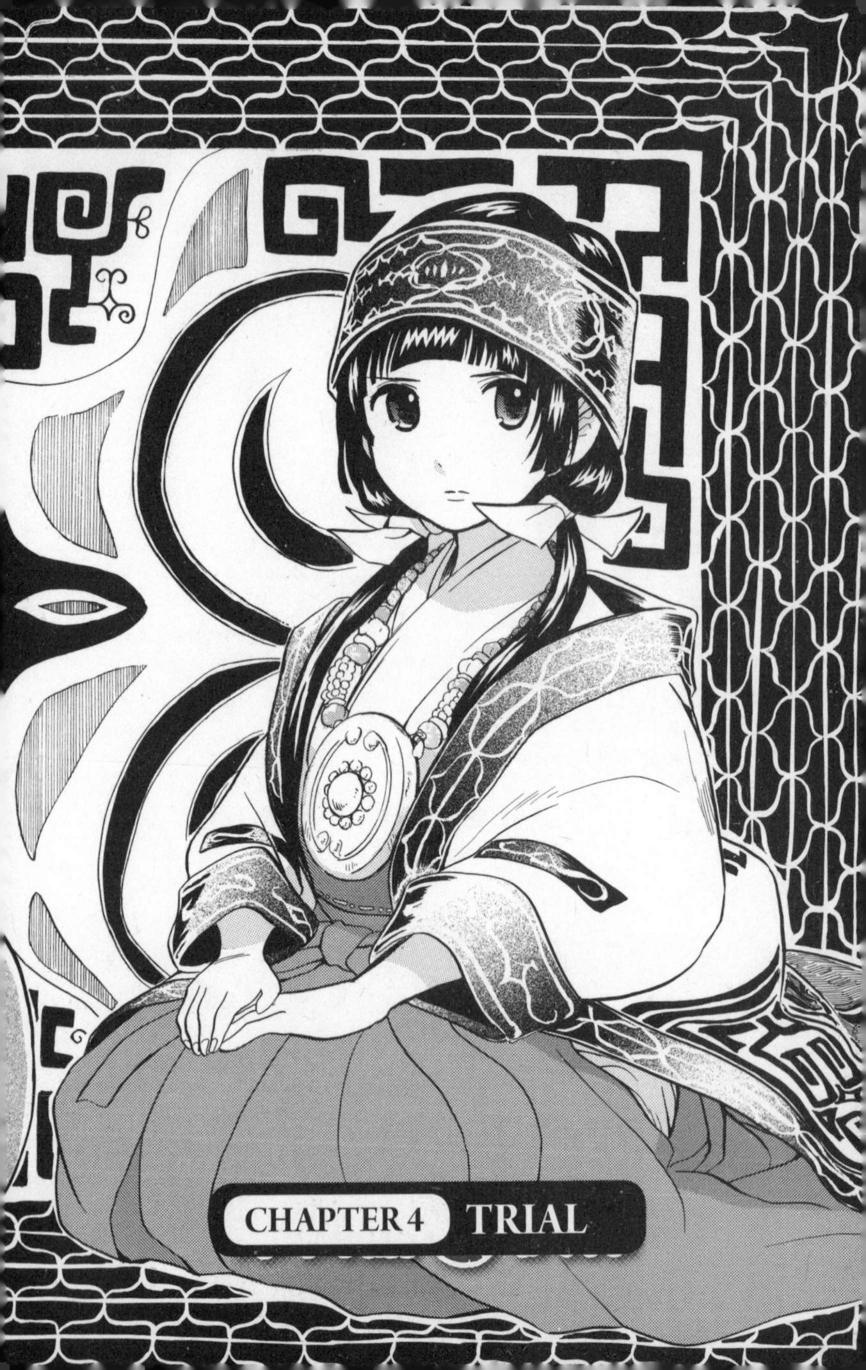
CHAPTER 4
TRIAL

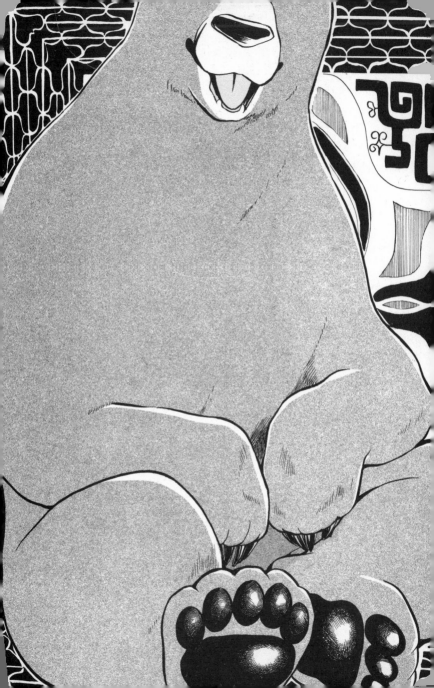

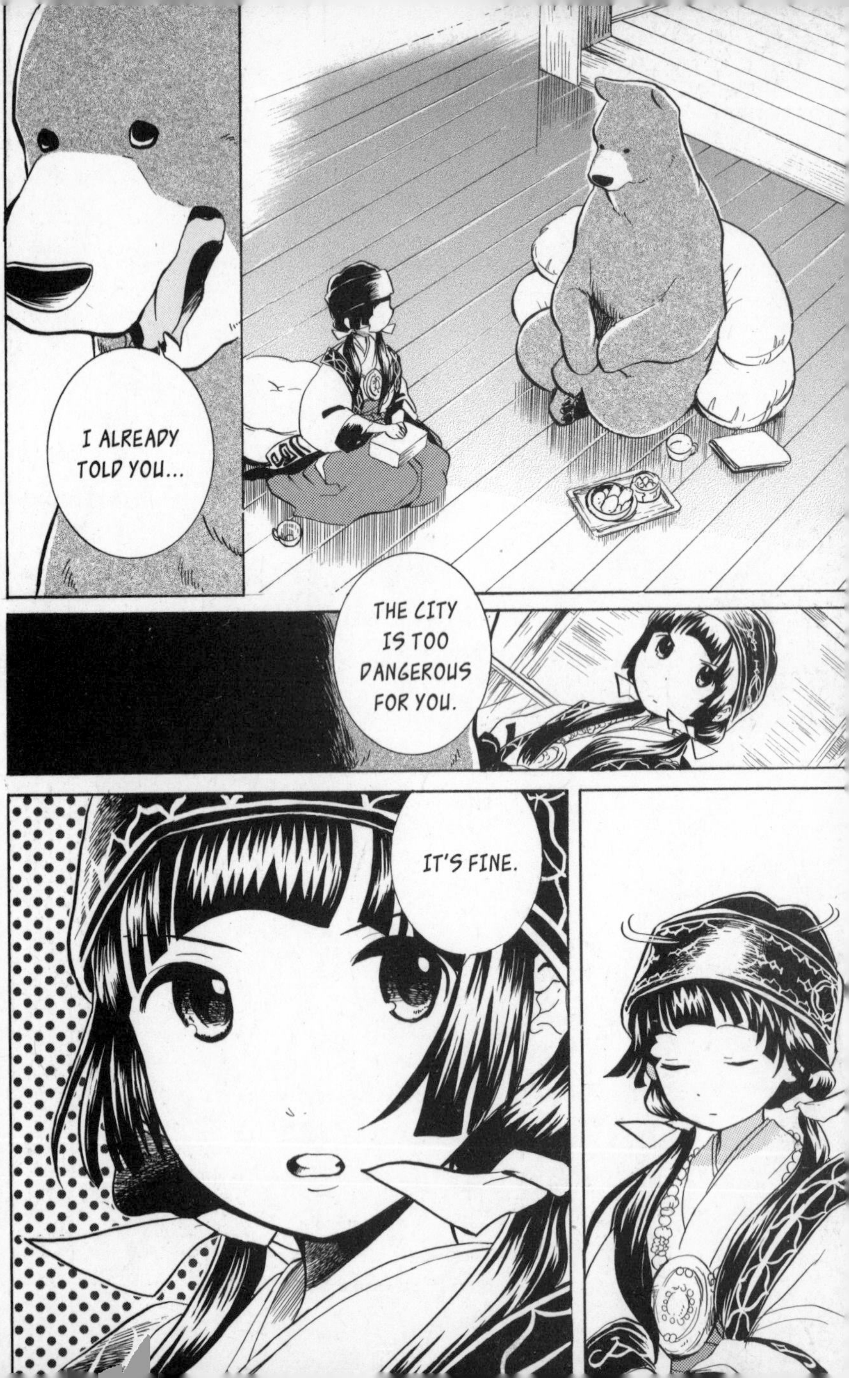
I ALREADY TOLD YOU...
THE CITY IS TOO DANGEROUS FOR YOU.
IT'S FINE.

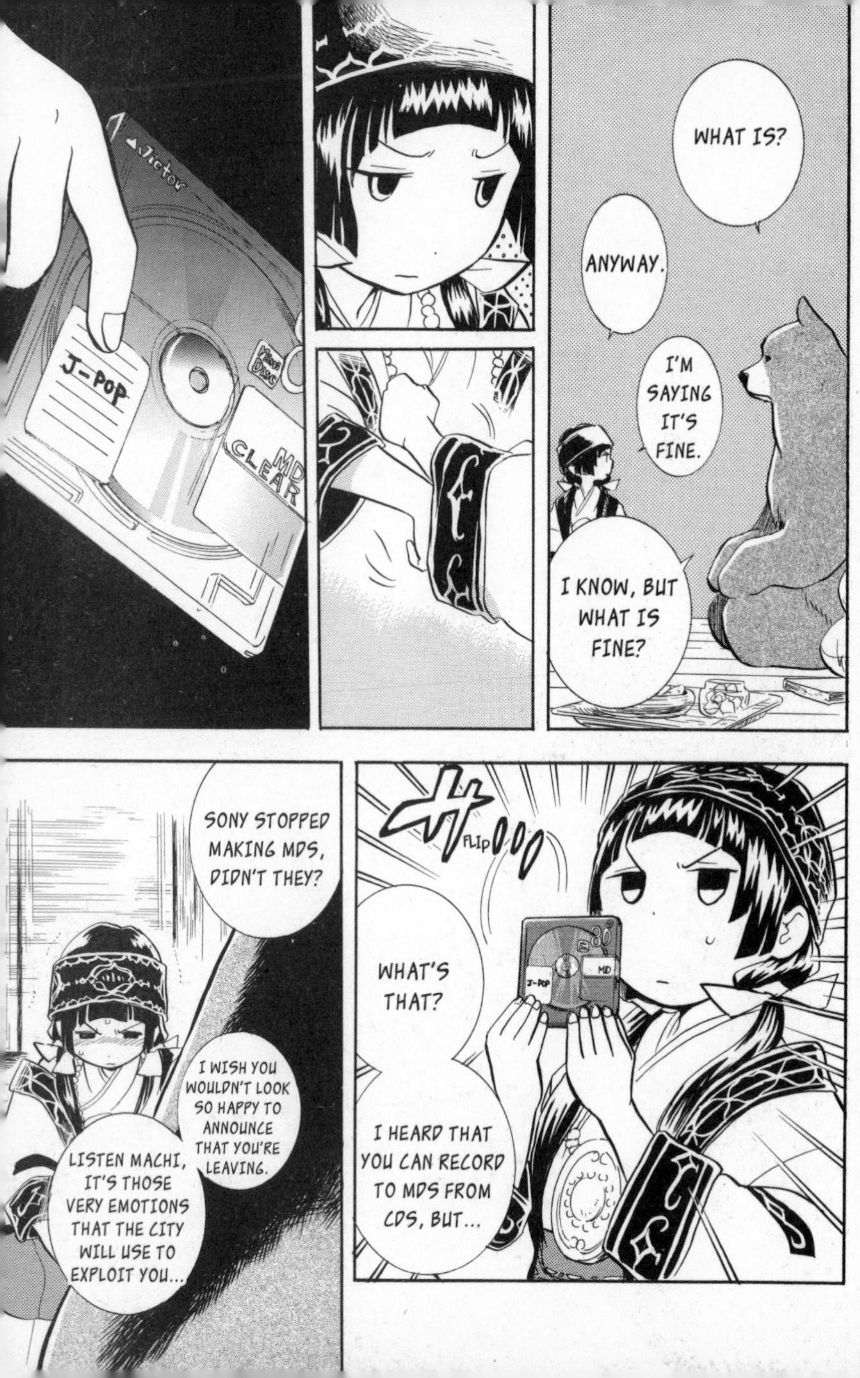
WHAT IS?
ANYWAY.
I'M SAYING IT'S FINE.
I KNOW, BUT WHAT IS FINE?
Victor
J-POP
MD CLEAR
FLIP
WHAT'S THAT?
I HEARD THAT YOU CAN RECORD TO MDS FROM CDS, BUT...
J-POP
MD
SONY STOPPED MAKING MDS, DIDN'T THEY?
I WISH YOU WOULDN'T LOOK SO HAPPY TO ANNOUNCE THAT YOU'RE LEAVING.
LISTEN MACHI, IT'S THOSE VERY EMOTIONS THAT THE CITY WILL USE TO EXPLOIT YOU...

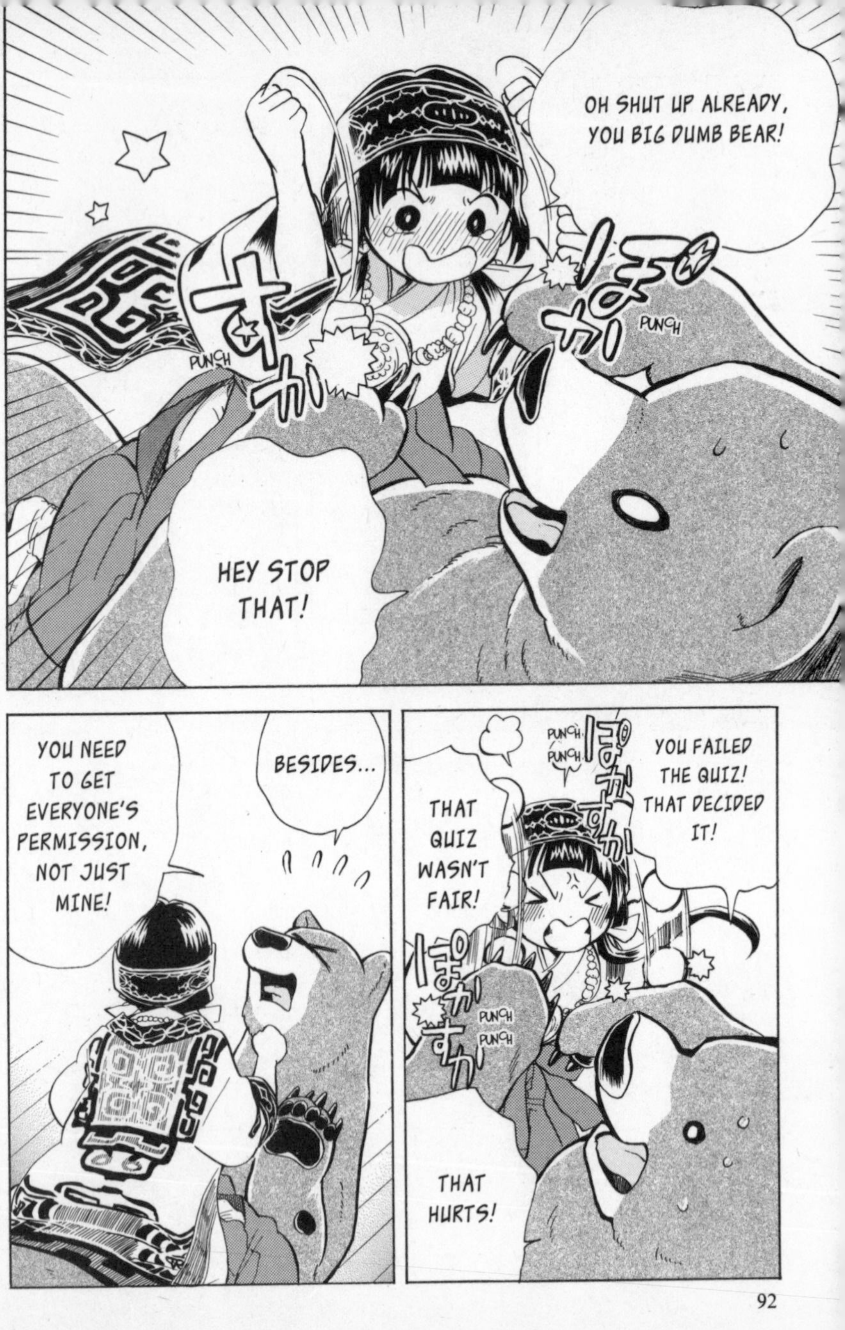
OH SHUT UP ALREADY, YOU BIG DUMB BEAR!
ぽか
PUNCH
すか
PUNCH
HEY STOP THAT!
YOU FAILED THE QUIZ! THAT DECIDED IT!
ぽかすか
PUNCH PUNCH
THAT QUIZ WASN'T FAIR!
ぽかすか
PUNCH PUNCH
THAT HURTS!
BESIDES...
YOU NEED TO GET EVERYONE'S PERMISSION, NOT JUST MINE!

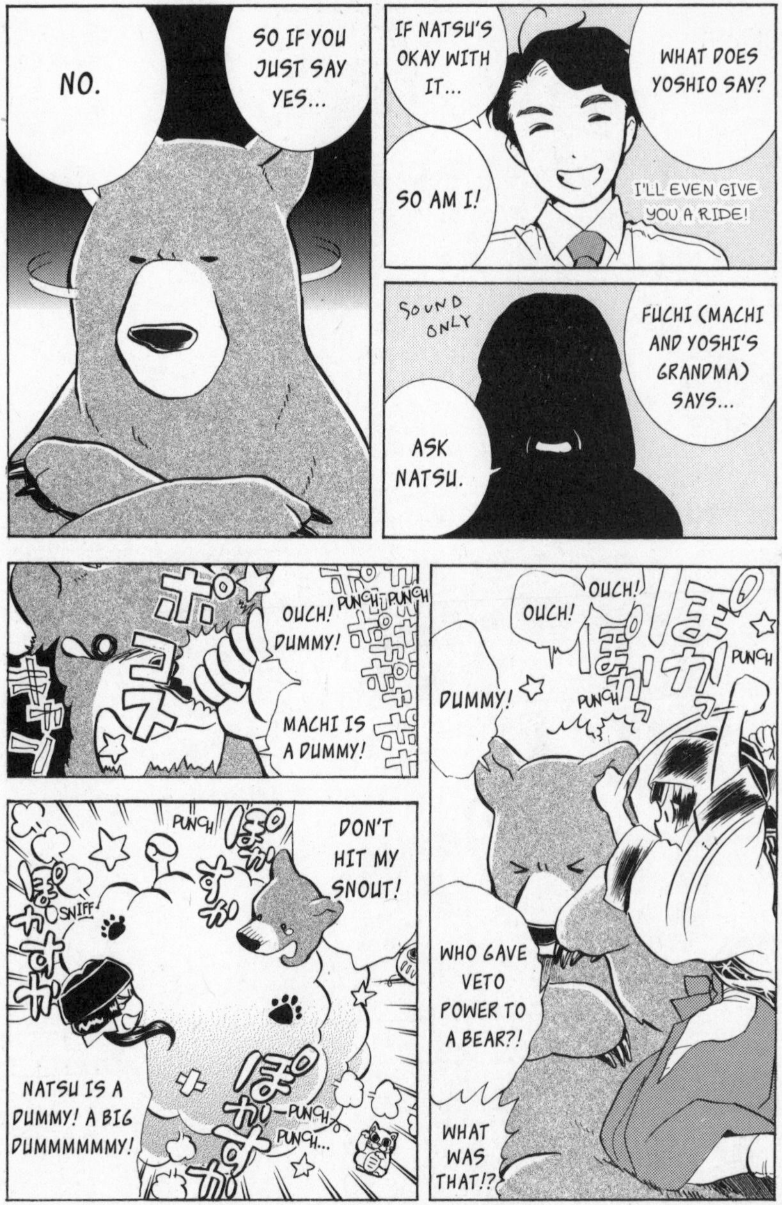
WHAT DOES YOSHIO SAY?
IF NATSU'S OKAY WITH IT...
SO AM I!
I'LL EVEN GIVE YOU A RIDE!
FUCHI (MACHI AND YOSHI'S GRANDMA) SAYS...
SOUND ONLY
ASK NATSU.
SO IF YOU JUST SAY YES...
NO.
OUCH!
OUCH!
PUNCH
PUNCH
DUMMY!
WHO GAVE VETO POWER TO A BEAR?!
WHAT WAS THAT!?
PUNCH PUNCH
OUCH! DUMMY!
MACHI IS A DUMMY!
DON'T HIT MY SNOUT!
PUNCH
SNIFF
NATSU IS A DUMMY! A BIG DUMMMMMMY!
PUNCH
PUNCH...

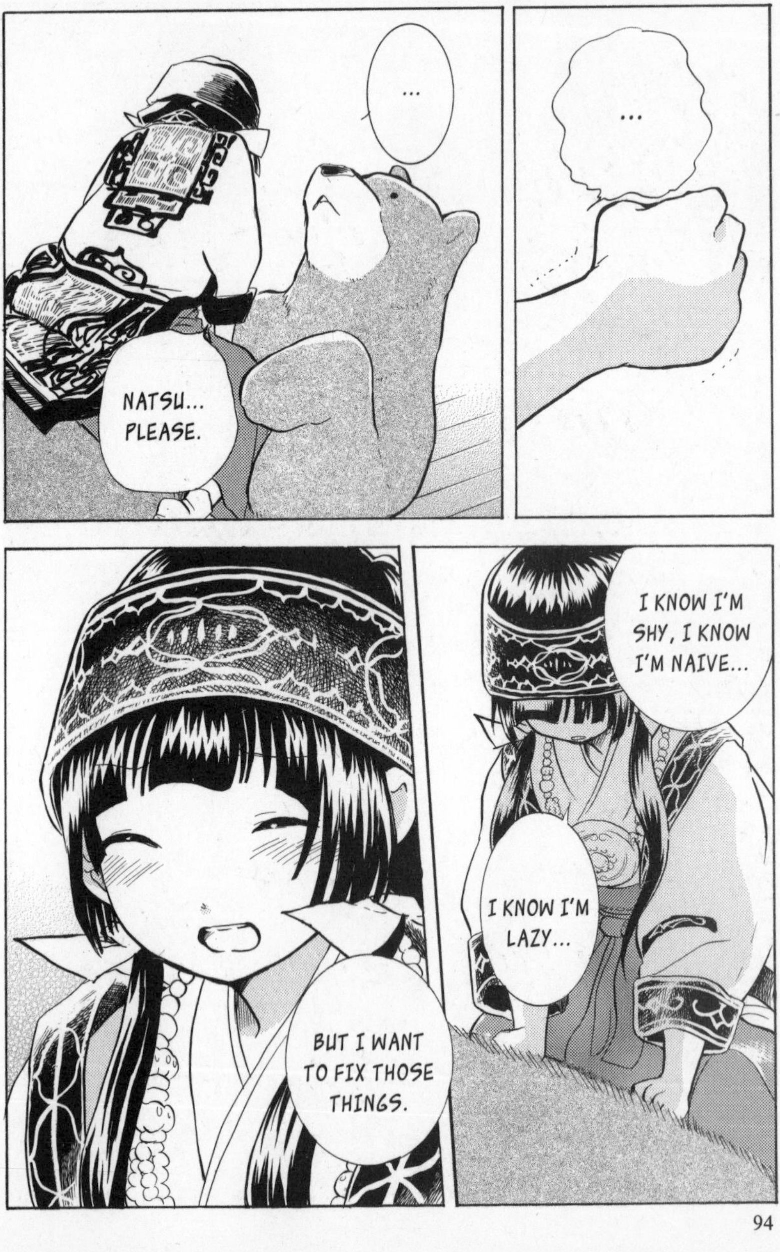
...
...
NATSU... PLEASE.
I KNOW I'M SHY, I KNOW I'M NAIVE...
I KNOW I'M LAZY...
BUT I WANT TO FIX THOSE THINGS.

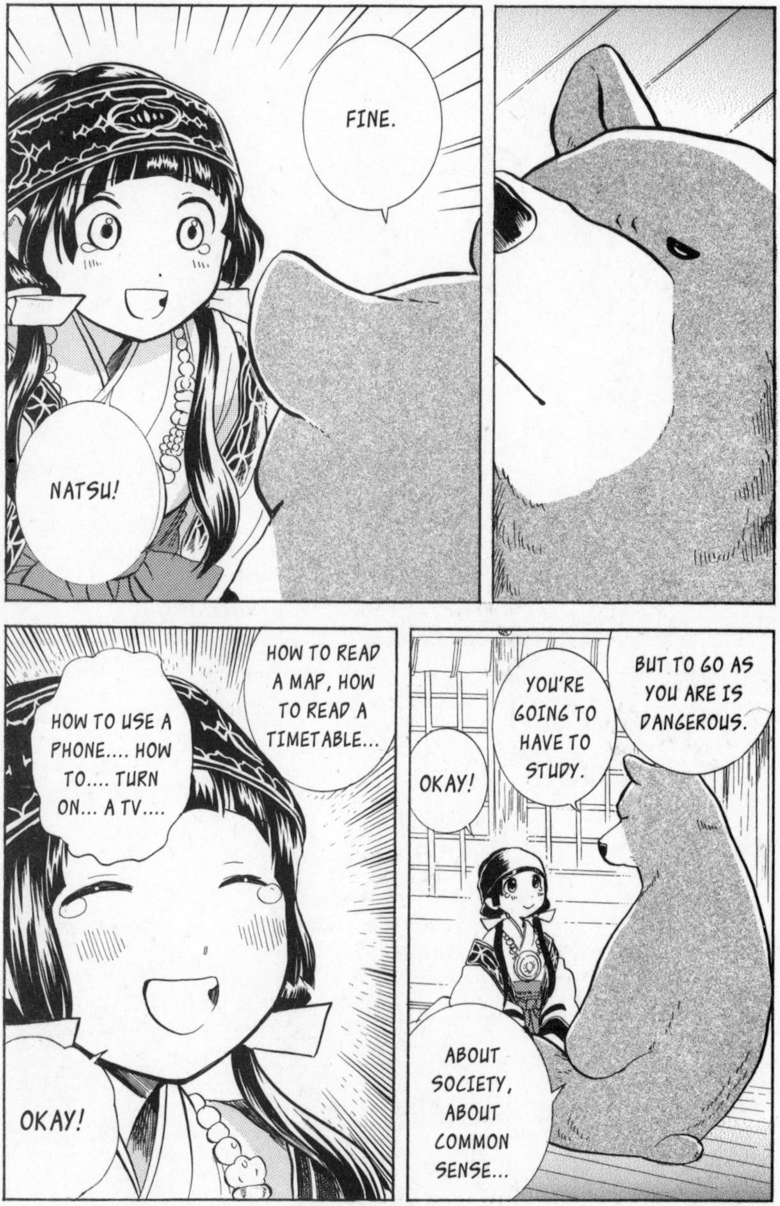
FINE.
NATSU!
BUT TO GO AS YOU ARE IS DANGEROUS.
YOU'RE GOING TO HAVE TO STUDY.
OKAY!
ABOUT SOCIETY, ABOUT COMMON SENSE...
HOW TO READ A MAP, HOW TO READ A TIMETABLE...
HOW TO USE A PHONE.... HOW TO.... TURN ON... A TV....
OKAY!

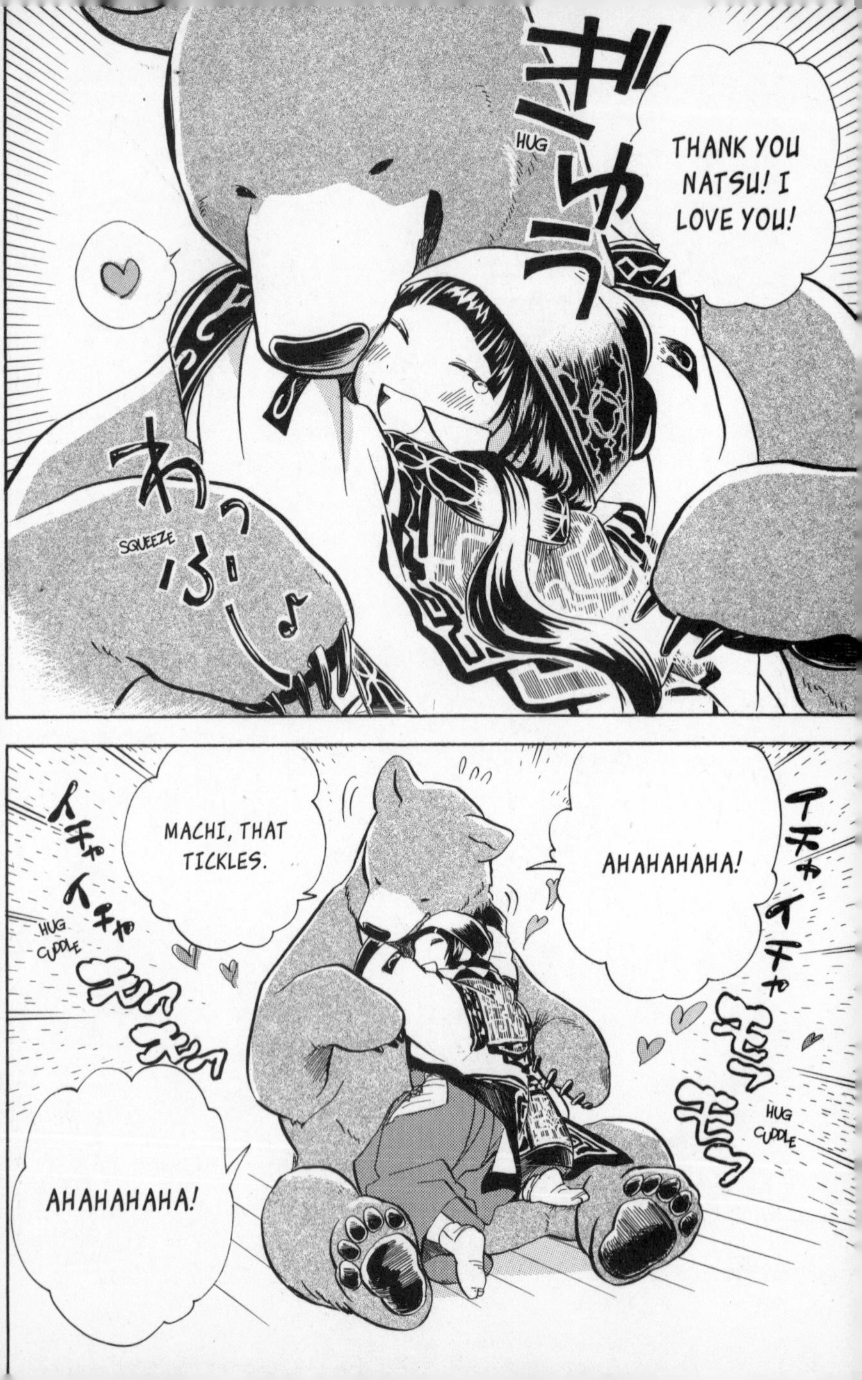
ぎゅう
HUG
THANK YOU NATSU! I LOVE YOU!
わふっ
SQUEEZE
AHAHAHAHA!
イチャイチャモフモフ
HUG CUDDLE
MACHI, THAT TICKLES.
イチャイチャモフモフ
HUG CUDDLE
AHAHAHAHA!

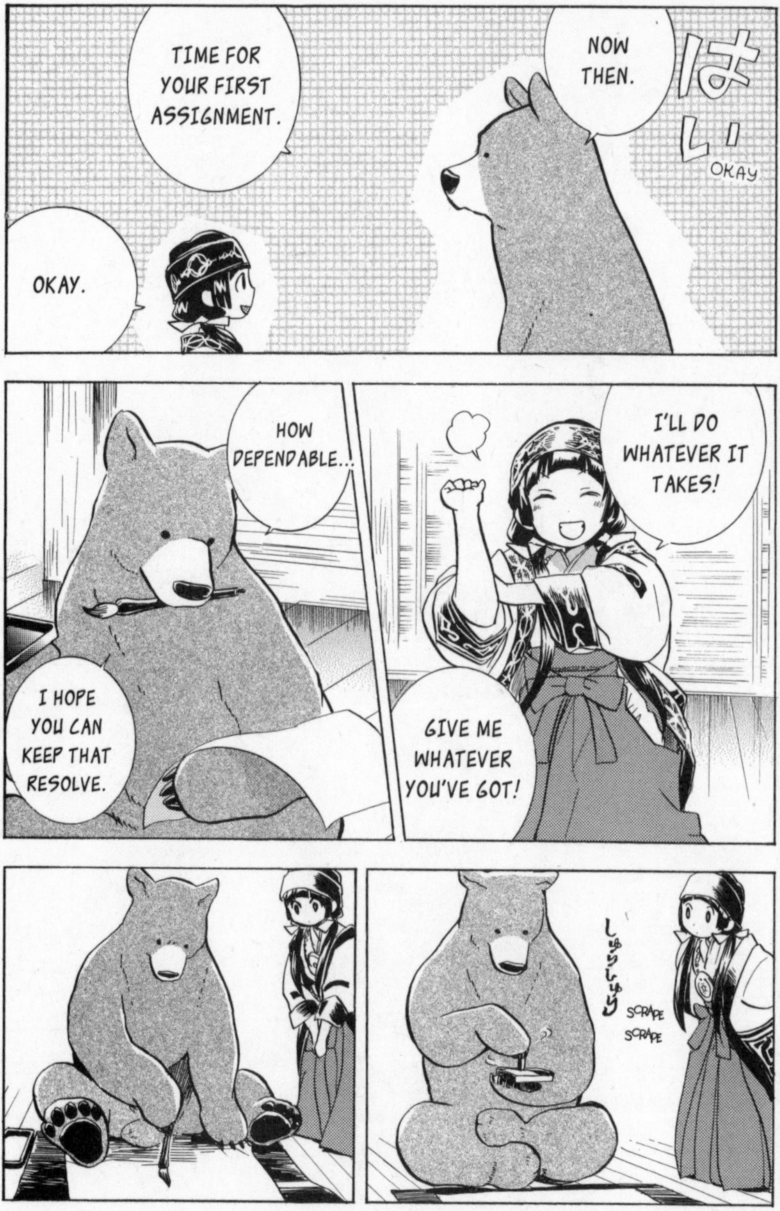
はい
OKAY
NOW THEN.
TIME FOR YOUR FIRST ASSIGNMENT.
OKAY.
I'LL DO WHATEVER IT TAKES!
GIVE ME WHATEVER YOU'VE GOT!
HOW DEPENDABLE...
I HOPE YOU CAN KEEP THAT RESOLVE.
SCRAPE
SCRAPE

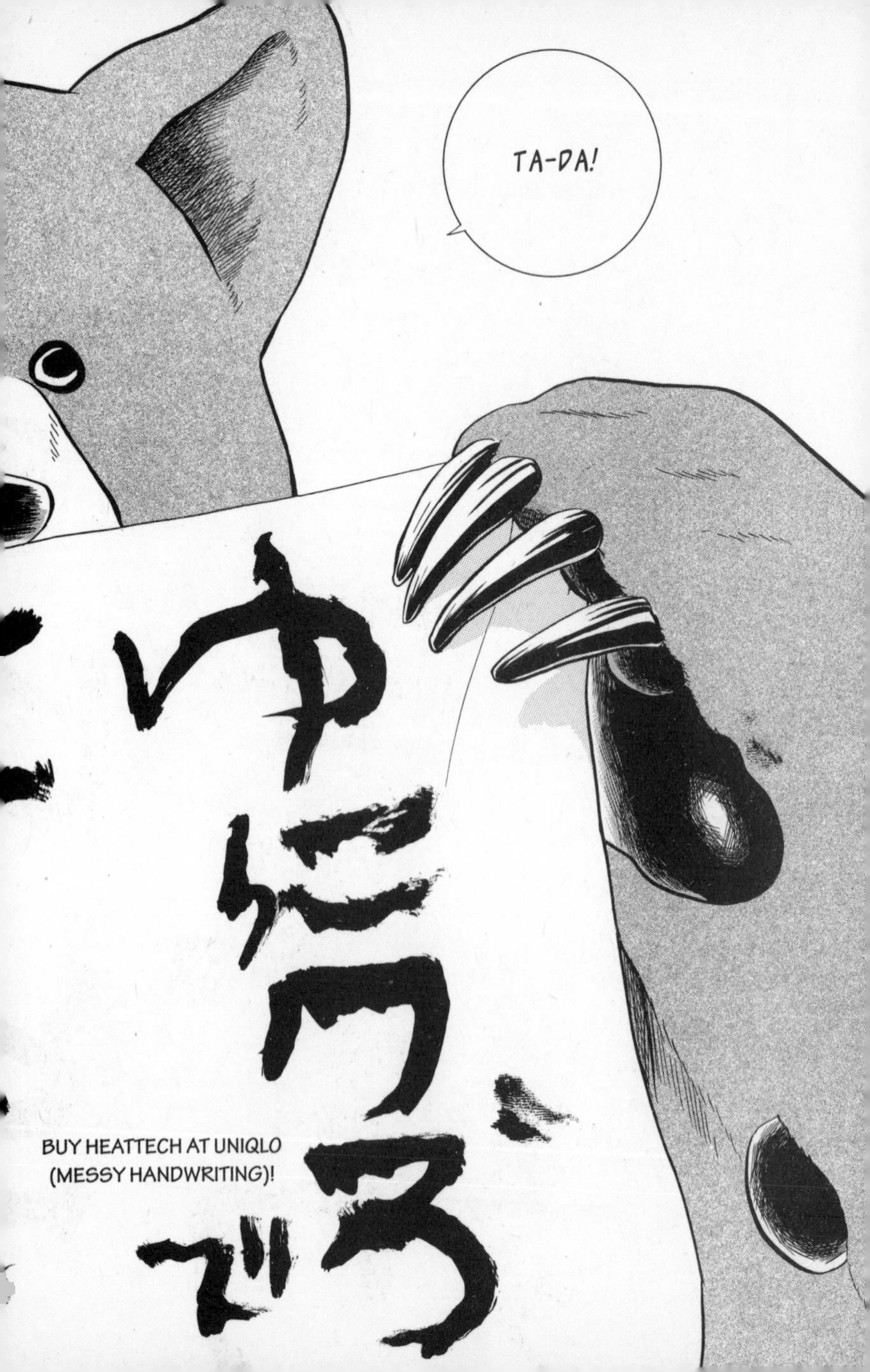
TA-DA!
ゆにクろ
BUY HEATTECH AT UNIQLO (MESSY HANDWRITING)!

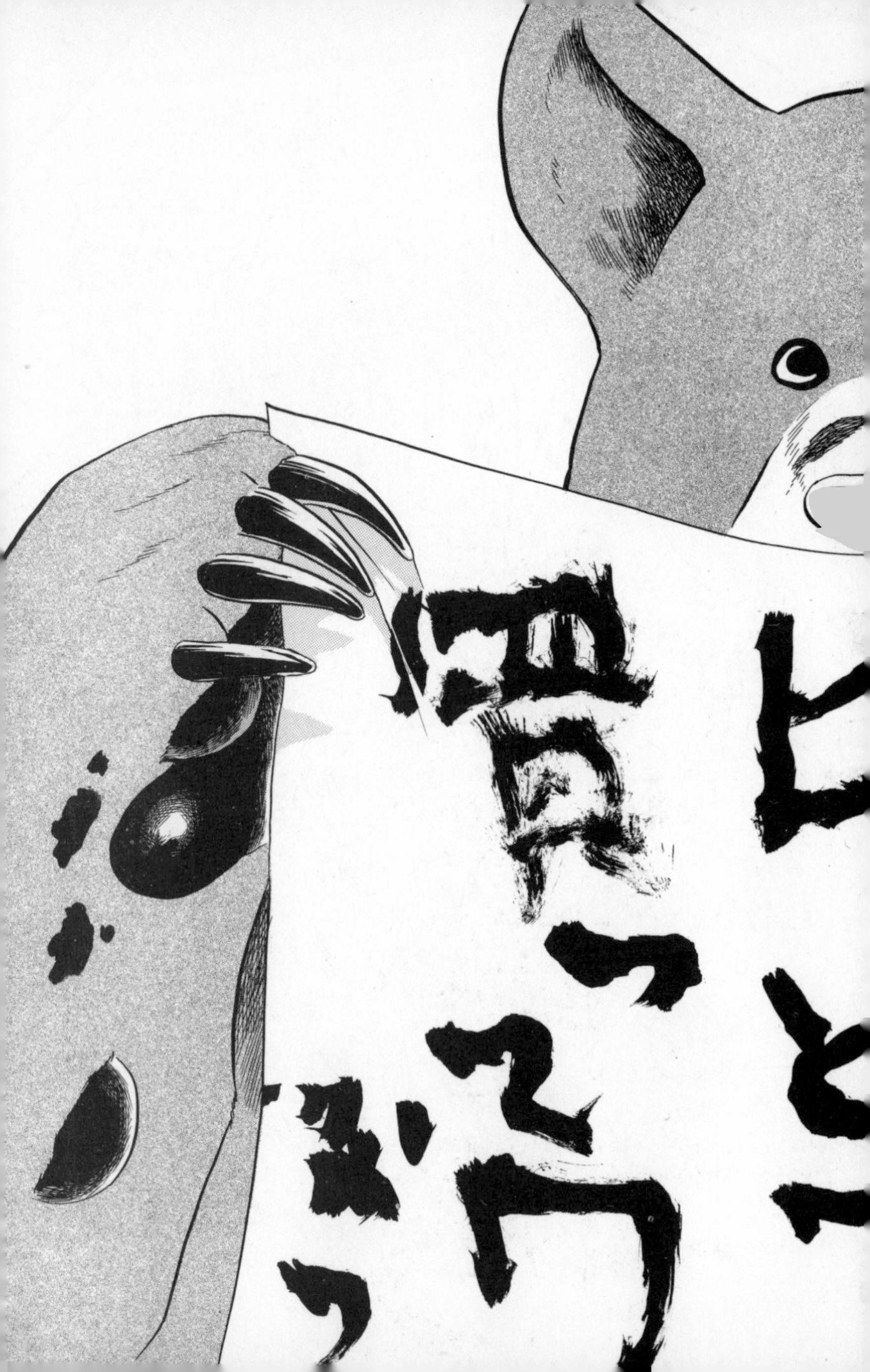
ヒと
骨っこ
ぶっ

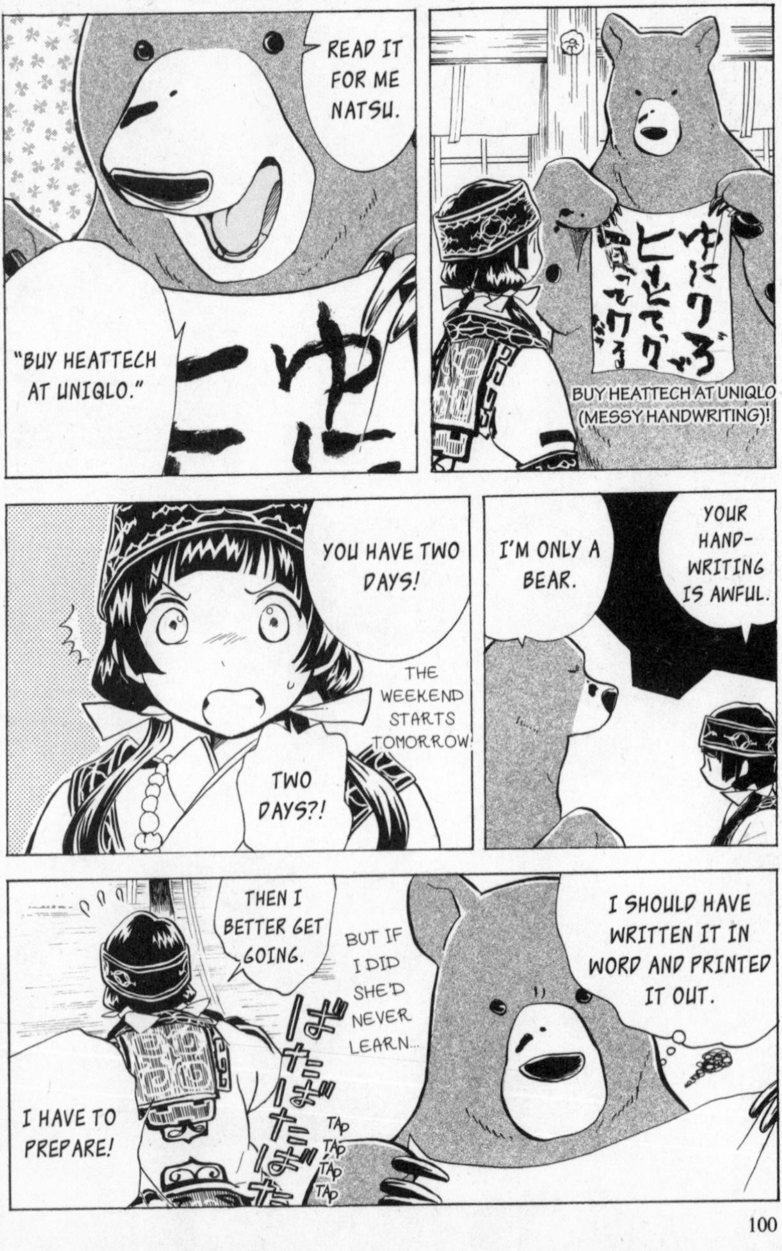
BUY HEATTECH AT UNIQLO (MESSY HANDWRITING)!
READ IT FOR ME NATSU.
“BUY HEATTECH AT UNIQLO.”
YOUR HAND-WRITING IS AWFUL.
I'M ONLY A BEAR.
YOU HAVE TWO DAYS!
THE WEEKEND STARTS TOMORROW!
TWO DAYS?!
I SHOULD HAVE WRITTEN IT IN WORD AND PRINTED IT OUT.
BUT IF I DID SHE'D NEVER LEARN...
THEN I BETTER GET GOING.
TAP TAP TAP TAP TAP
I HAVE TO PREPARE!

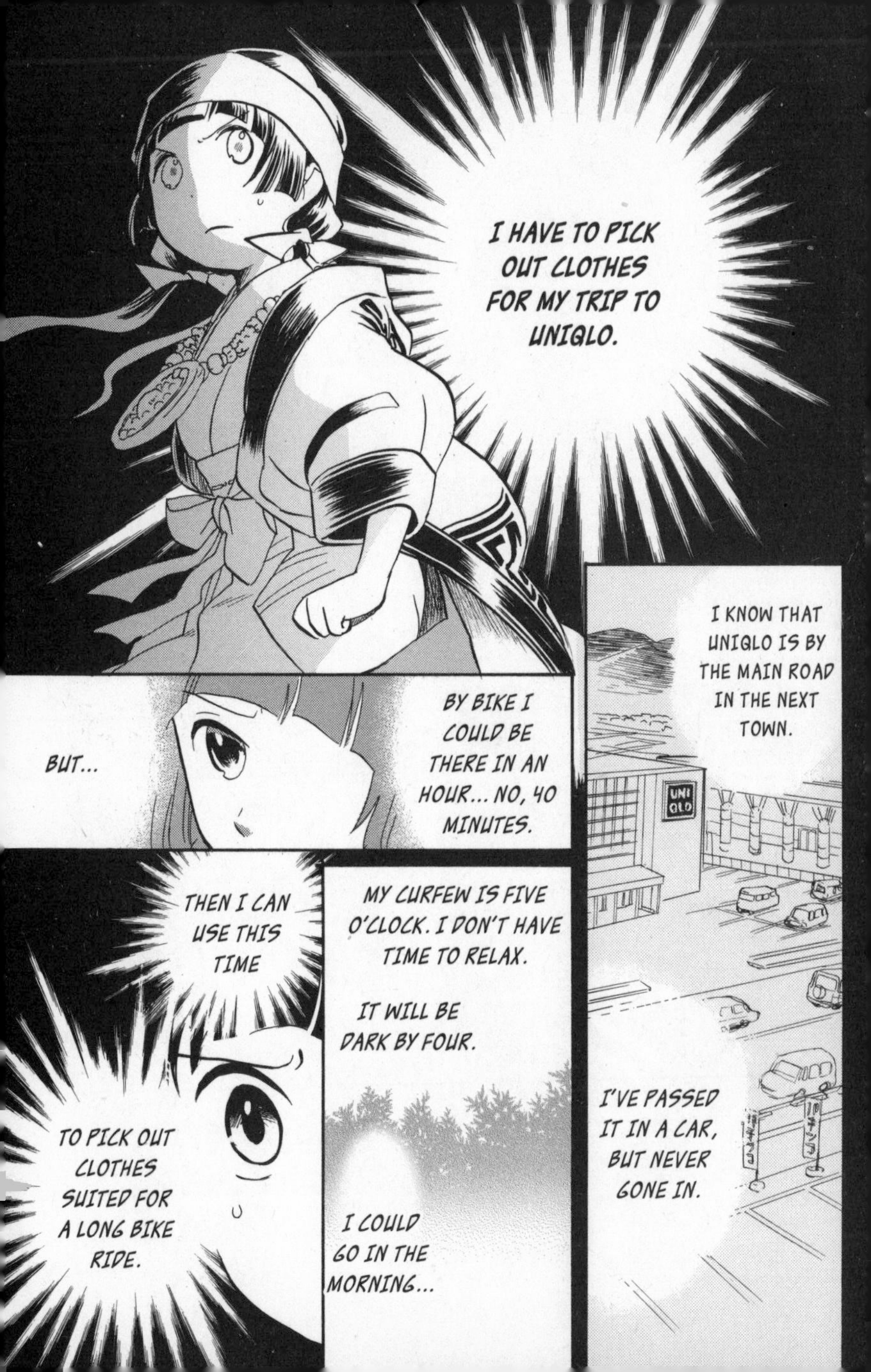
I HAVE TO PICK OUT CLOTHES FOR MY TRIP TO UNIQLO.
I KNOW THAT UNIQLO IS BY THE MAIN ROAD IN THE NEXT TOWN.
UNI QLO
I'VE PASSED IT IN A CAR, BUT NEVER GONE IN.
BY BIKE I COULD BE THERE IN AN HOUR... NO, 40 MINUTES.
BUT...
MY CURFEW IS FIVE O'CLOCK. I DON'T HAVE TIME TO RELAX.
IT WILL BE DARK BY FOUR.
I COULD GO IN THE MORNING...
THEN I CAN USE THIS TIME
TO PICK OUT CLOTHES SUITED FOR A LONG BIKE RIDE.

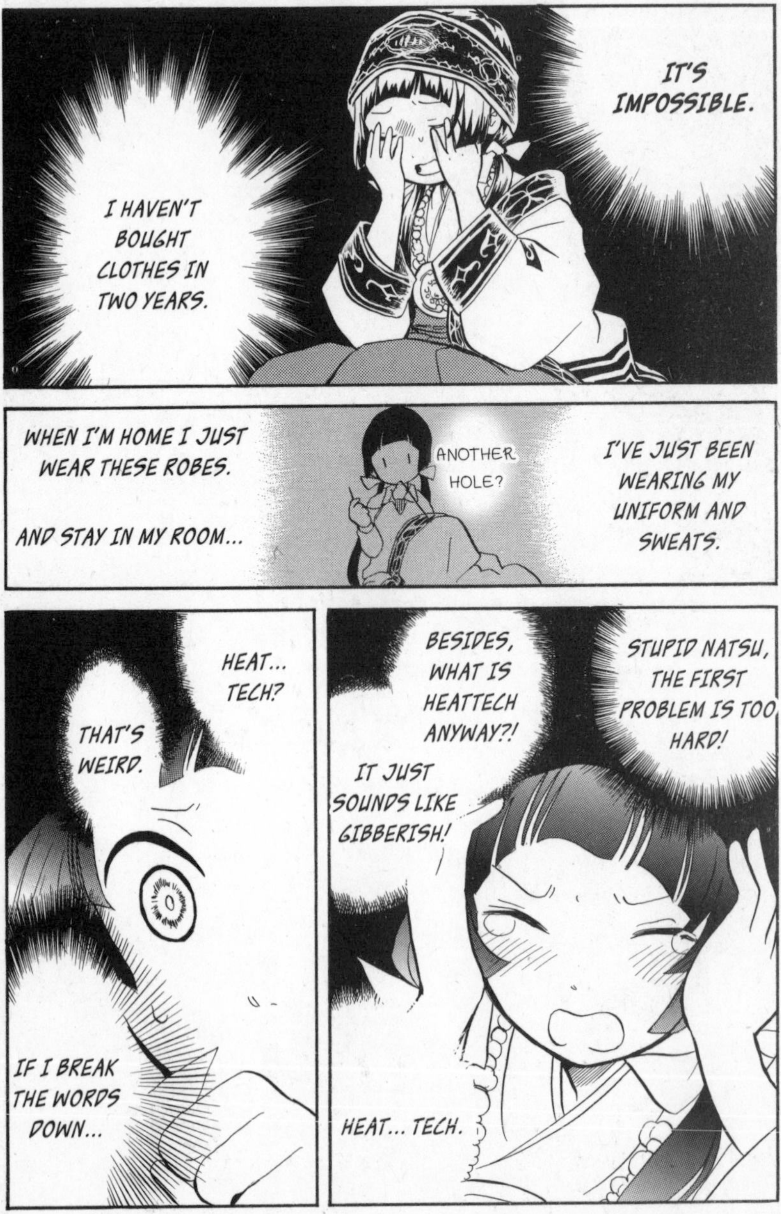
IT'S IMPOSSIBLE.
I HAVEN'T BOUGHT CLOTHES IN TWO YEARS.
I'VE JUST BEEN WEARING MY UNIFORM AND SWEATS.
ANOTHER HOLE?
WHEN I'M HOME I JUST WEAR THESE ROBES.
AND STAY IN MY ROOM...
STUPID NATSU, THE FIRST PROBLEM IS TOO HARD!
BESIDES, WHAT IS HEATTECH ANYWAY?!
IT JUST SOUNDS LIKE GIBBERISH!
HEAT... TECH.
HEAT... TECH?
THAT'S WEIRD.
IF I BREAK THE WORDS DOWN...

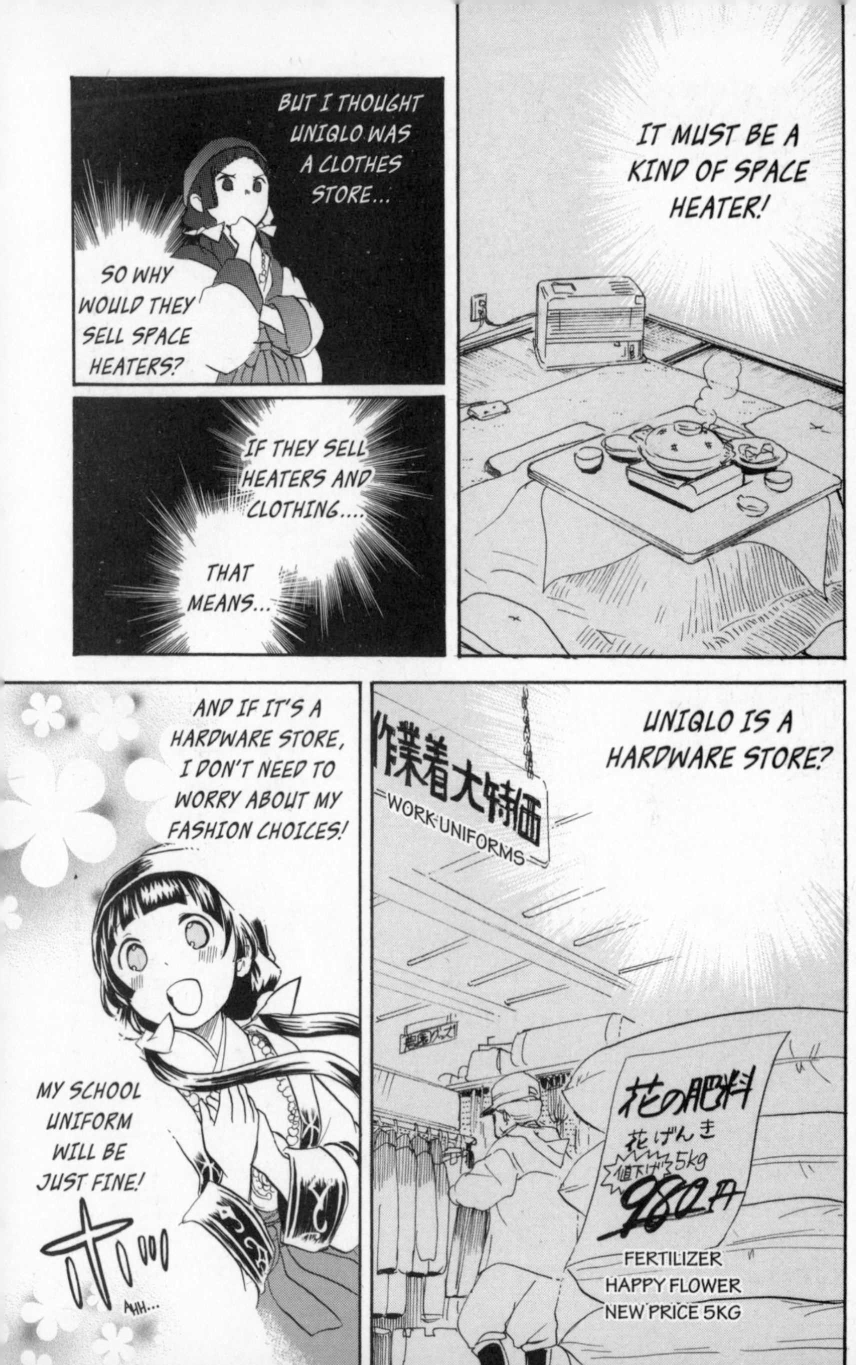
IT MUST BE A KIND OF SPACE HEATER!
BUT I THOUGHT UNIQLO WAS A CLOTHES STORE...
SO WHY WOULD THEY SELL SPACE HEATERS?
IF THEY SELL HEATERS AND CLOTHING....
THAT MEANS...
UNIQLO IS A HARDWARE STORE?
作業着大特価
WORK UNIFORMS
花の肥料
花げんき
値下げ 5kg
980円
FERTILIZER
HAPPY FLOWER
NEW PRICE 5KG
AND IF IT'S A HARDWARE STORE, I DON'T NEED TO WORRY ABOUT MY FASHION CHOICES!
MY SCHOOL UNIFORM WILL BE JUST FINE!
AHH...

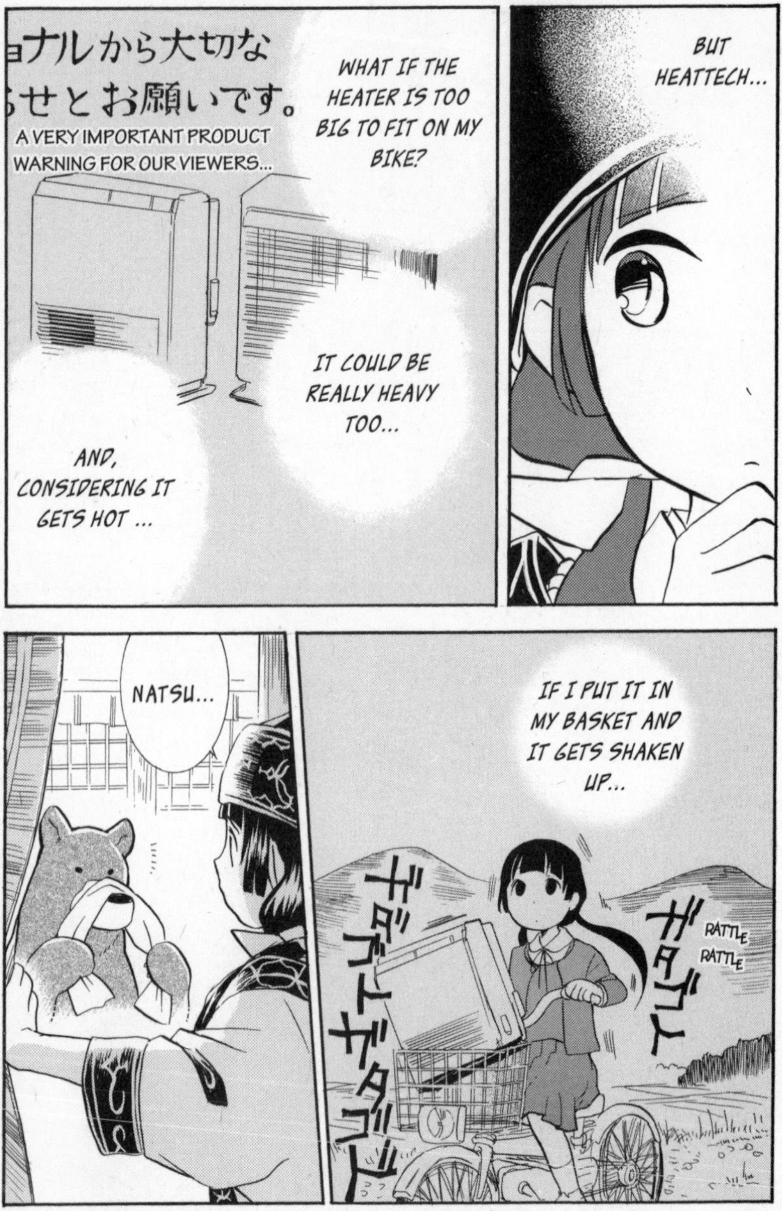
BUT HEATTECH...
WHAT IF THE HEATER IS TOO BIG TO FIT ON MY BIKE?
ョナルから大切な
せとお願いです。
A VERY IMPORTANT PRODUCT WARNING FOR OUR VIEWERS...
IT COULD BE REALLY HEAVY TOO...
AND, CONSIDERING IT GETS HOT ...
IF I PUT IT IN MY BASKET AND IT GETS SHAKEN UP...
ガタゴト
RATTLE RATTLE
ガタゴトガタゴト
NATSU...

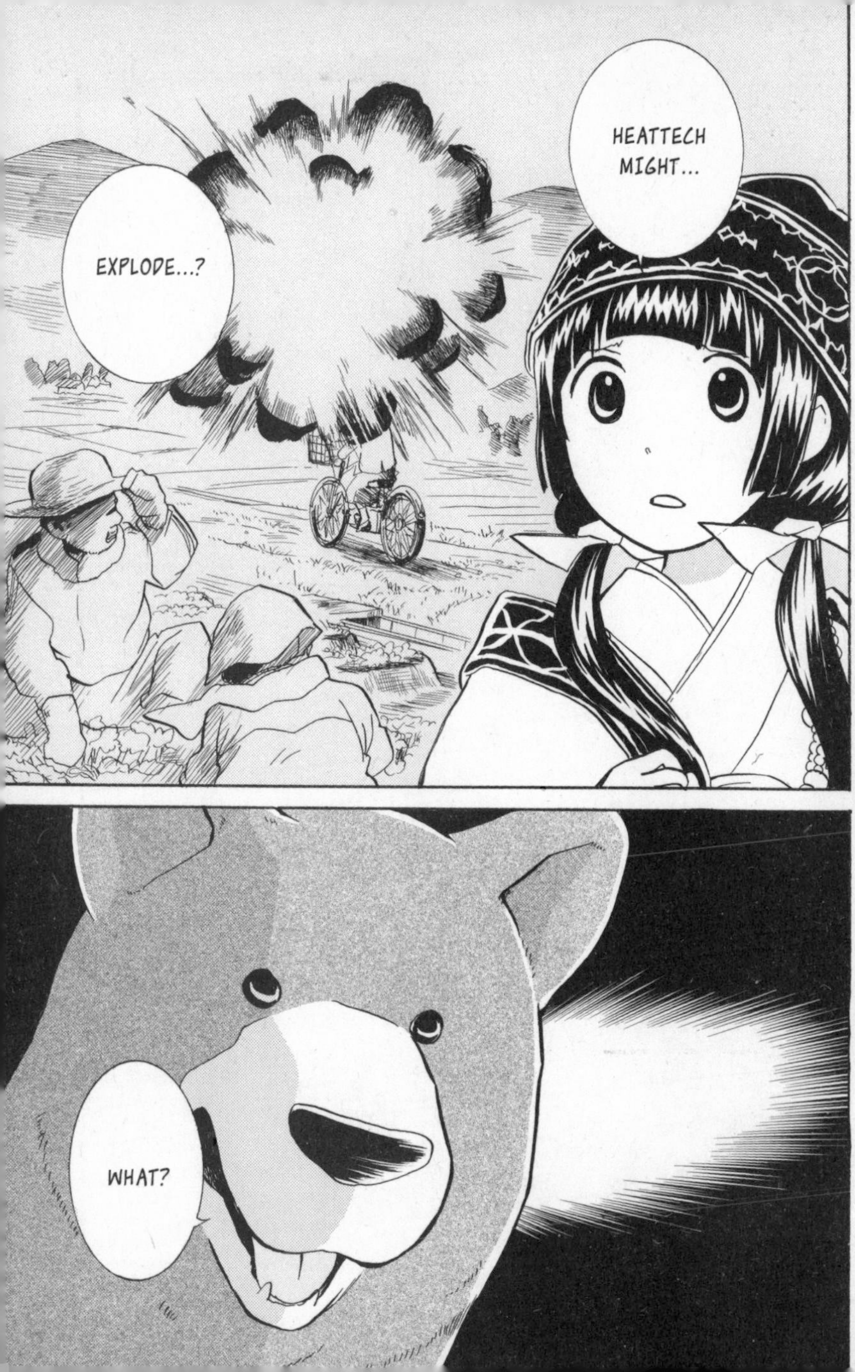
HEATTECH MIGHT...
EXPLODE...?
WHAT?

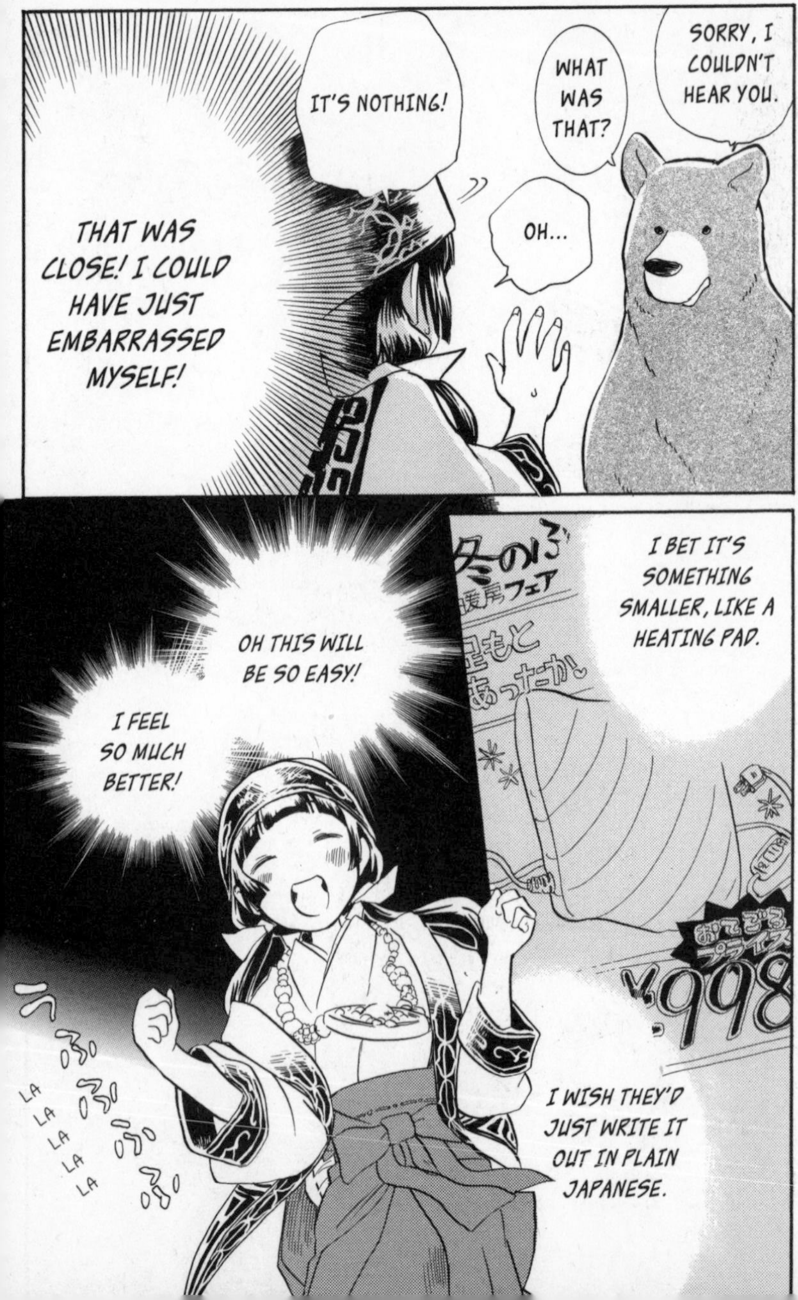
SORRY, I COULDN'T HEAR YOU.
WHAT WAS THAT?
IT'S NOTHING!
OH...
THAT WAS CLOSE! I COULD HAVE JUST EMBARRASSED MYSELF!
I BET IT'S SOMETHING SMALLER, LIKE A HEATING PAD.
暖房フェア
おてごろプライス
¥998
OH THIS WILL BE SO EASY!
I FEEL SO MUCH BETTER!
I WISH THEY'D JUST WRITE IT OUT IN PLAIN JAPANESE.
LA LA LA LA LA

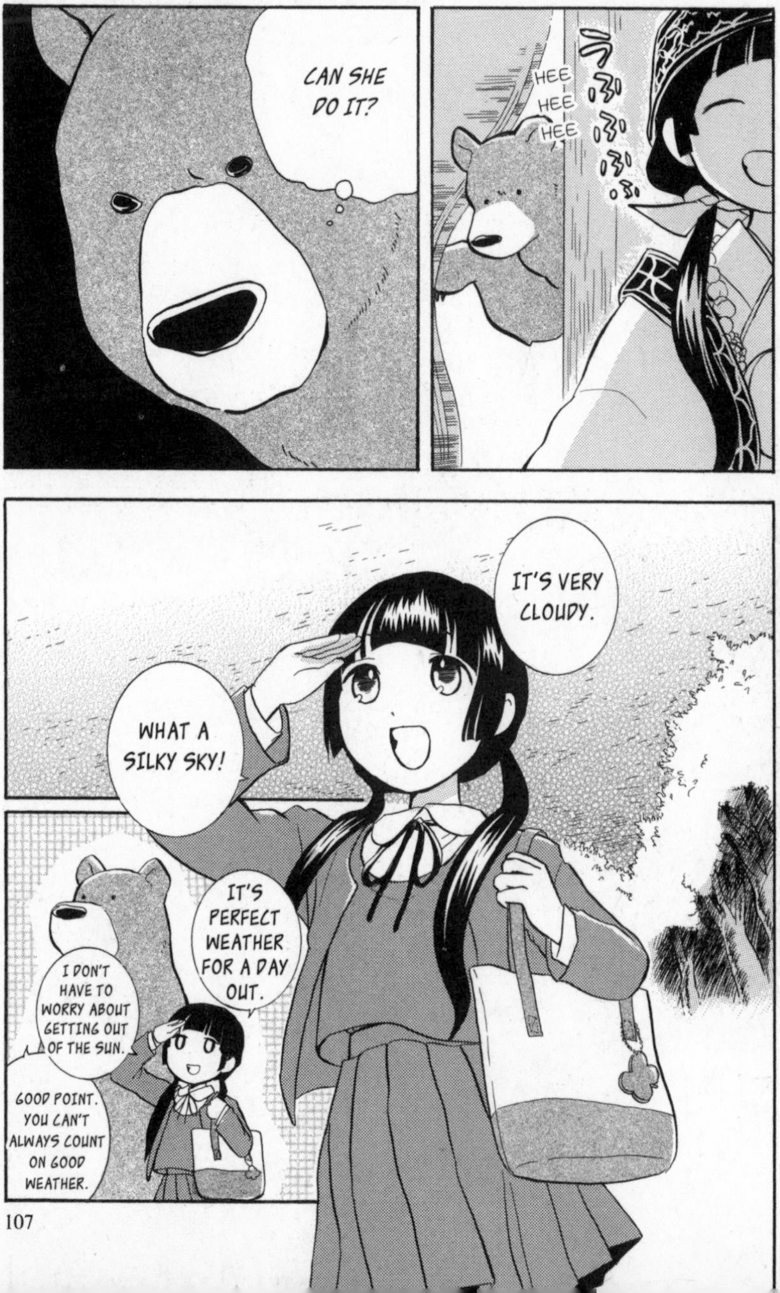
HEE HEE HEE
CAN SHE DO IT?
IT'S VERY CLOUDY.
WHAT A SILKY SKY!
IT'S PERFECT WEATHER FOR A DAY OUT.
I DON'T HAVE TO WORRY ABOUT GETTING OUT OF THE SUN.
GOOD POINT. YOU CAN'T ALWAYS COUNT ON GOOD WEATHER.

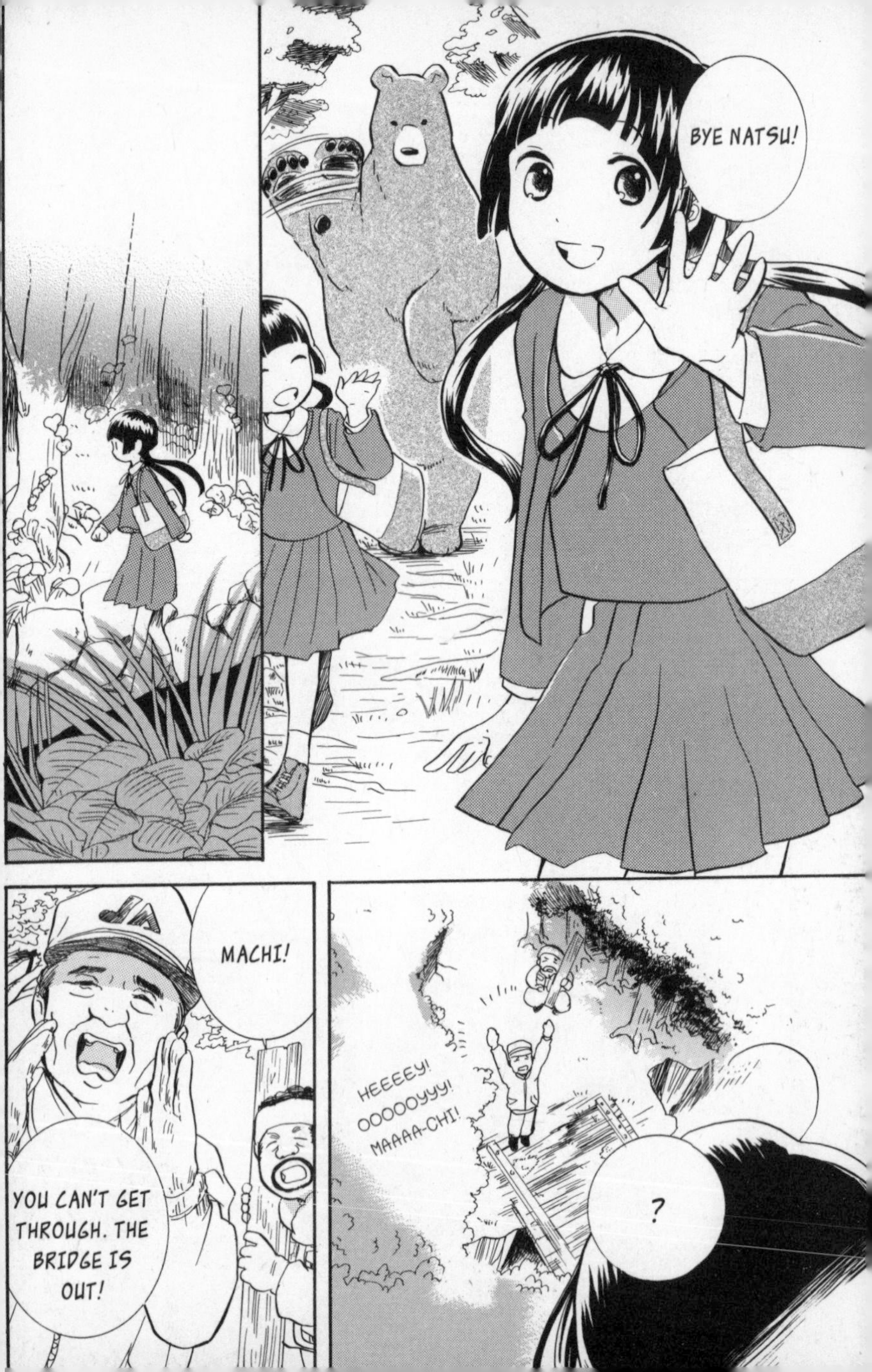
BYE NATSU!
HEEEEY! OOOOOYYY! MAAAA-CHI!
?
MACHI!
YOU CAN'T GET THROUGH. THE BRIDGE IS OUT!

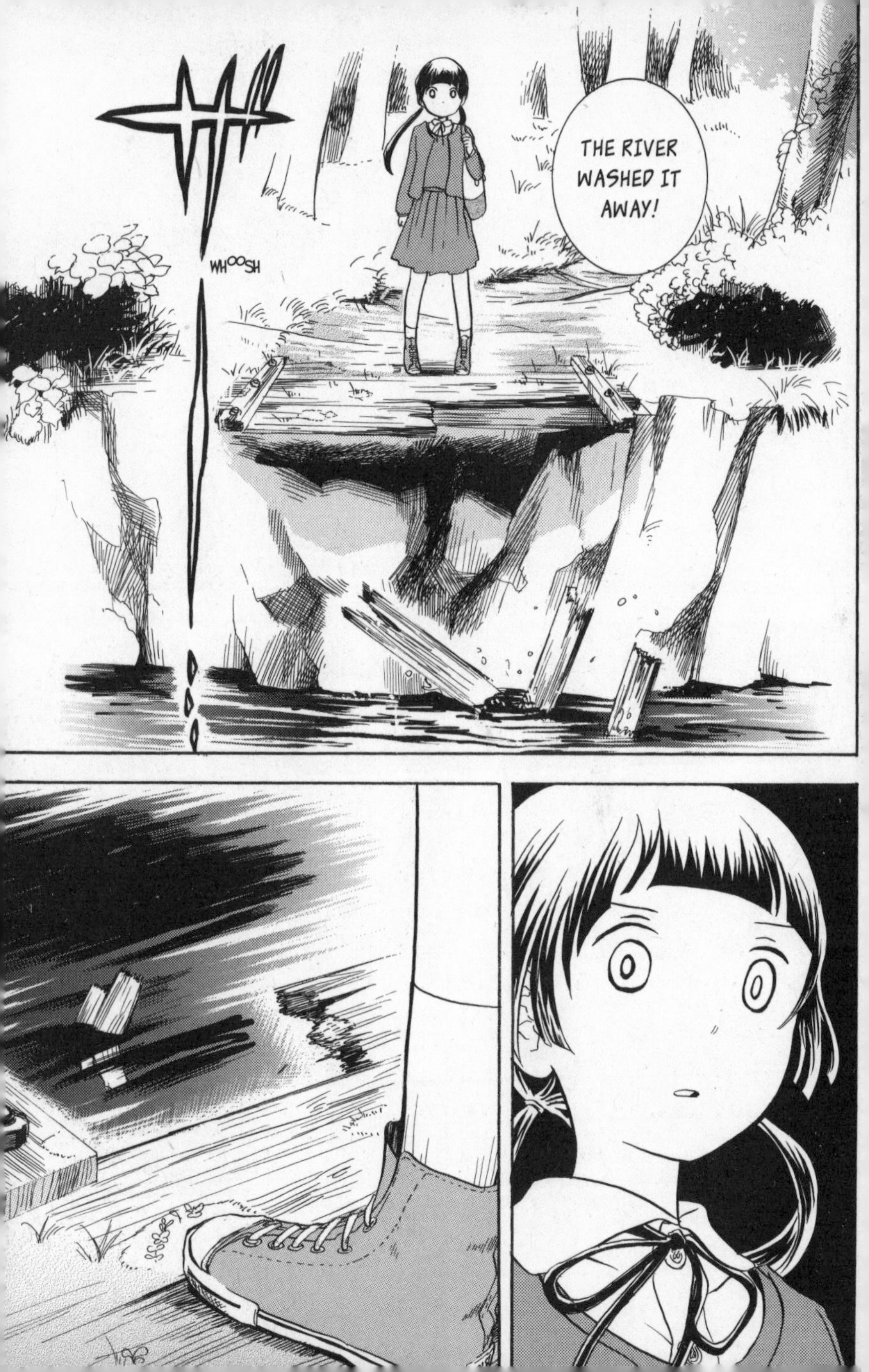
THE RIVER WASHED IT AWAY!
WHOOSH

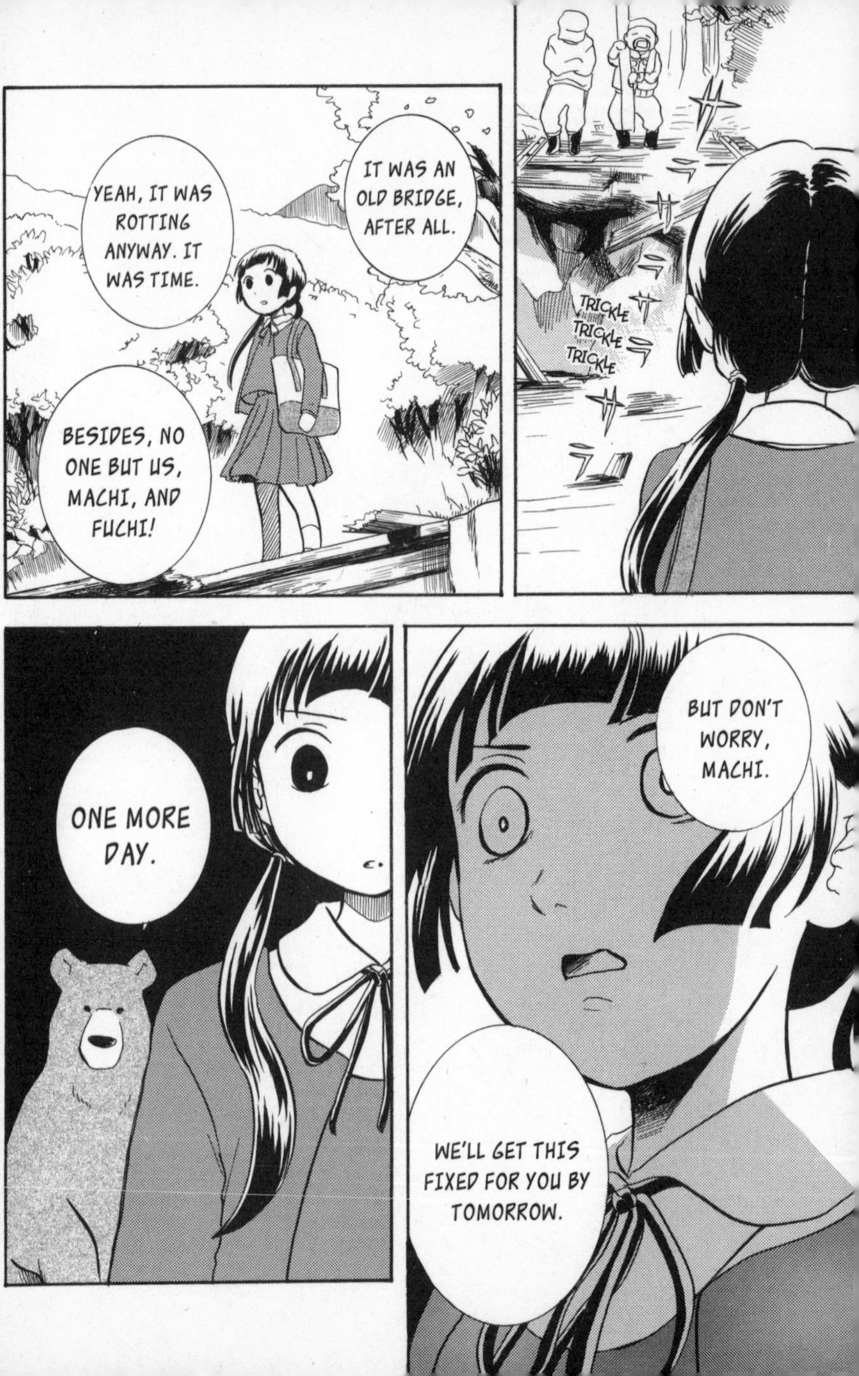
TRICKLE TRICKLE TRICKLE
IT WAS AN OLD BRIDGE, AFTER ALL.
YEAH, IT WAS ROTTING ANYWAY. IT WAS TIME.
BESIDES, NO ONE BUT US, MACHI, AND FUCHI!
BUT DON'T WORRY, MACHI.
WE'LL GET THIS FIXED FOR YOU BY TOMORROW.
ONE MORE DAY.

晴れたらいいね… HOPE THE SUN COMES OUT...

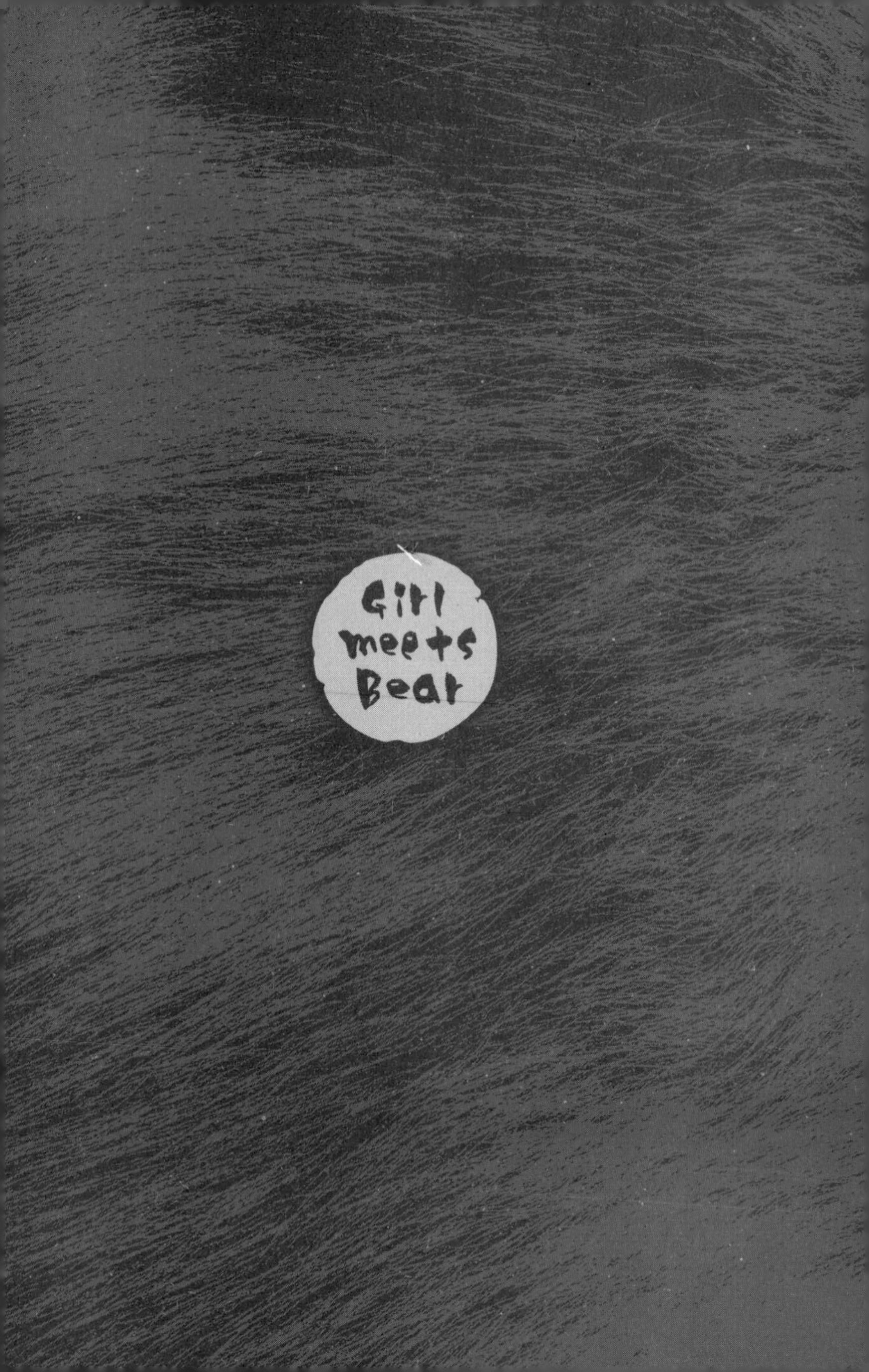
Girl
meets
Bear

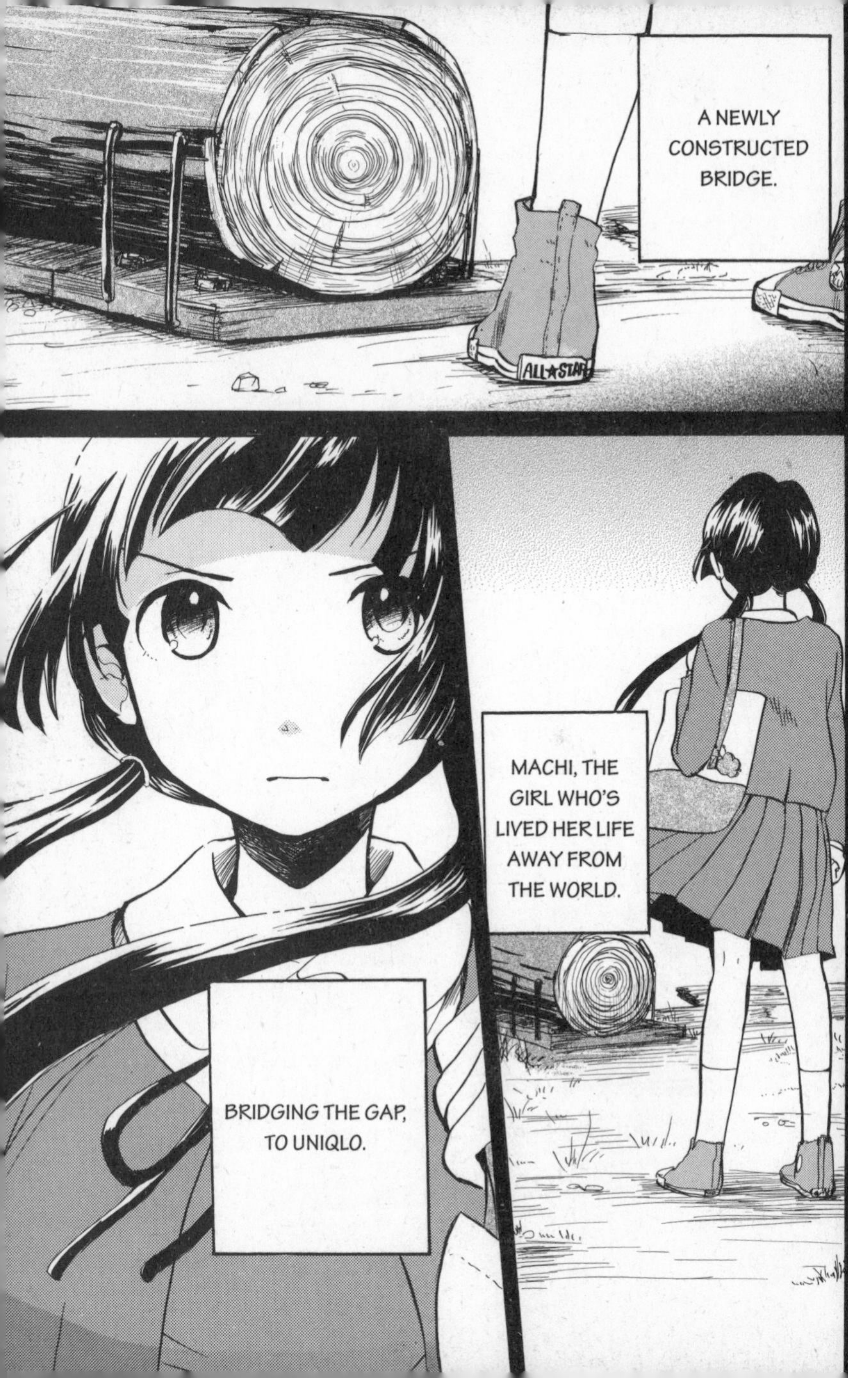
A NEWLY CONSTRUCTED BRIDGE.
ALL★STAR
MACHI, THE GIRL WHO'S LIVED HER LIFE AWAY FROM THE WORLD.
BRIDGING THE GAP, TO UNIQLO.

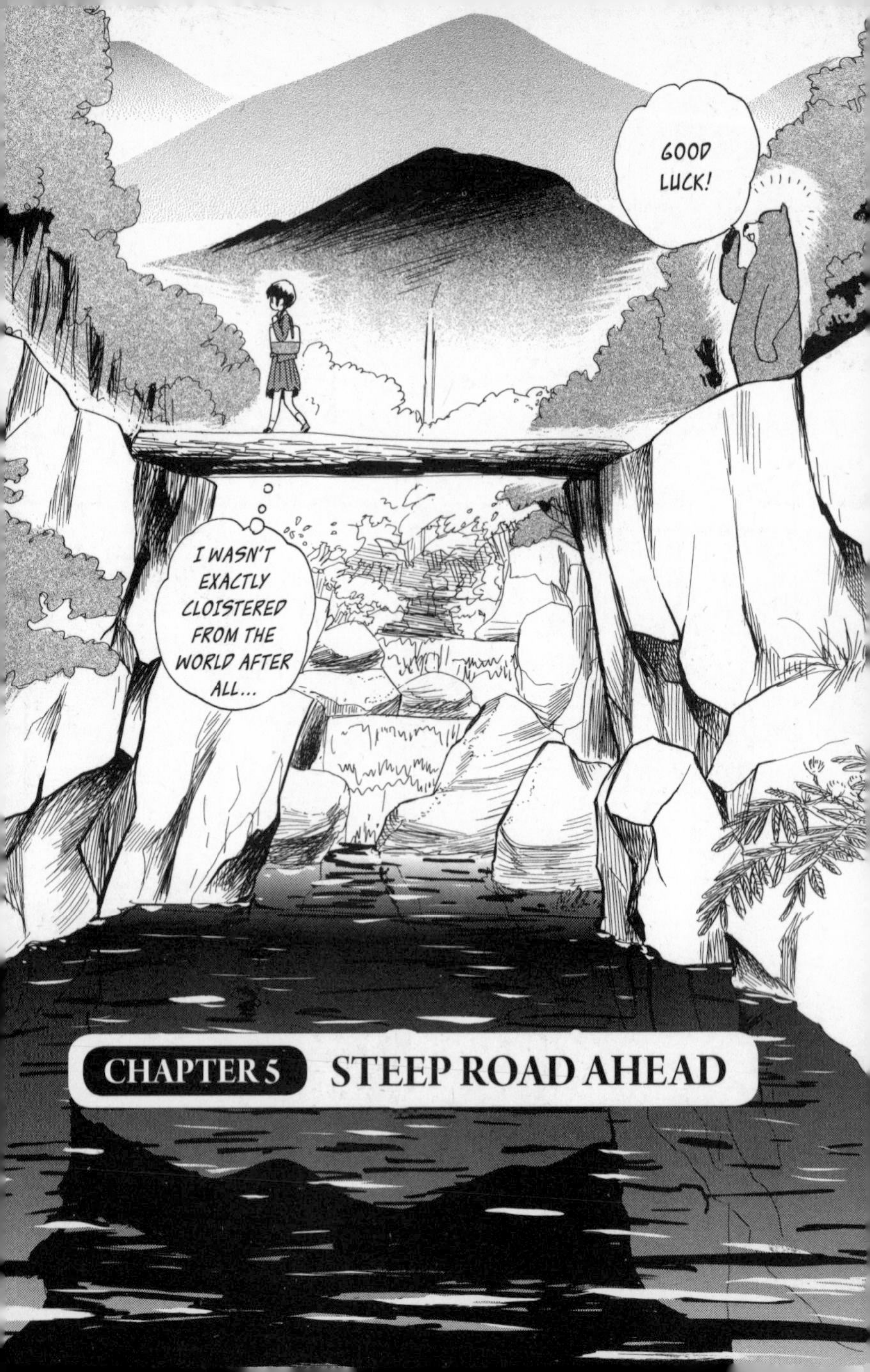
GOOD LUCK!
I WASN'T EXACTLY CLOISTERED FROM THE WORLD AFTER ALL...

CHAPTER 5 STEEP ROAD AHEAD

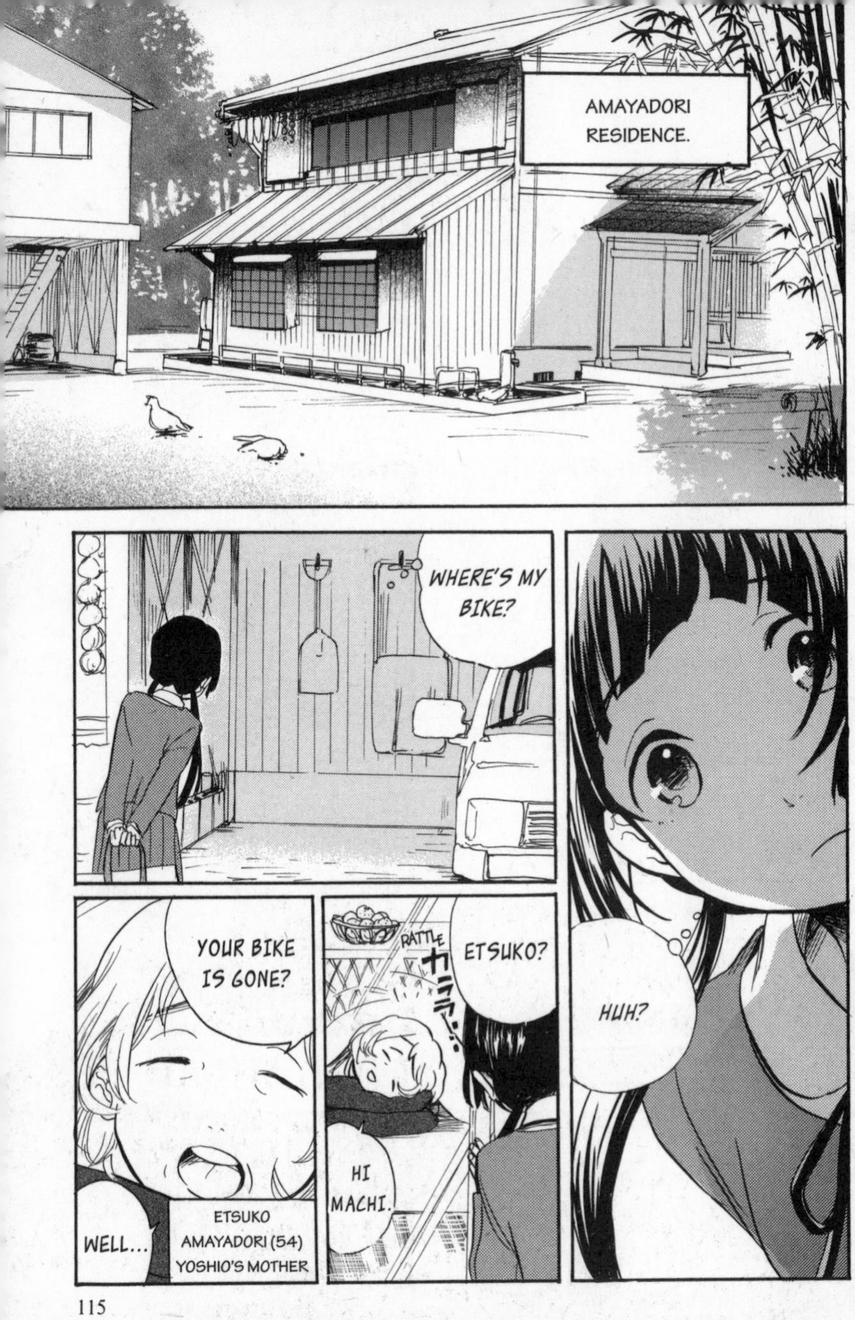
AMAYADORI RESIDENCE.
HUH?
WHERE'S MY BIKE?
ETSUKO?
RATTLE
HI MACHI.
YOUR BIKE IS GONE?
WELL...
ETSUKO AMAYADORI (54) YOSHIO'S MOTHER

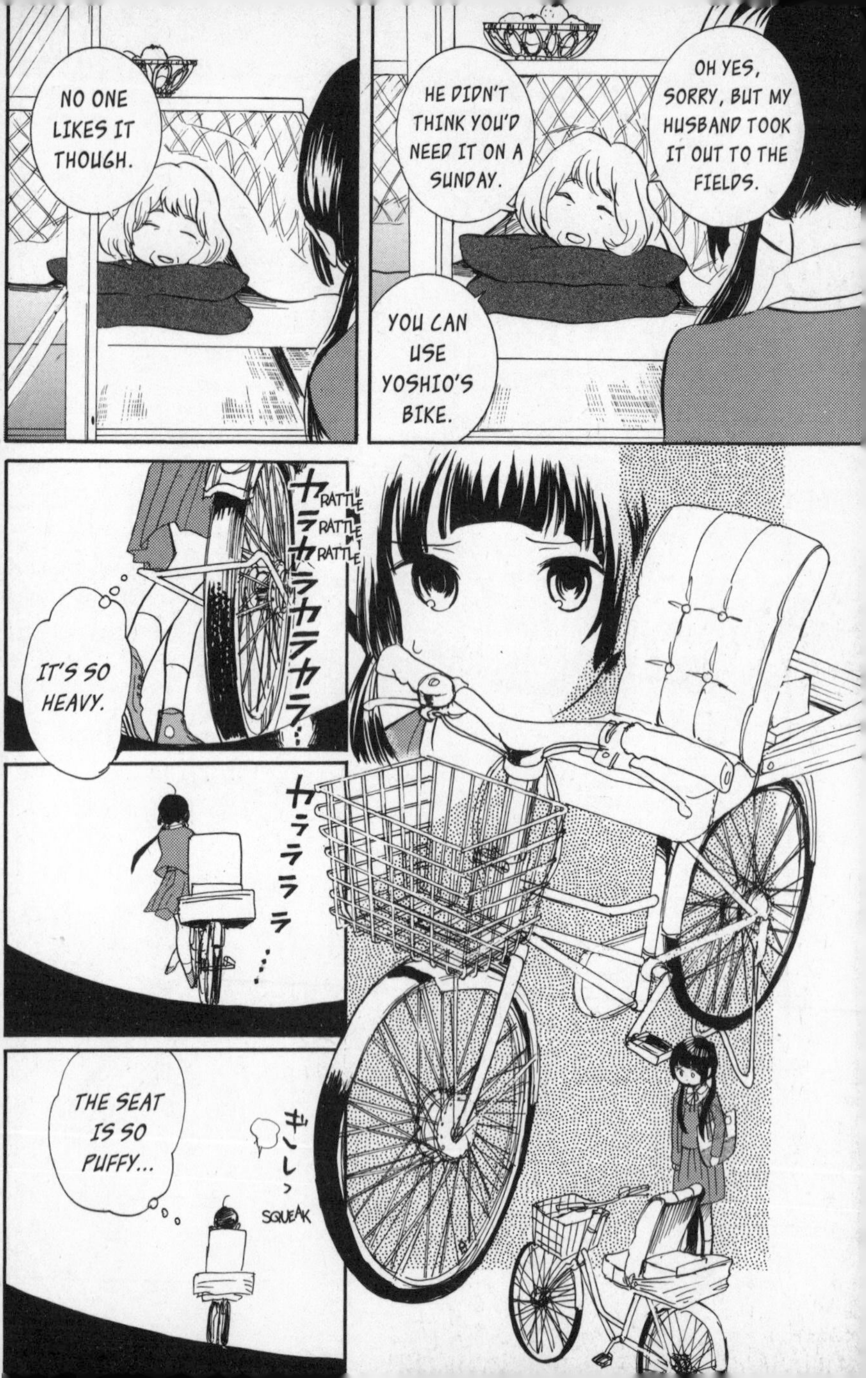

OH YES, SORRY, BUT MY HUSBAND TOOK IT OUT TO THE FIELDS.
HE DIDN'T THINK YOU'D NEED IT ON A SUNDAY.
YOU CAN USE YOSHIO'S BIKE.
NO ONE LIKES IT THOUGH.
カラカラカラカラ…
RATTLE RATTLE RATTLE
IT'S SO HEAVY.
カラララ…
THE SEAT IS SO PUFFY...
ぎしっ
SQUEAK

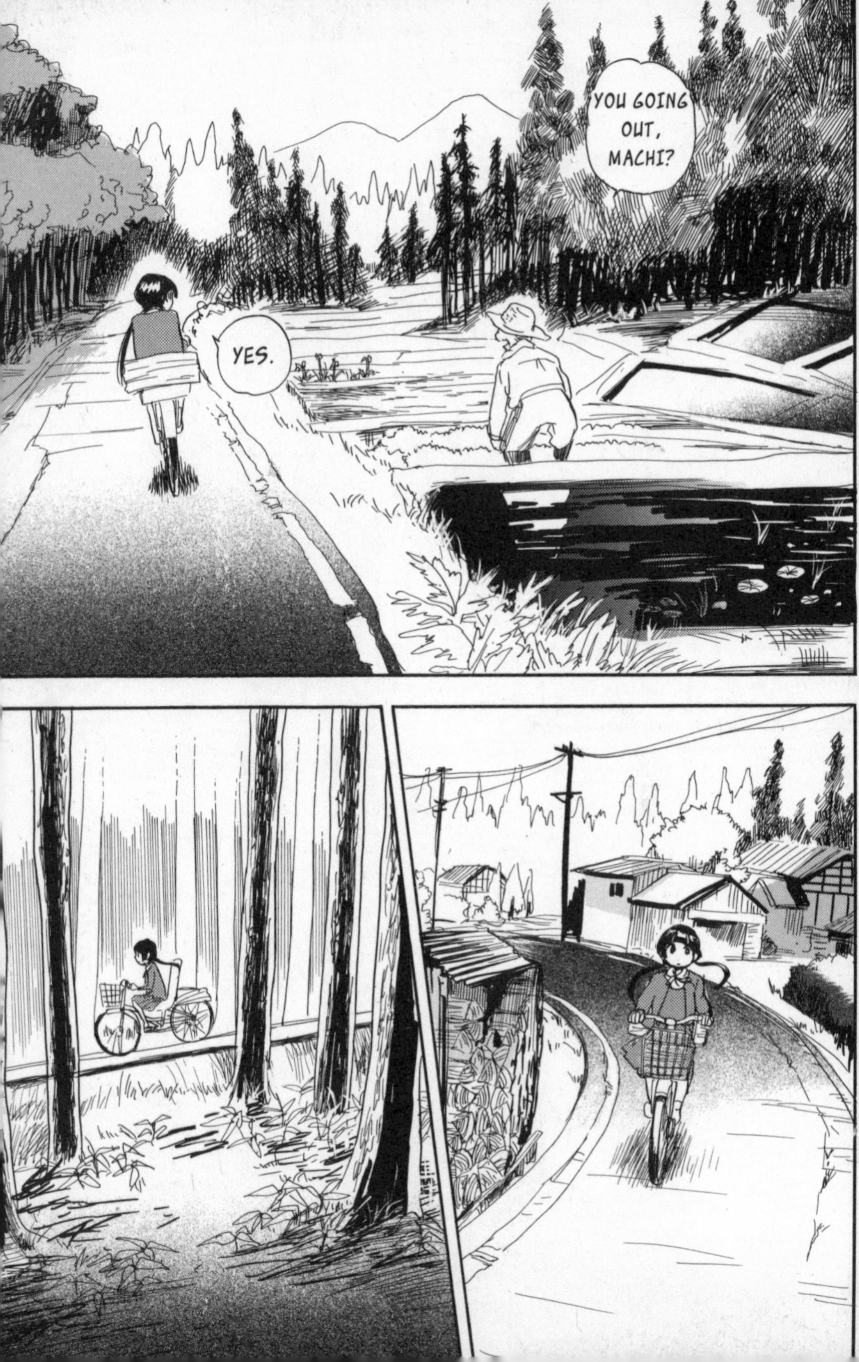
YOU GOING OUT, MACHI?
YES.

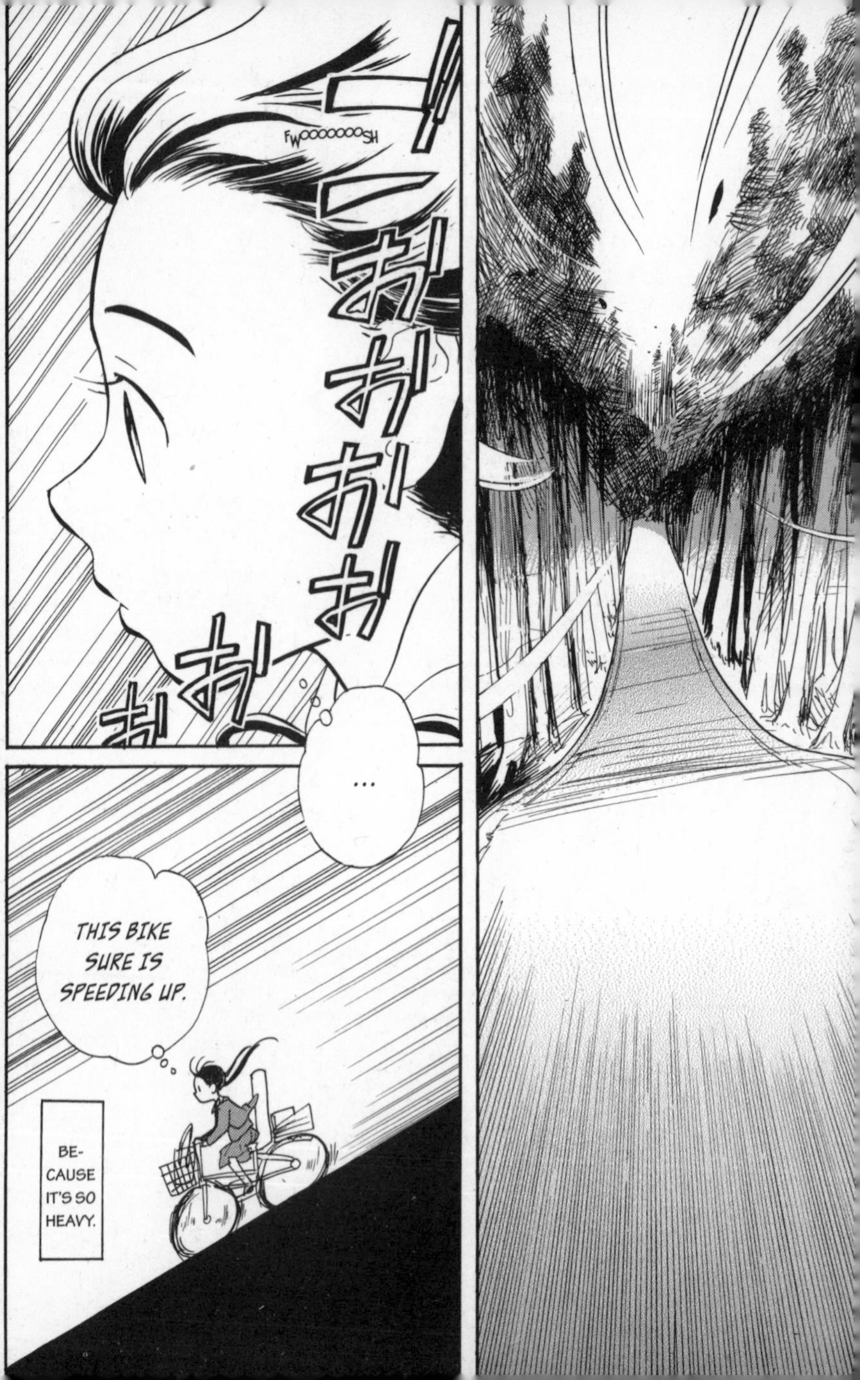
ごおおおおお
FWOOOOOOOOSH
...
THIS BIKE SURE IS SPEEDING UP.
BE-CAUSE IT'S SO HEAVY.

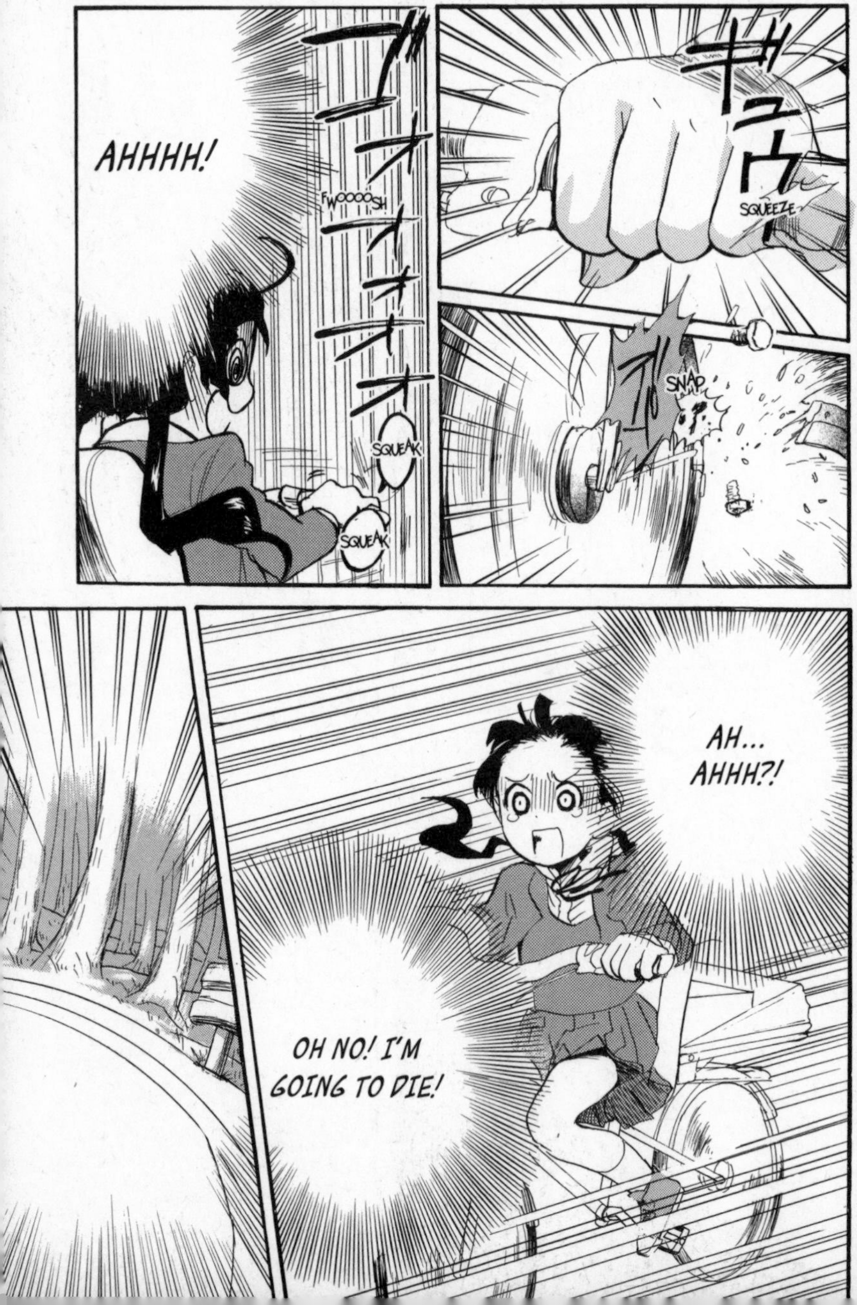
ギュウ
SQUEEZE
SNAP
AHHHH!
FWOOOOSH
SQUEAK
SQUEAK
AH... AHHH?!
OH NO! I'M GOING TO DIE!

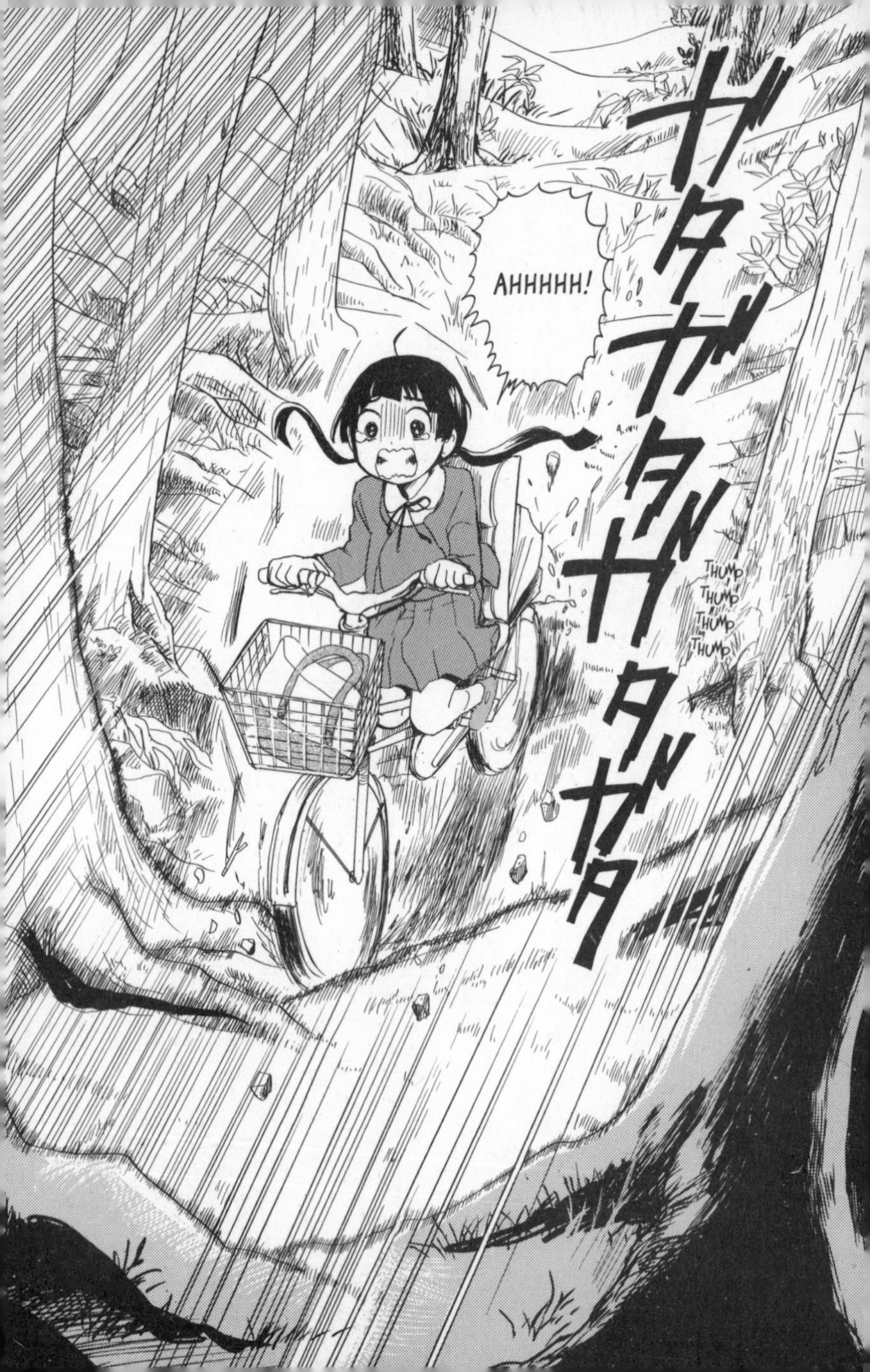
AHHHHH!
THUMP THUMP THUMP THUMP

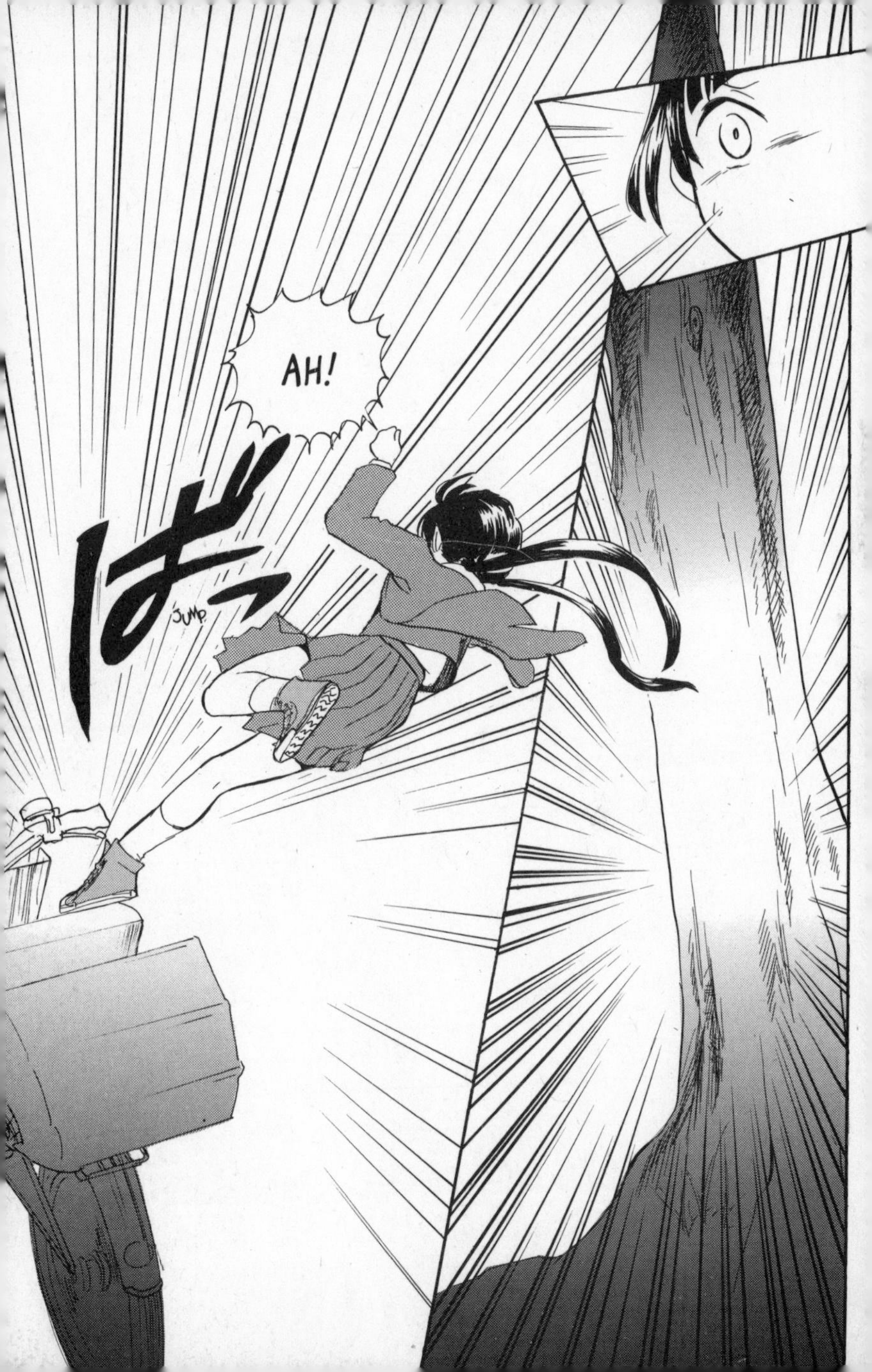
AH!
ばっ
JUMP

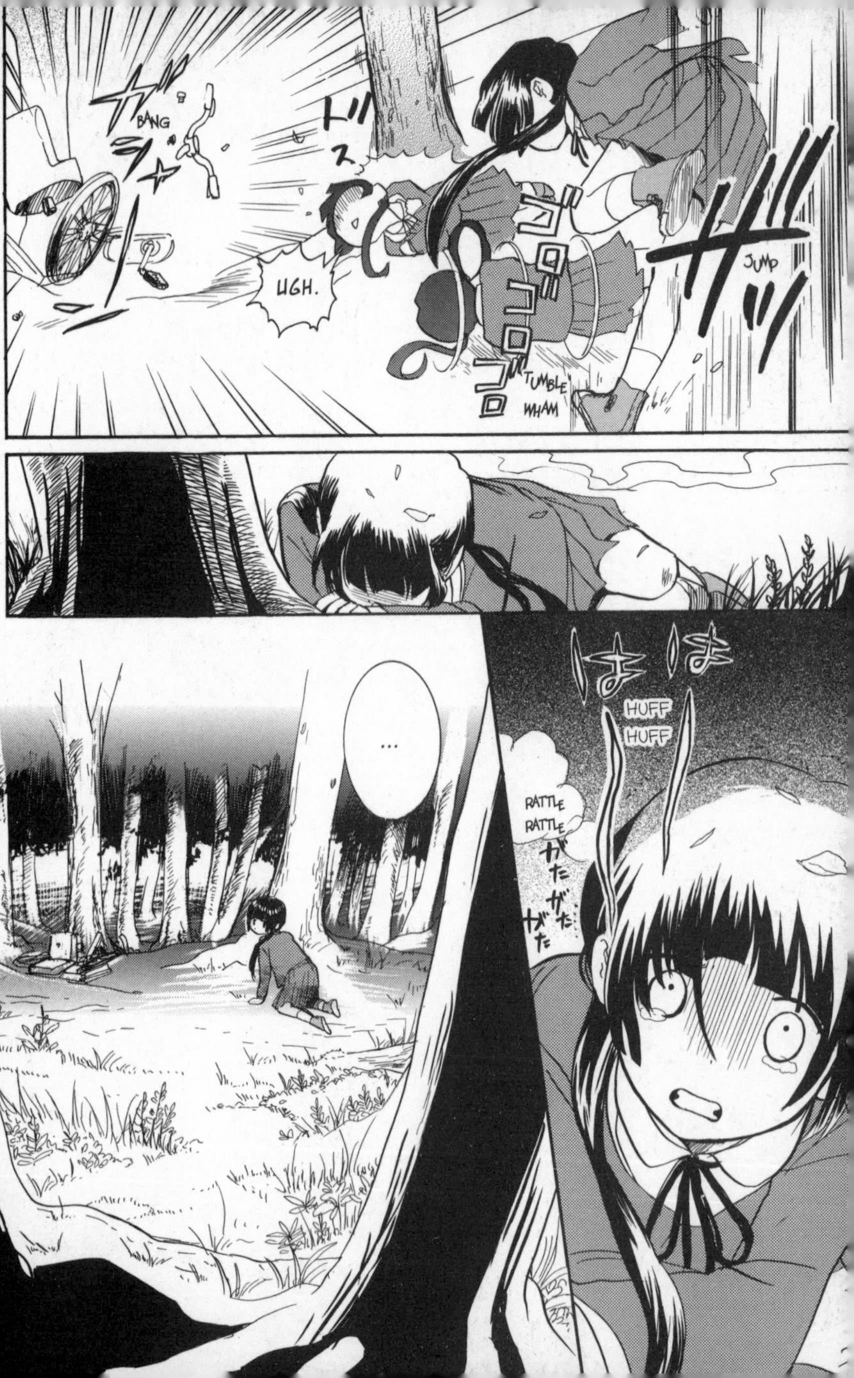
ザッ
JUMP
ゴロゴロゴロ
TUMBLE
WHAM
ドス
UGH.
ガシャ
BANG
はぁはぁ
HUFF HUFF
がたがたがた
RATTLE RATTLE
...

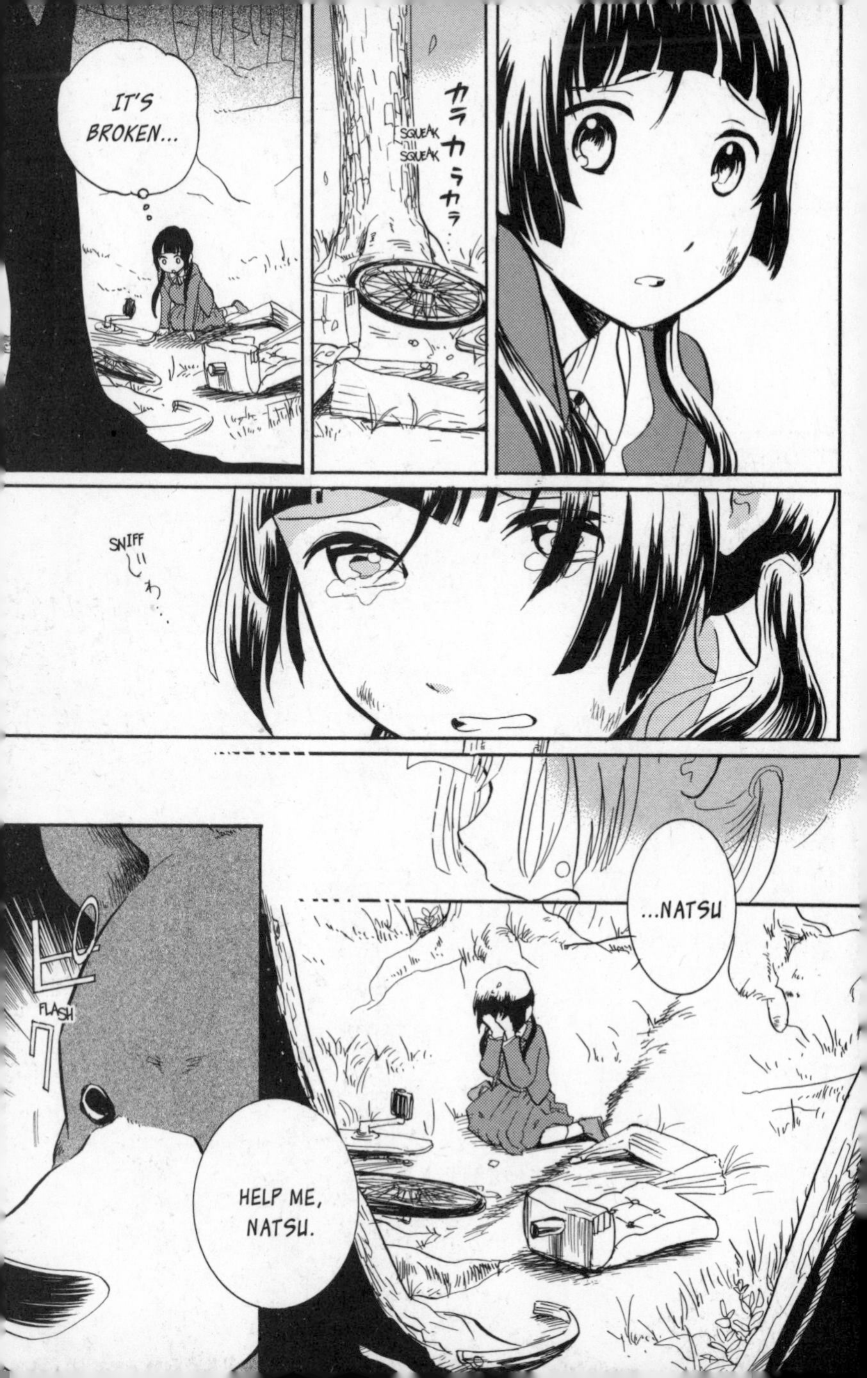
カラカラカラ...
SQUEAK SQUEAK
IT'S BROKEN...
SNIFF
じわ...
...NATSU
FLASH
HELP ME, NATSU.

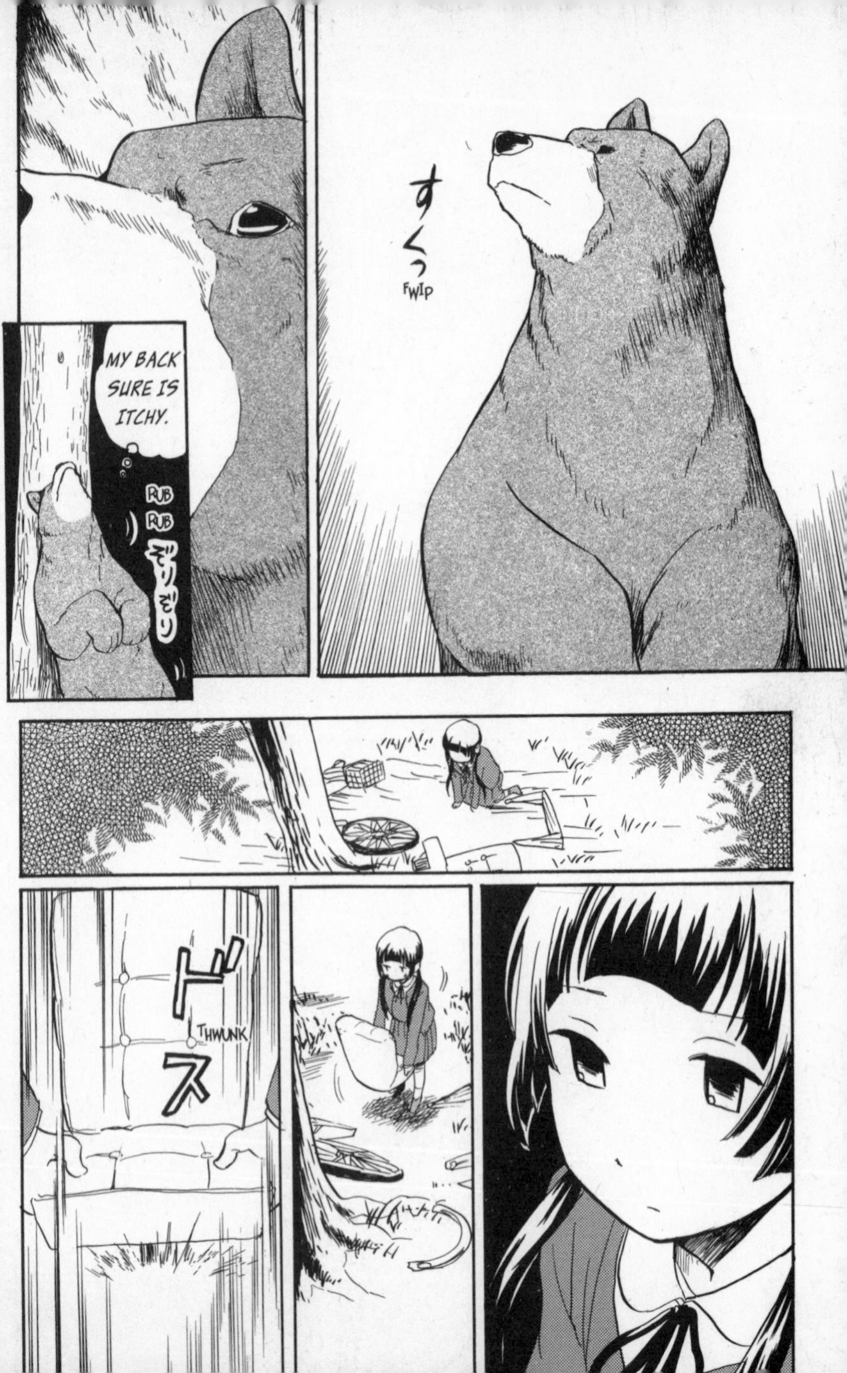
すくっ
FWIP
MY BACK SURE IS ITCHY.
RUB RUB
ぞりぞり
...
ドス
THWUNK

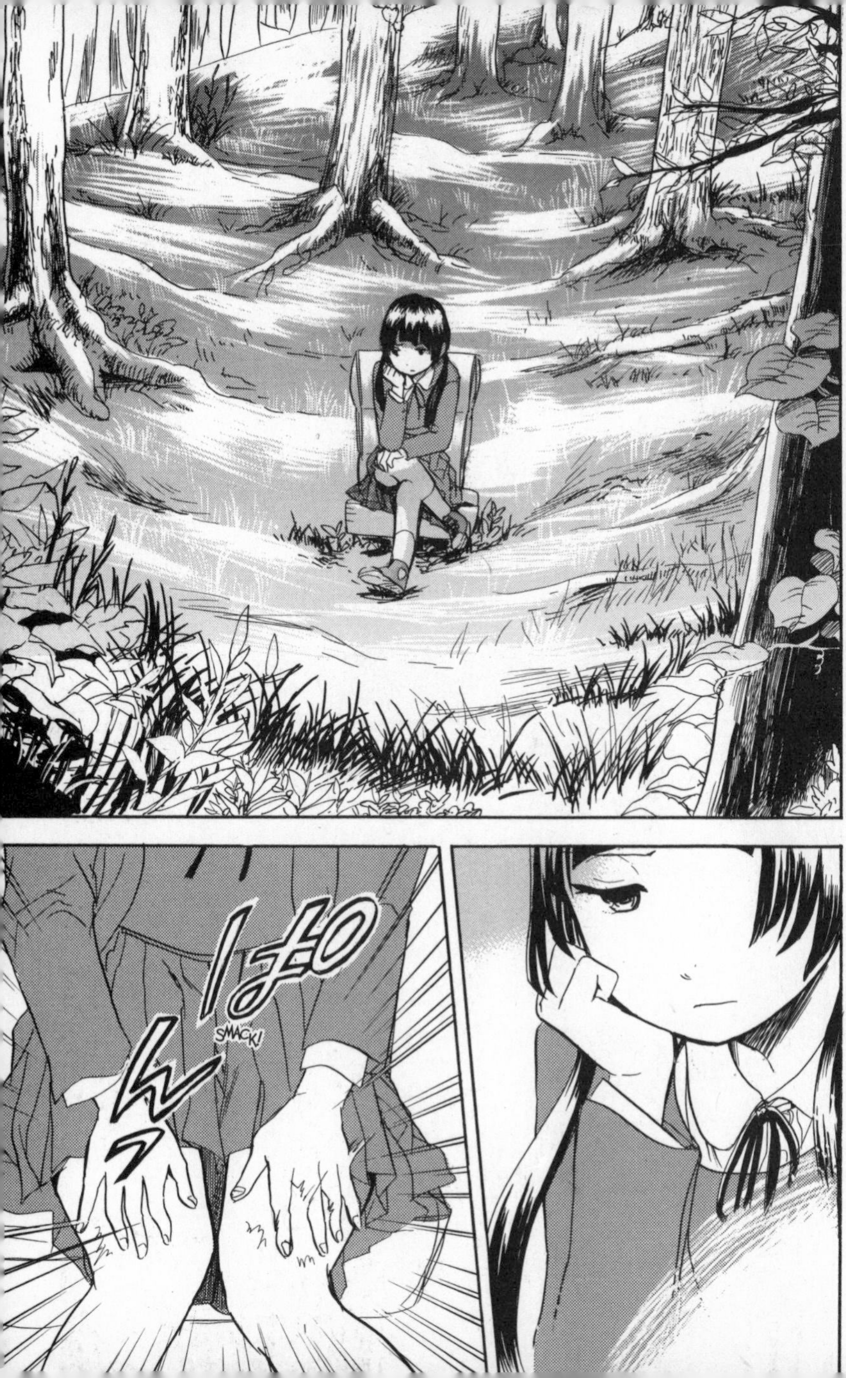
ぱんっ
SMACK!

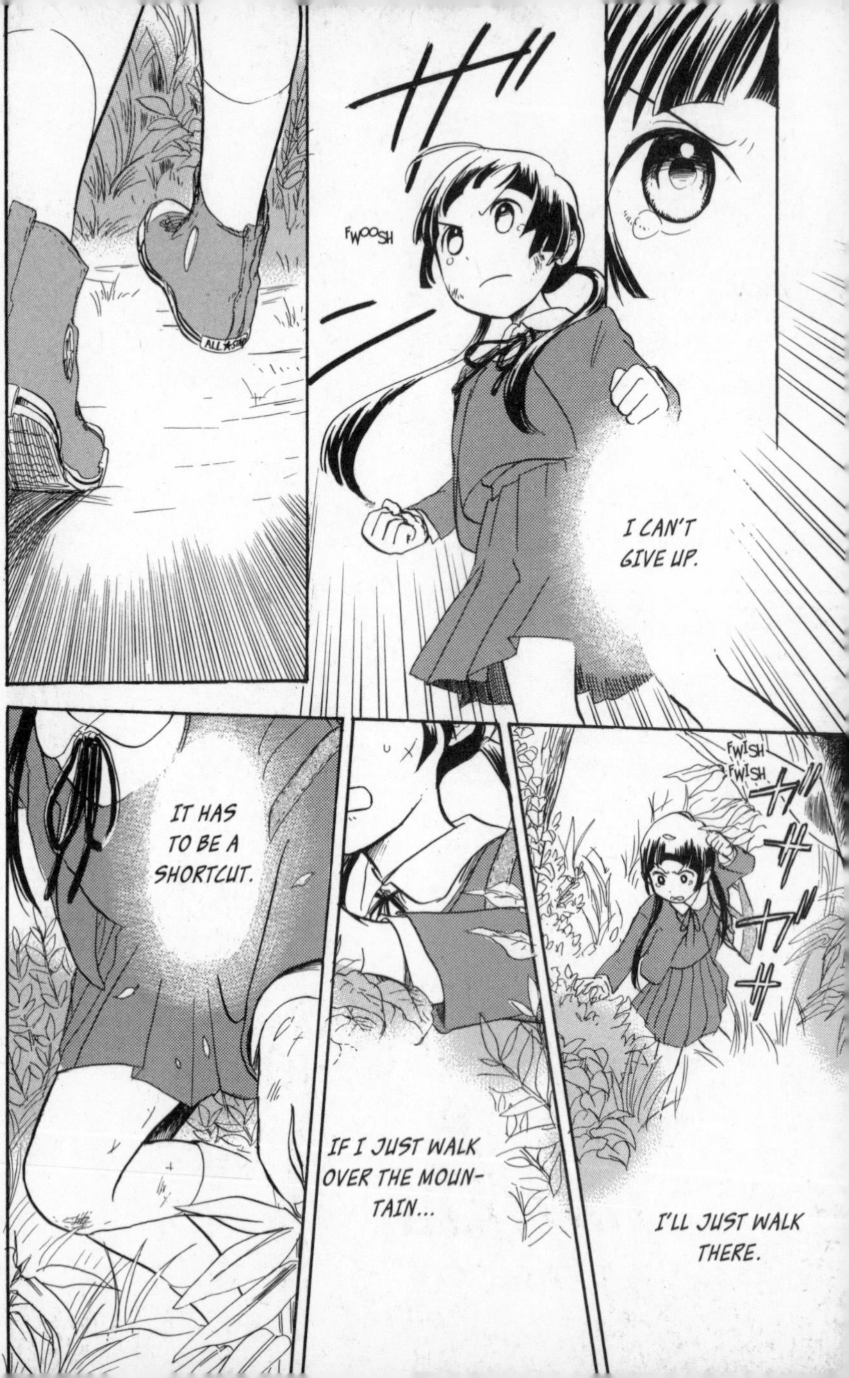
FWOOSH
I CAN'T GIVE UP.
FWISH FWISH
I'LL JUST WALK THERE.
IF I JUST WALK OVER THE MOUN-TAIN...
IT HAS TO BE A SHORTCUT.

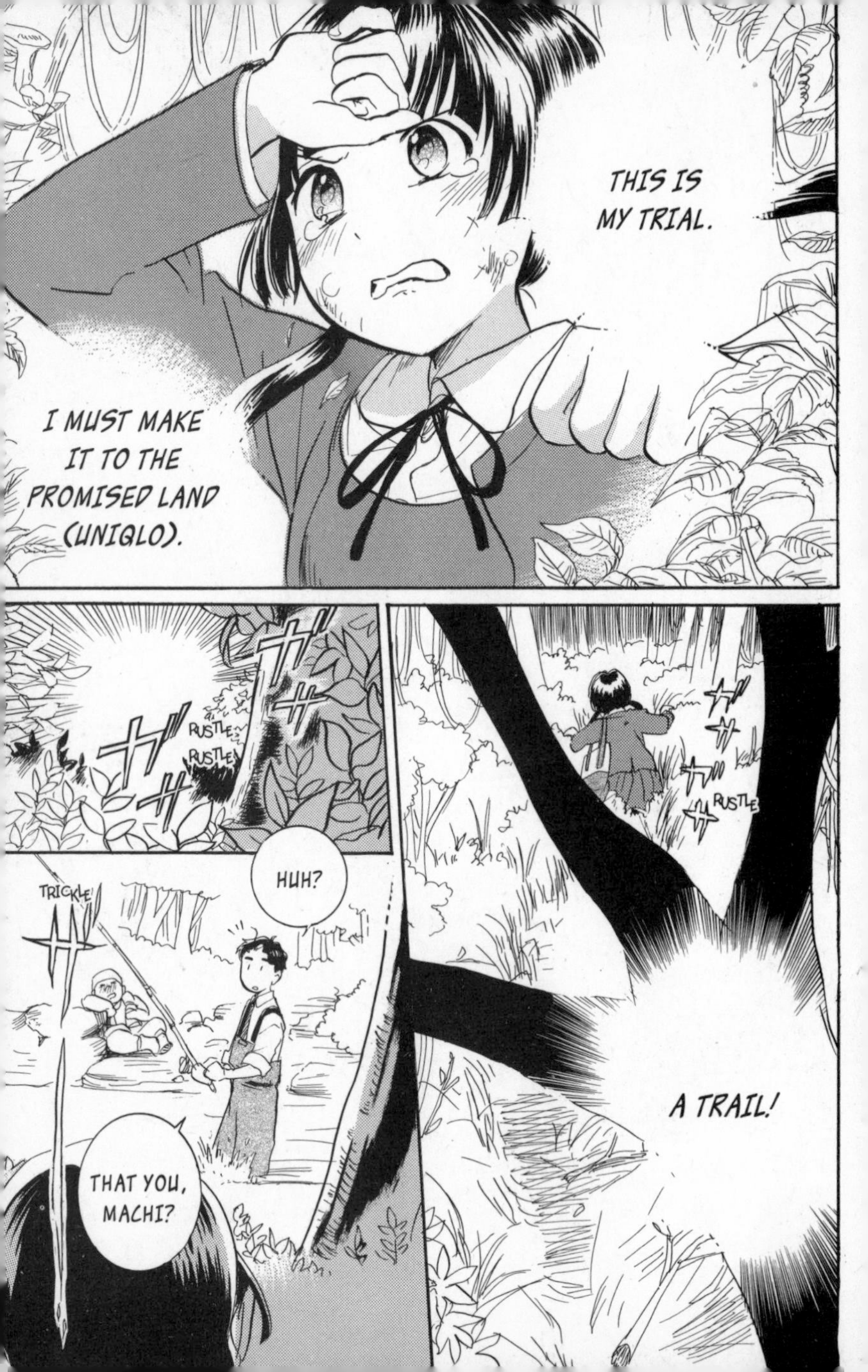
THIS IS MY TRIAL.
I MUST MAKE IT TO THE PROMISED LAND (UNIQLO).
RUSTLE
A TRAIL!
RUSTLE
RUSTLE
HUH?
TRICKLE
THAT YOU, MACHI?

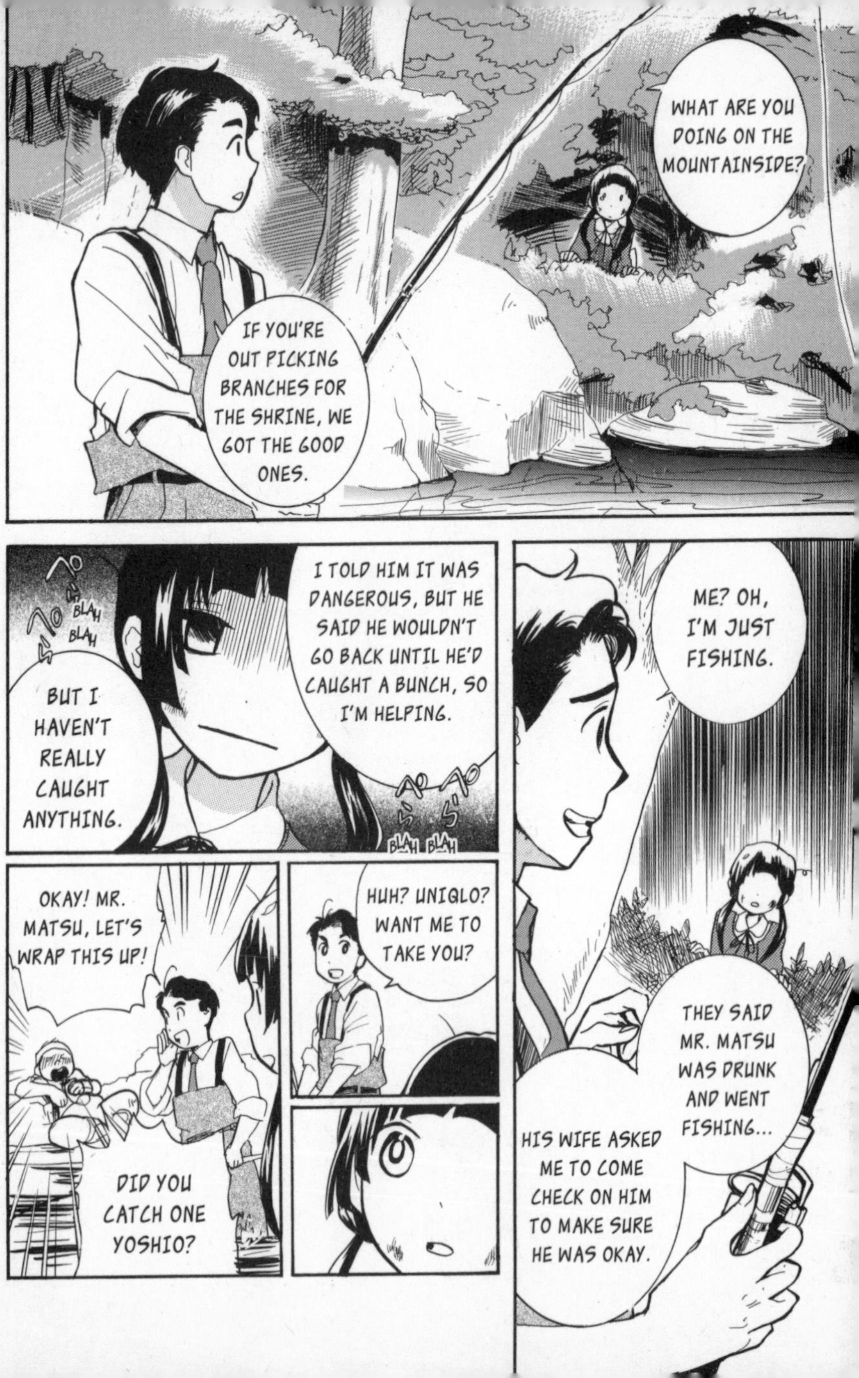
WHAT ARE YOU DOING ON THE MOUNTAINSIDE?
IF YOU'RE OUT PICKING BRANCHES FOR THE SHRINE, WE GOT THE GOOD ONES.
ME? OH, I'M JUST FISHING.
THEY SAID MR. MATSU WAS DRUNK AND WENT FISHING...
HIS WIFE ASKED ME TO COME CHECK ON HIM TO MAKE SURE HE WAS OKAY.
I TOLD HIM IT WAS DANGEROUS, BUT HE SAID HE WOULDN'T GO BACK UNTIL HE'D CAUGHT A BUNCH, SO I'M HELPING.
BLAH BLAH
BUT I HAVEN'T REALLY CAUGHT ANYTHING.
BLAH BLAH
HUH? UNIQLO? WANT ME TO TAKE YOU?
OKAY! MR. MATSU, LET'S WRAP THIS UP!
DID YOU CATCH ONE YOSHIO?

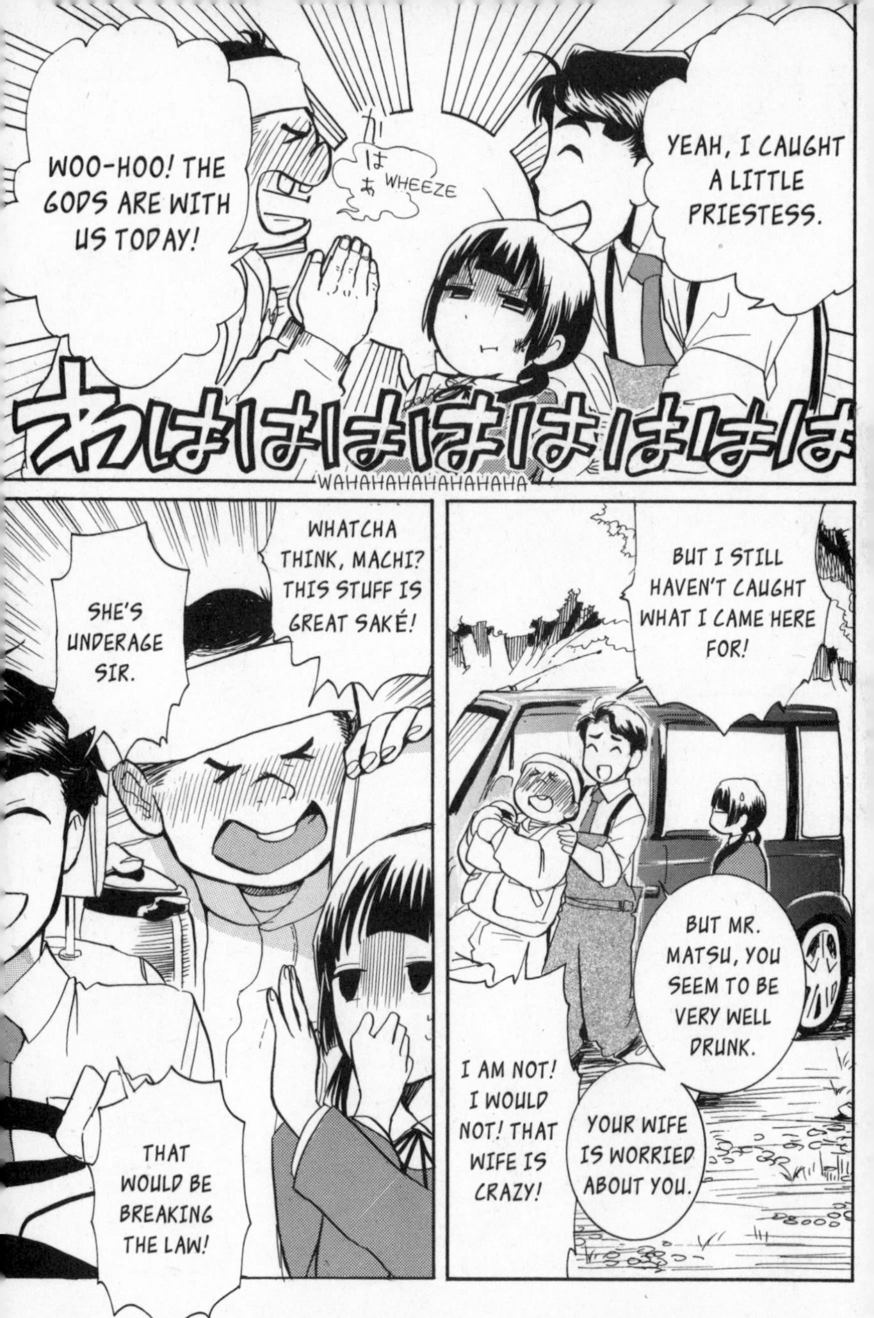
YEAH, I CAUGHT A LITTLE PRIESTESS.
かはあ
WHEEZE
WOO-HOO! THE GODS ARE WITH US TODAY!
あはははははははは
WAHAHAHAHAHAHAHA
BUT I STILL HAVEN'T CAUGHT WHAT I CAME HERE FOR!
BUT MR. MATSU, YOU SEEM TO BE VERY WELL DRUNK.
YOUR WIFE IS WORRIED ABOUT YOU.
I AM NOT! I WOULD NOT! THAT WIFE IS CRAZY!
WHATCHA THINK, MACHI? THIS STUFF IS GREAT SAKÉ!
SHE'S UNDERAGE SIR.
THAT WOULD BE BREAKING THE LAW!

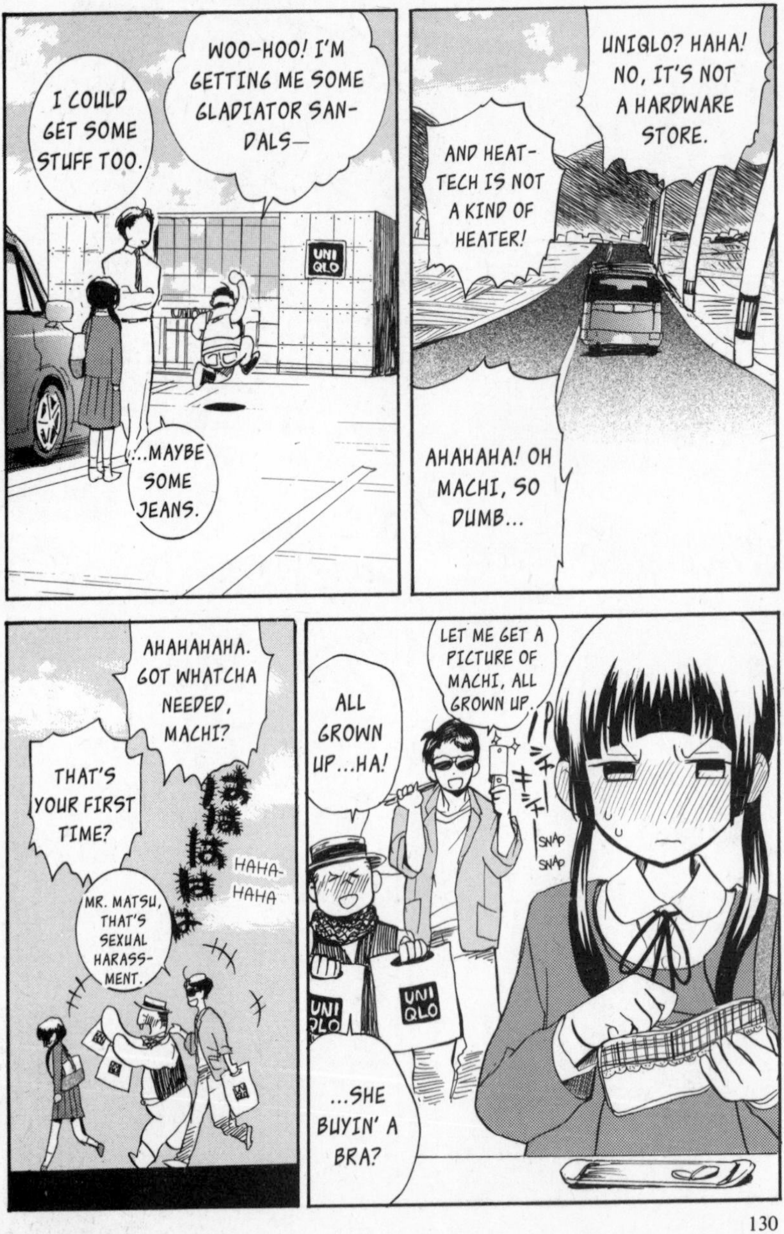
UNIQLO? HAHA! NO, IT'S NOT A HARDWARE STORE.
AND HEAT-TECH IS NOT A KIND OF HEATER!
AHAHAHA! OH MACHI, SO DUMB...
WOO-HOO! I'M GETTING ME SOME GLADIATOR SAN-DALS—
UNI QLO
I COULD GET SOME STUFF TOO.
...MAYBE SOME JEANS.
LET ME GET A PICTURE OF MACHI, ALL GROWN UP.
ALL GROWN UP...HA!
SNAP SNAP
UNI QLO
...SHE BUYIN' A BRA?
AHAHAHAHA. GOT WHATCHA NEEDED, MACHI?
THAT'S YOUR FIRST TIME?
ははははは
HAHA-HAHA
MR. MATSU, THAT'S SEXUAL HARASS-MENT.

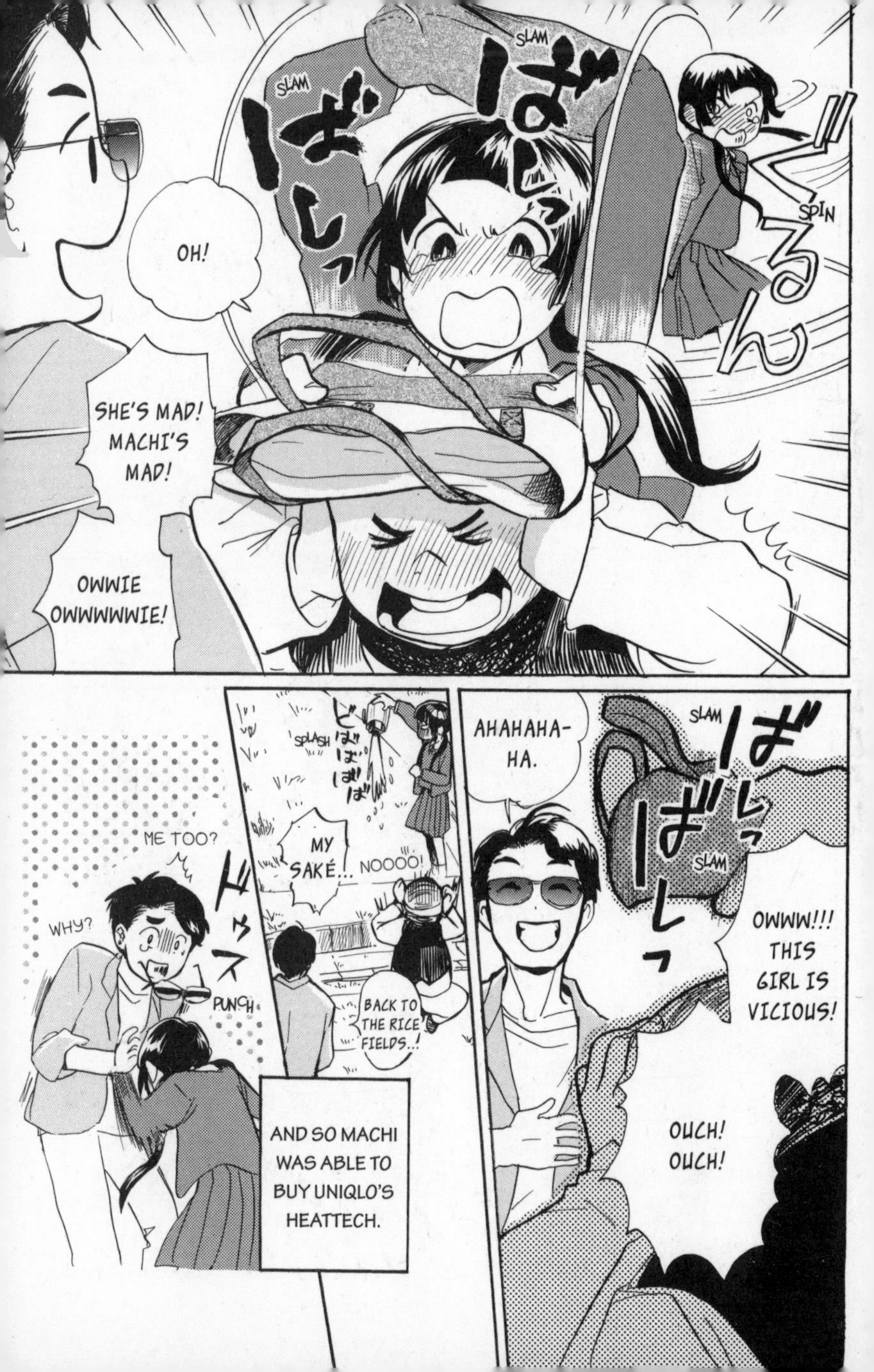
SPIN
くるん
SLAM
ばしっ
SLAM
ばしっ
OH!
SHE'S MAD! MACHI'S MAD!
OWWIE OWWWWIE!
AHAHAHA-HA.
SLAM
ばしっ
SLAM
ばしっ
OWWW!!! THIS GIRL IS VICIOUS!
OUCH! OUCH!
SPLASH
MY SAKÉ...
NOOOO!
BACK TO THE RICE FIELDS...!
PUNCH
ME TOO?
WHY?
AND SO MACHI WAS ABLE TO BUY UNIQLO'S HEATTECH.

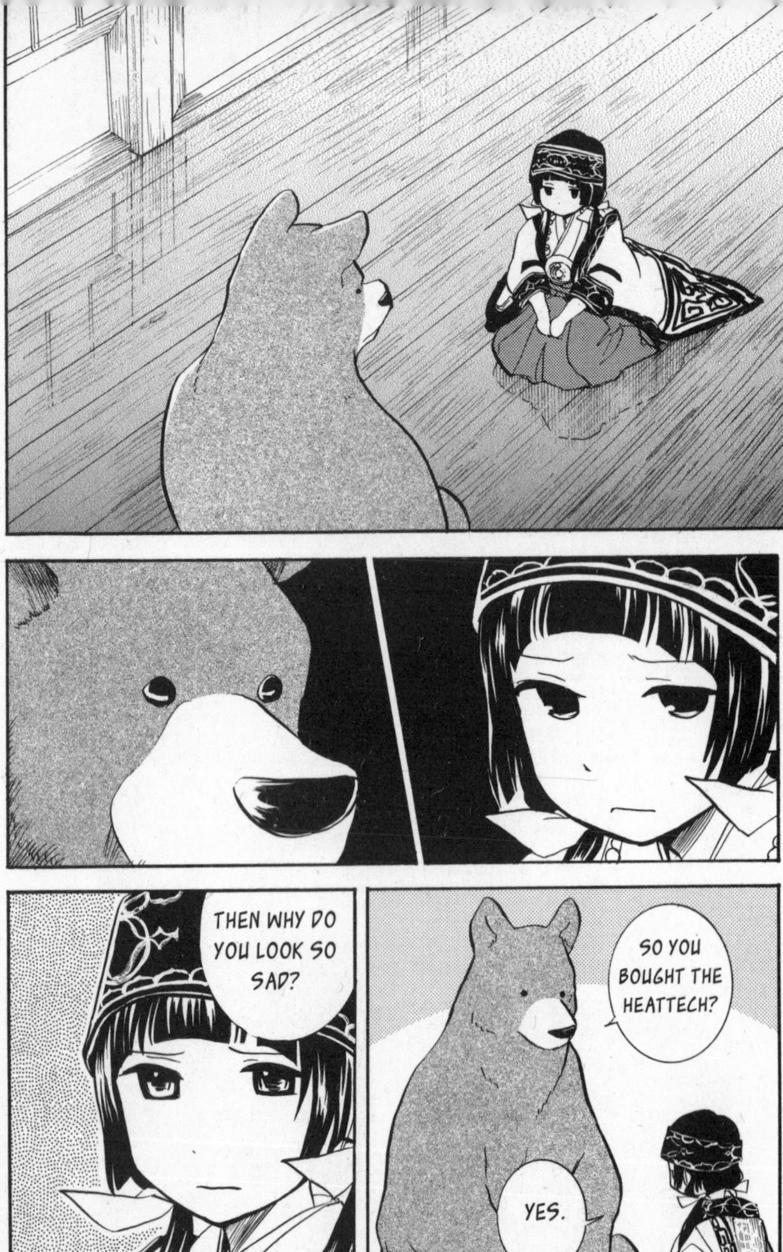
SO YOU BOUGHT THE HEATTECH?
YES.
THEN WHY DO YOU LOOK SO SAD?

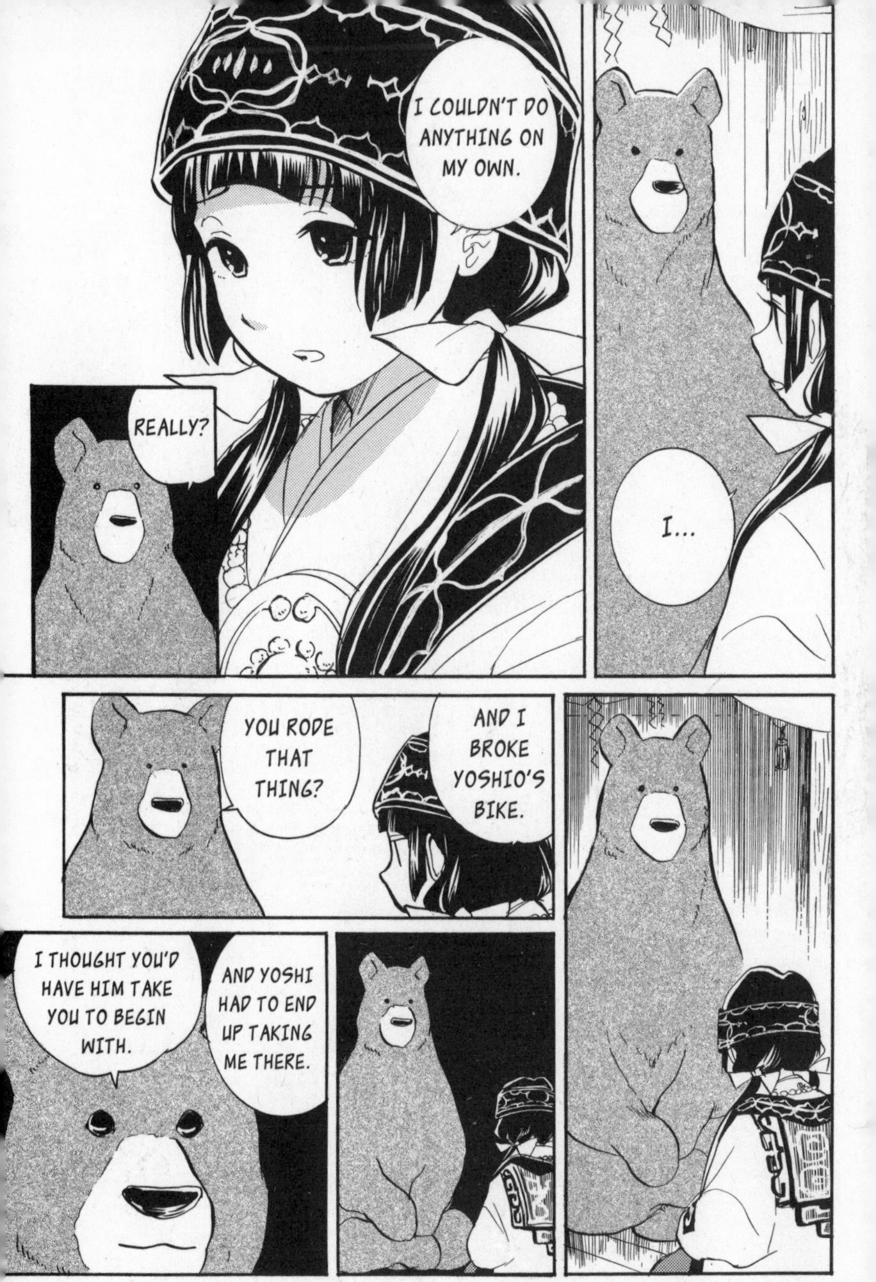
I...
I COULDN'T DO ANYTHING ON MY OWN.
REALLY?
AND I BROKE YOSHIO'S BIKE.
YOU RODE THAT THING?
AND YOSHI HAD TO END UP TAKING ME THERE.
I THOUGHT YOU'D HAVE HIM TAKE YOU TO BEGIN WITH.

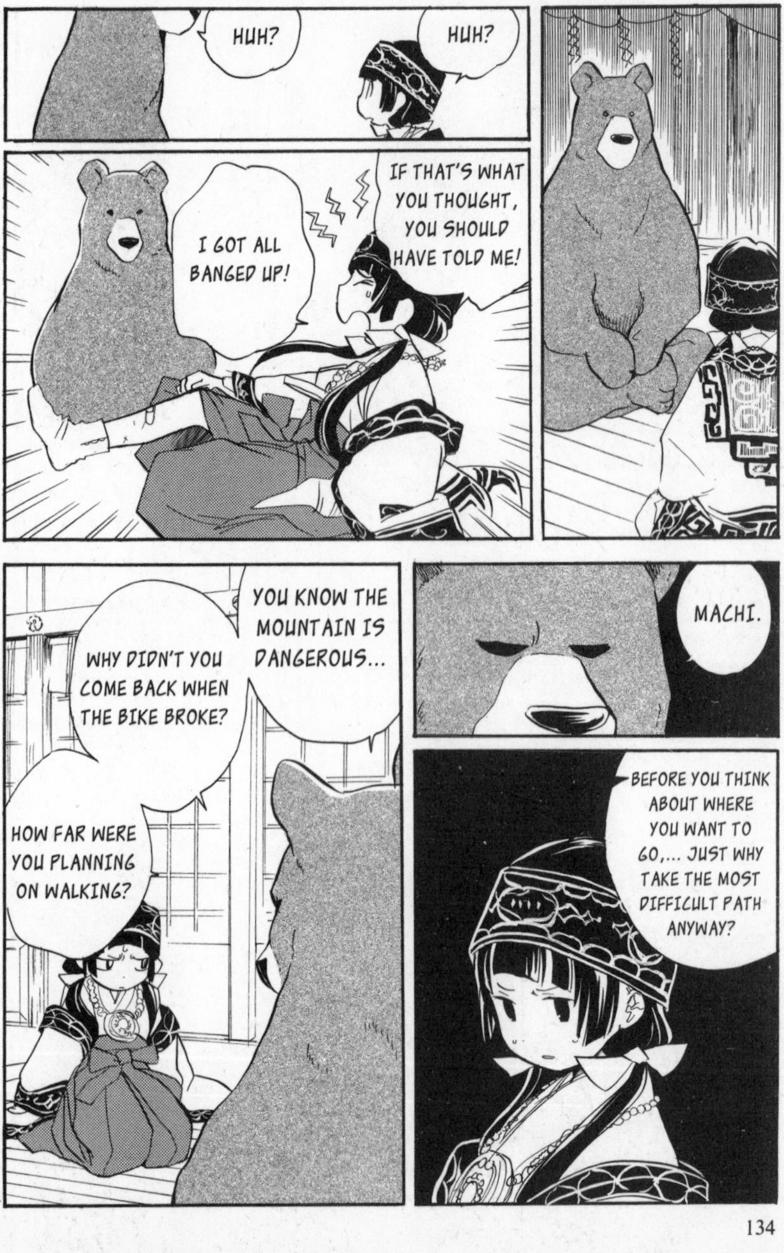
HUH?
HUH?
IF THAT'S WHAT YOU THOUGHT, YOU SHOULD HAVE TOLD ME!
I GOT ALL BANGED UP!
MACHI.
BEFORE YOU THINK ABOUT WHERE YOU WANT TO GO,... JUST WHY TAKE THE MOST DIFFICULT PATH ANYWAY?
YOU KNOW THE MOUNTAIN IS DANGEROUS...
WHY DIDN'T YOU COME BACK WHEN THE BIKE BROKE?
HOW FAR WERE YOU PLANNING ON WALKING?

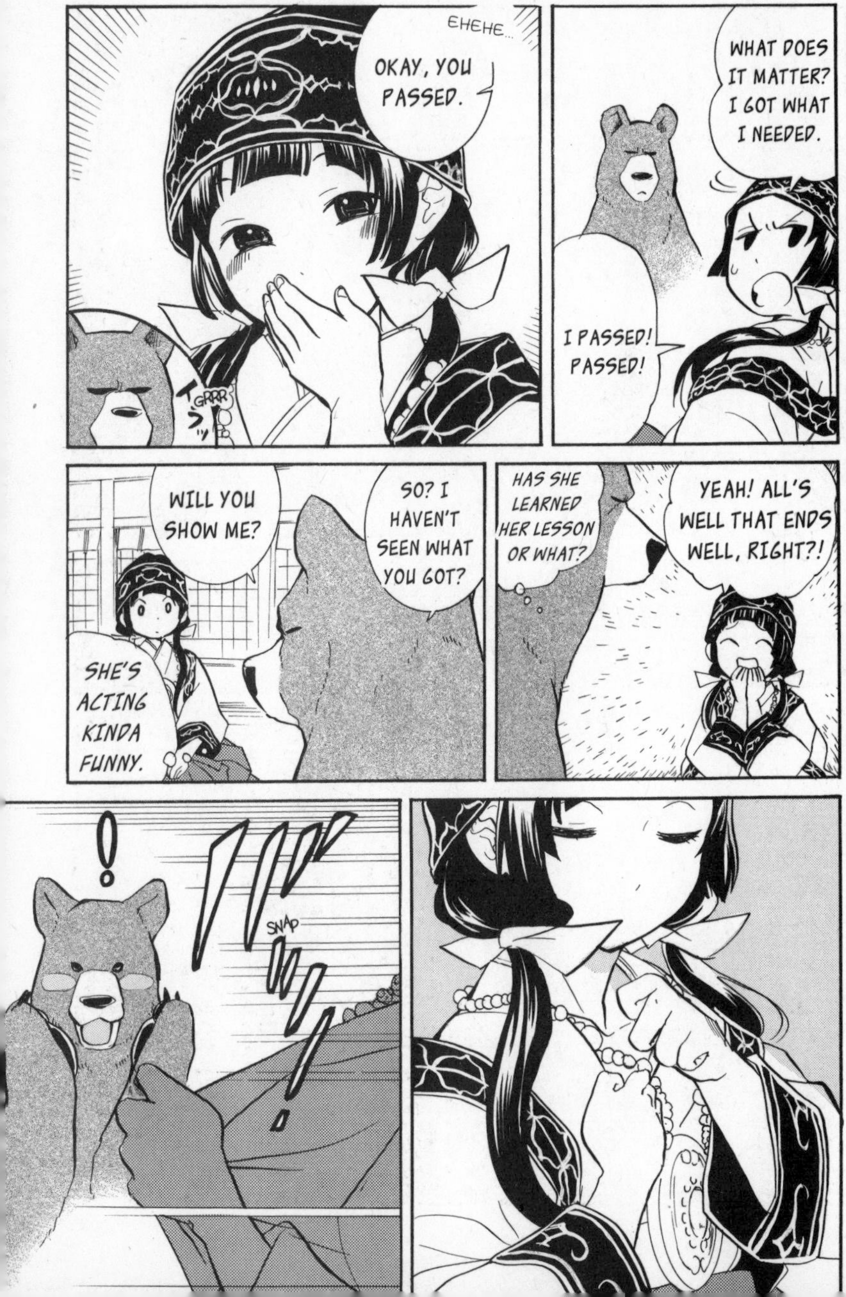
WHAT DOES IT MATTER? I GOT WHAT I NEEDED.
I PASSED! PASSED!
EHEHE...
OKAY, YOU PASSED.
GRRR
YEAH! ALL'S WELL THAT ENDS WELL, RIGHT?!
HAS SHE LEARNED HER LESSON OR WHAT?
SO? I HAVEN'T SEEN WHAT YOU GOT?
WILL YOU SHOW ME?
SHE'S ACTING KINDA FUNNY.
!
SNAP

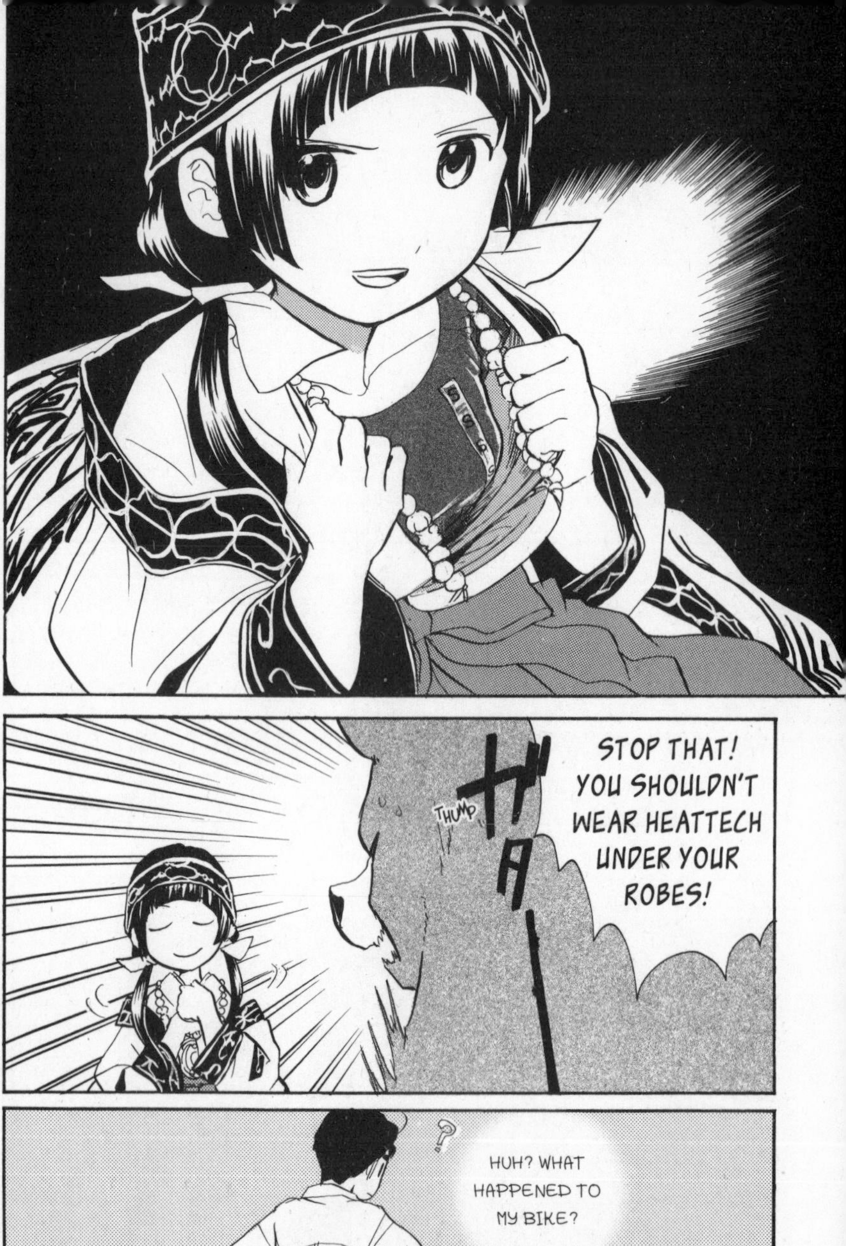
THUMP
STOP THAT! YOU SHOULDN'T WEAR HEATTECH UNDER YOUR ROBES!
HUH? WHAT HAPPENED TO MY BIKE?

CHAPTER 6
PROTECTOR OF TRADITION

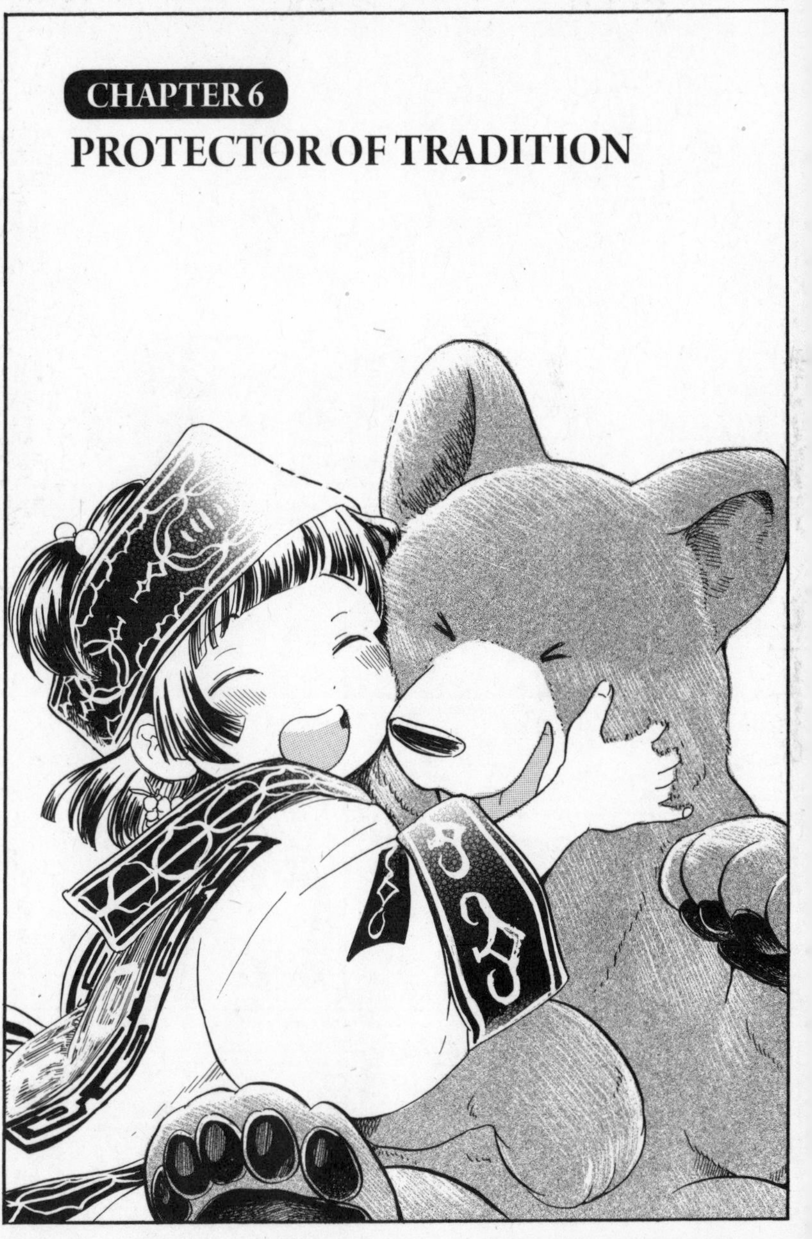

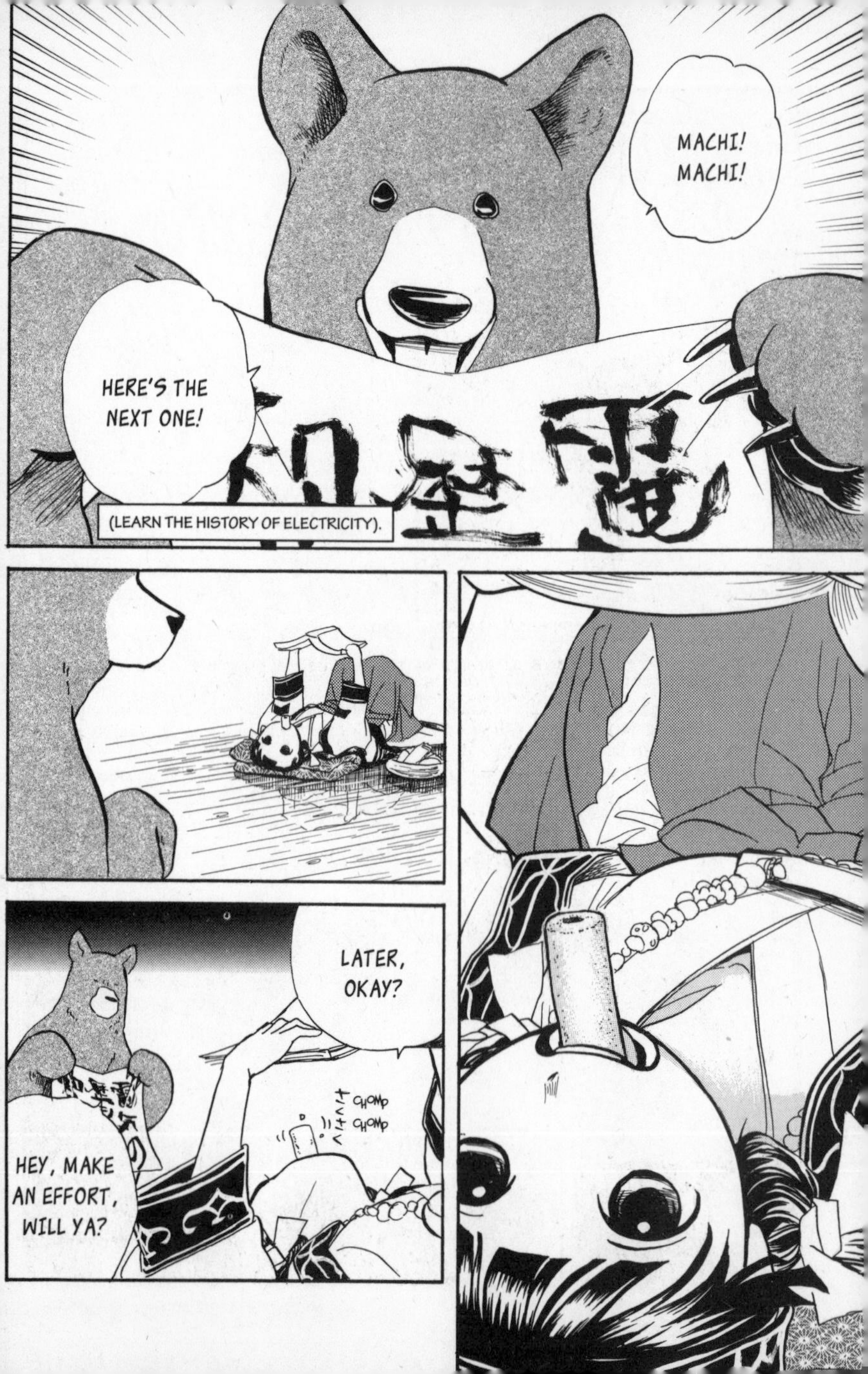
MACHI! MACHI!
HERE'S THE NEXT ONE!
(LEARN THE HISTORY OF ELECTRICITY).
LATER, OKAY?
CHOMP CHOMP
HEY, MAKE AN EFFORT, WILL YA?

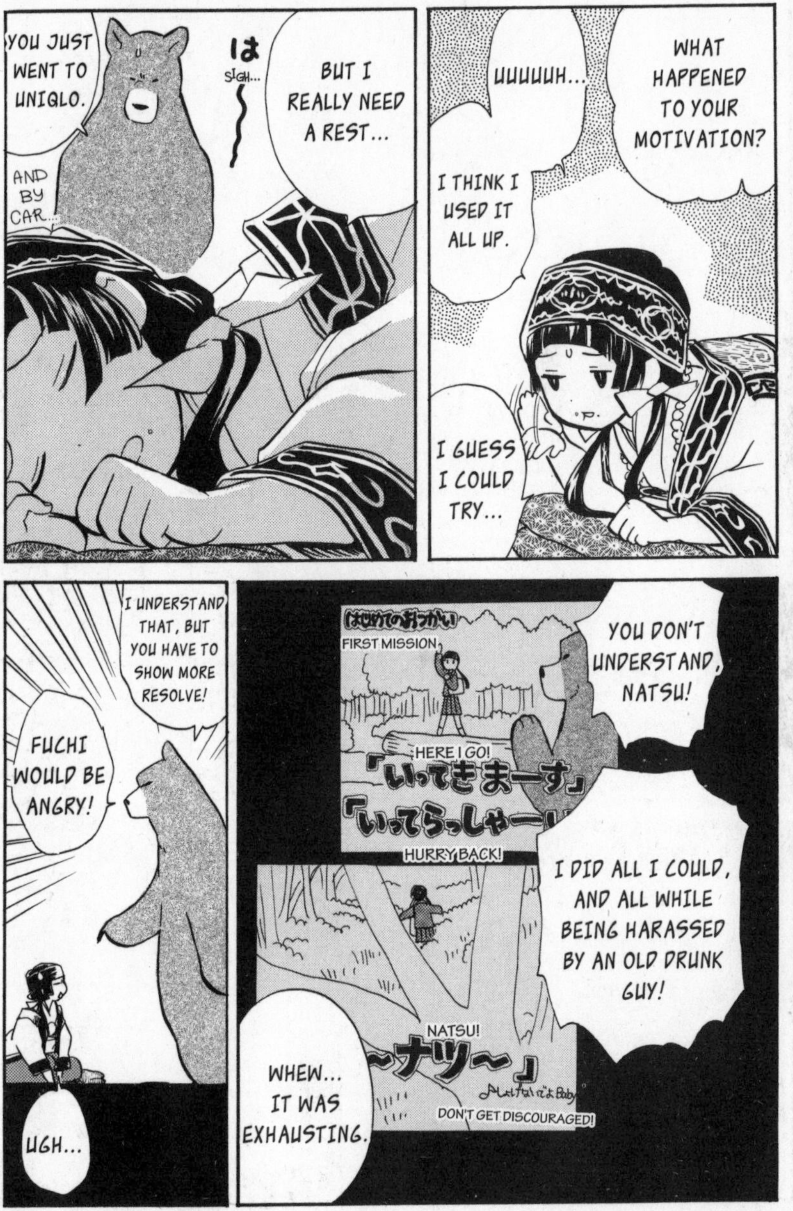
WHAT HAPPENED TO YOUR MOTIVATION?
UUUUUH...
I THINK I USED IT ALL UP.
I GUESS I COULD TRY...
BUT I REALLY NEED A REST...
は
SIGH...
YOU JUST WENT TO UNIQLO.
AND BY CAR...
YOU DON'T UNDERSTAND, NATSU!
はじめてのおつかい
FIRST MISSION
HERE I GO!
「いってきまーす」
「いってらっしゃー
HURRY BACK!
I DID ALL I COULD, AND ALL WHILE BEING HARASSED BY AN OLD DRUNK GUY!
NATSU!
〜ナツ〜」
しょげないでよBaby
DON'T GET DISCOURAGED!
WHEW... IT WAS EXHAUSTING.
I UNDERSTAND THAT, BUT YOU HAVE TO SHOW MORE RESOLVE!
FUCHI WOULD BE ANGRY!
UGH...

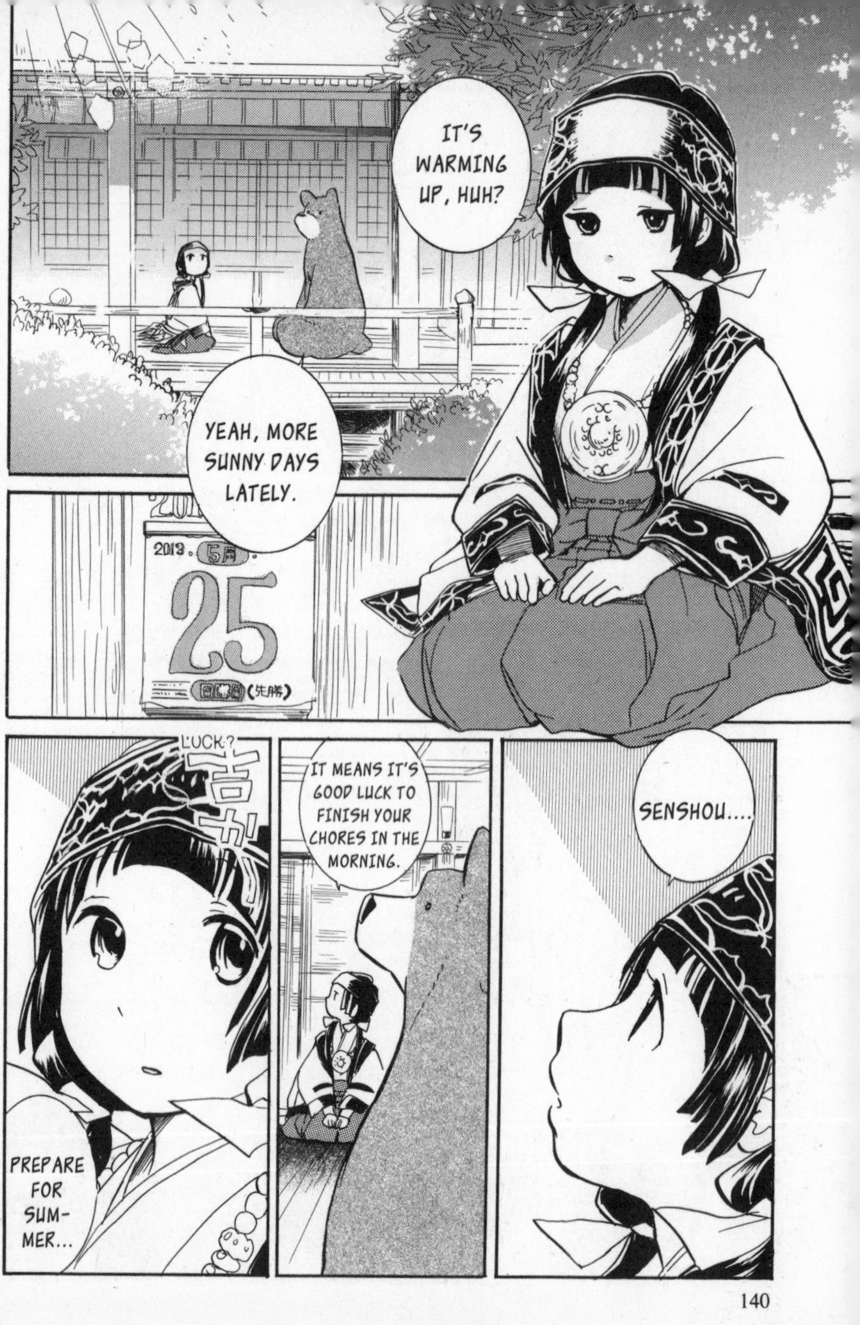
IT'S WARMING UP, HUH?
YEAH, MORE SUNNY DAYS LATELY.
2013 5月
25
(先勝)
SENSHOU....
IT MEANS IT'S GOOD LUCK TO FINISH YOUR CHORES IN THE MORNING.
LUCK?
吉か
PREPARE FOR SUM-MER...

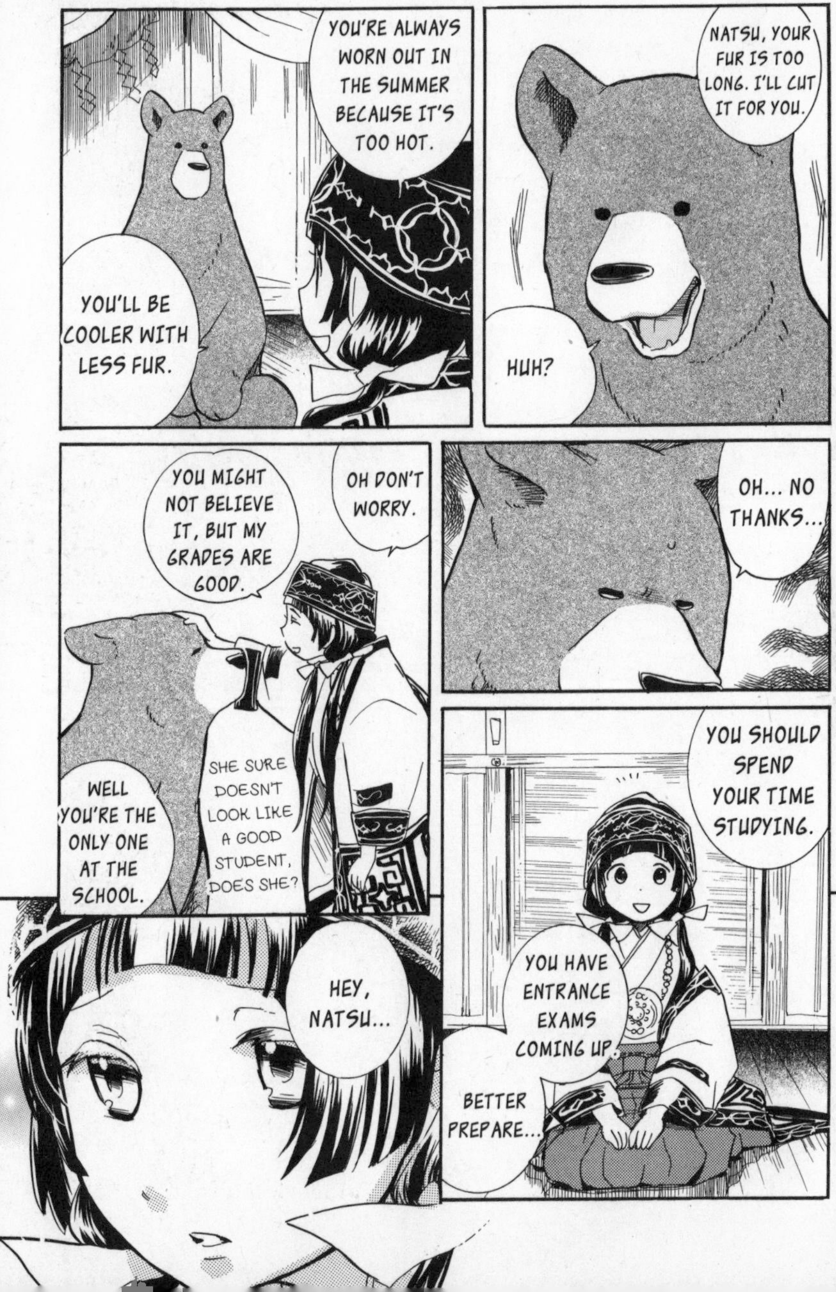
NATSU, YOUR FUR IS TOO LONG. I'LL CUT IT FOR YOU.
HUH?
YOU'RE ALWAYS WORN OUT IN THE SUMMER BECAUSE IT'S TOO HOT.
YOU'LL BE COOLER WITH LESS FUR.
OH... NO THANKS...
OH DON'T WORRY.
YOU MIGHT NOT BELIEVE IT, BUT MY GRADES ARE GOOD.
SHE SURE DOESN'T LOOK LIKE A GOOD STUDENT, DOES SHE?
WELL YOU'RE THE ONLY ONE AT THE SCHOOL.
YOU SHOULD SPEND YOUR TIME STUDYING.
YOU HAVE ENTRANCE EXAMS COMING UP.
BETTER PREPARE...
HEY, NATSU...

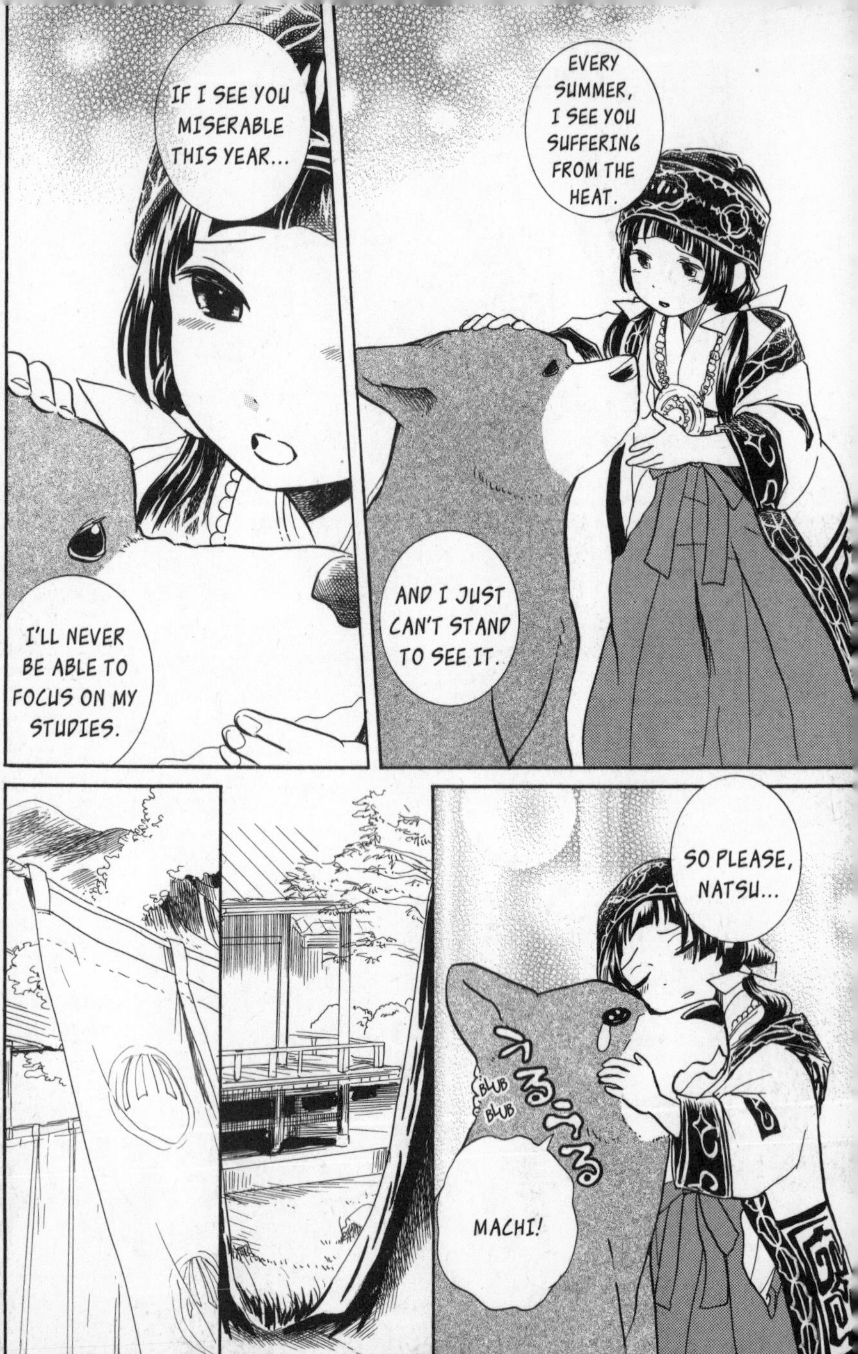
EVERY SUMMER, I SEE YOU SUFFERING FROM THE HEAT.
AND I JUST CAN'T STAND TO SEE IT.
IF I SEE YOU MISERABLE THIS YEAR...
I'LL NEVER BE ABLE TO FOCUS ON MY STUDIES.
SO PLEASE, NATSU...
BLUB BLUB
MACHI!

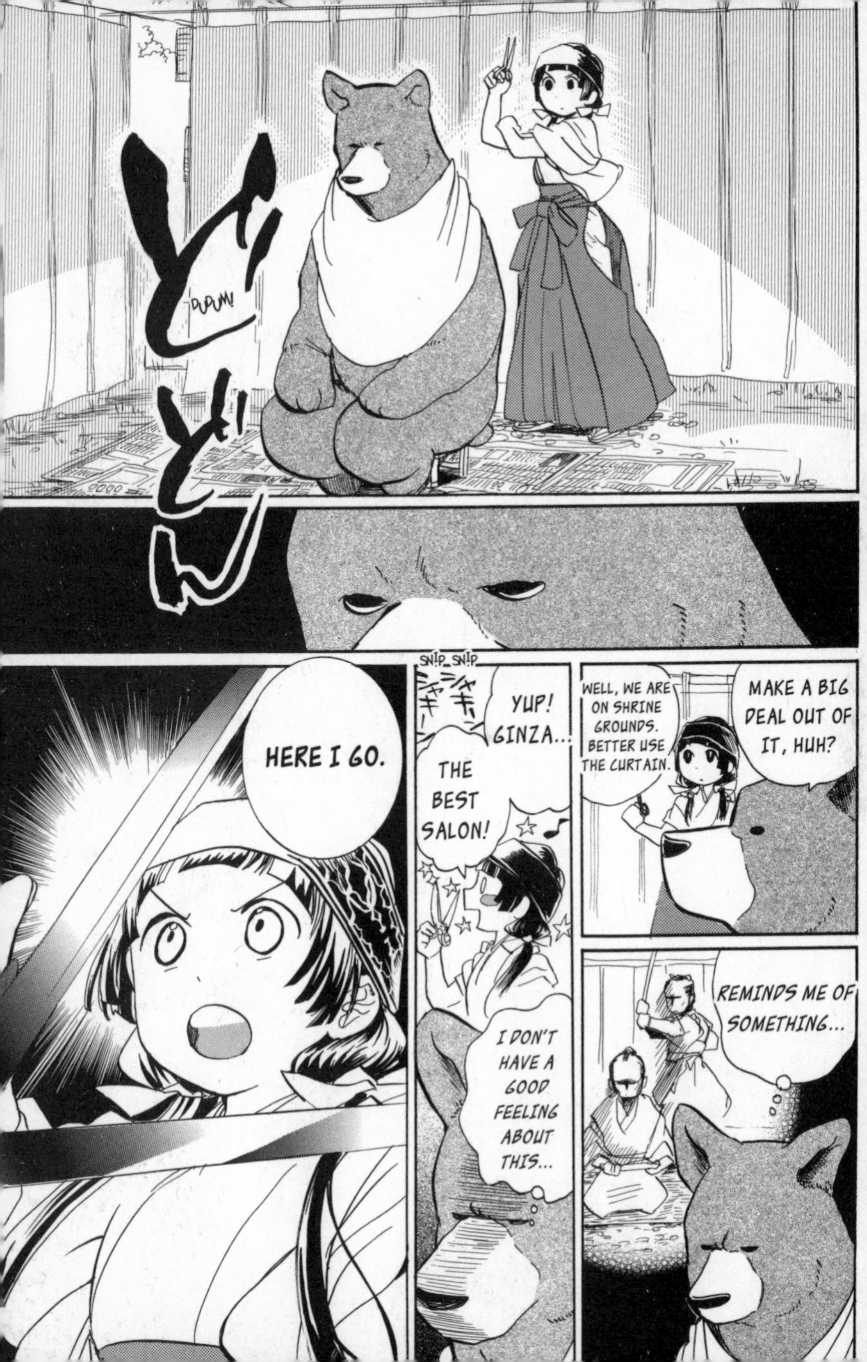
どどん
DUDUM!
MAKE A BIG DEAL OUT OF IT, HUH?
WELL, WE ARE ON SHRINE GROUNDS. BETTER USE THE CURTAIN.
REMINDS ME OF SOMETHING...
SNIP SNIP
シャキ シャキ
YUP! GINZA...
THE BEST SALON!
I DON'T HAVE A GOOD FEELING ABOUT THIS...
HERE I GO.

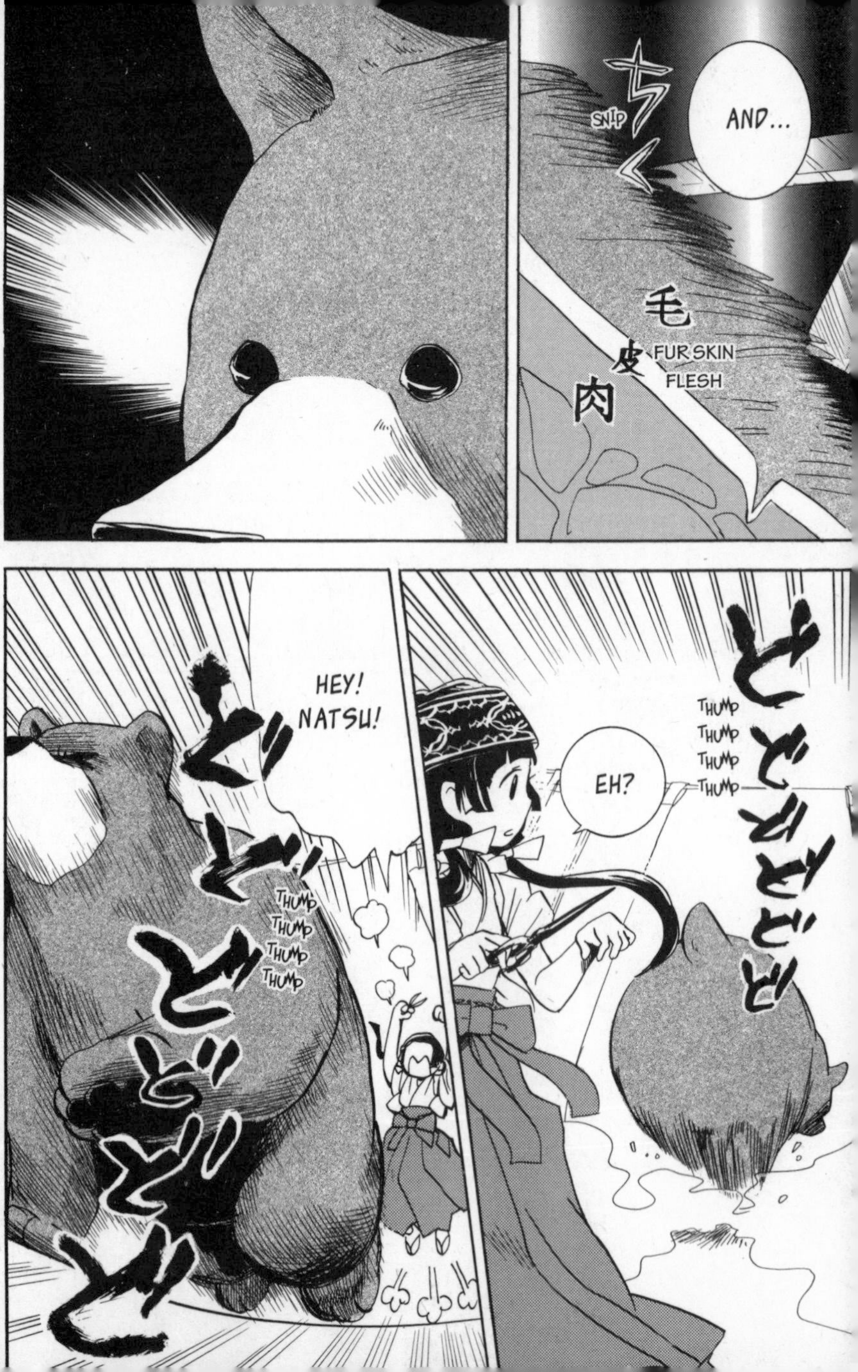
AND...
ちく
SNIP
毛
皮
肉
FUR SKIN
FLESH
THUMP
THUMP
THUMP
THUMP
EH?
HEY! NATSU!
THUMP
THUMP
THUMP
THUMP

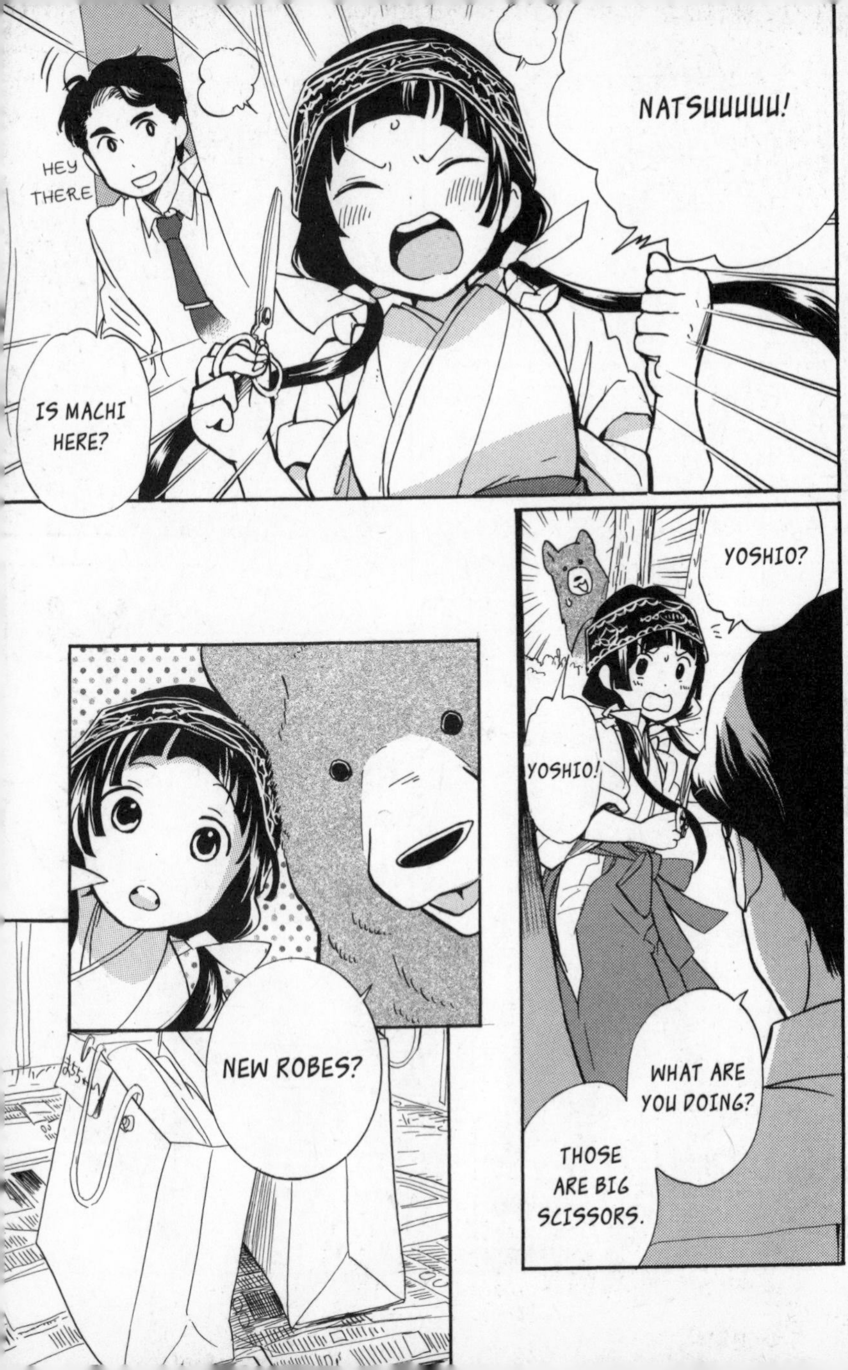
NATSUUUUU!
HEY THERE
IS MACHI HERE?
YOSHIO?
YOSHIO!
WHAT ARE YOU DOING?
THOSE ARE BIG SCISSORS.
NEW ROBES?

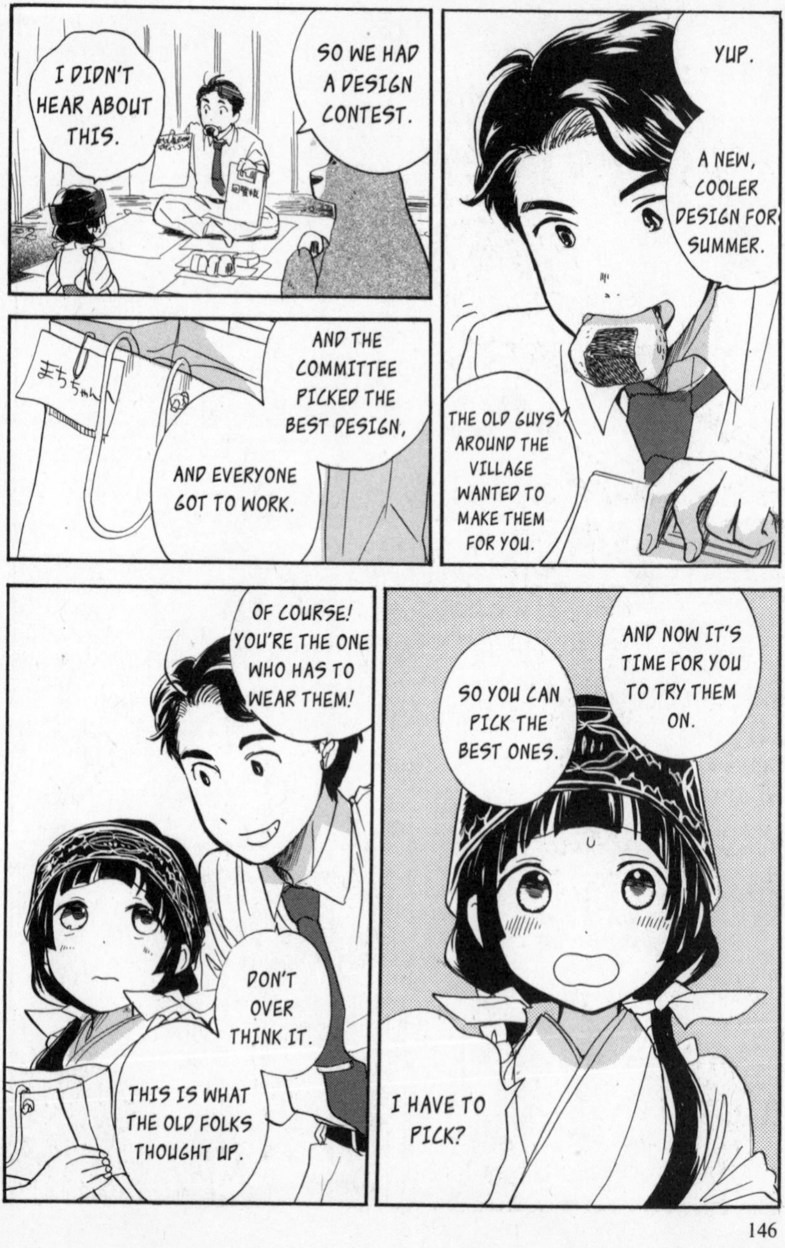
YUP.
A NEW, COOLER DESIGN FOR SUMMER.
THE OLD GUYS AROUND THE VILLAGE WANTED TO MAKE THEM FOR YOU.
SO WE HAD A DESIGN CONTEST.
I DIDN'T HEAR ABOUT THIS.
まちちゃんへ
AND THE COMMITTEE PICKED THE BEST DESIGN,
AND EVERYONE GOT TO WORK.
AND NOW IT'S TIME FOR YOU TO TRY THEM ON.
SO YOU CAN PICK THE BEST ONES.
I HAVE TO PICK?
OF COURSE! YOU'RE THE ONE WHO HAS TO WEAR THEM!
DON'T OVER THINK IT.
THIS IS WHAT THE OLD FOLKS THOUGHT UP.

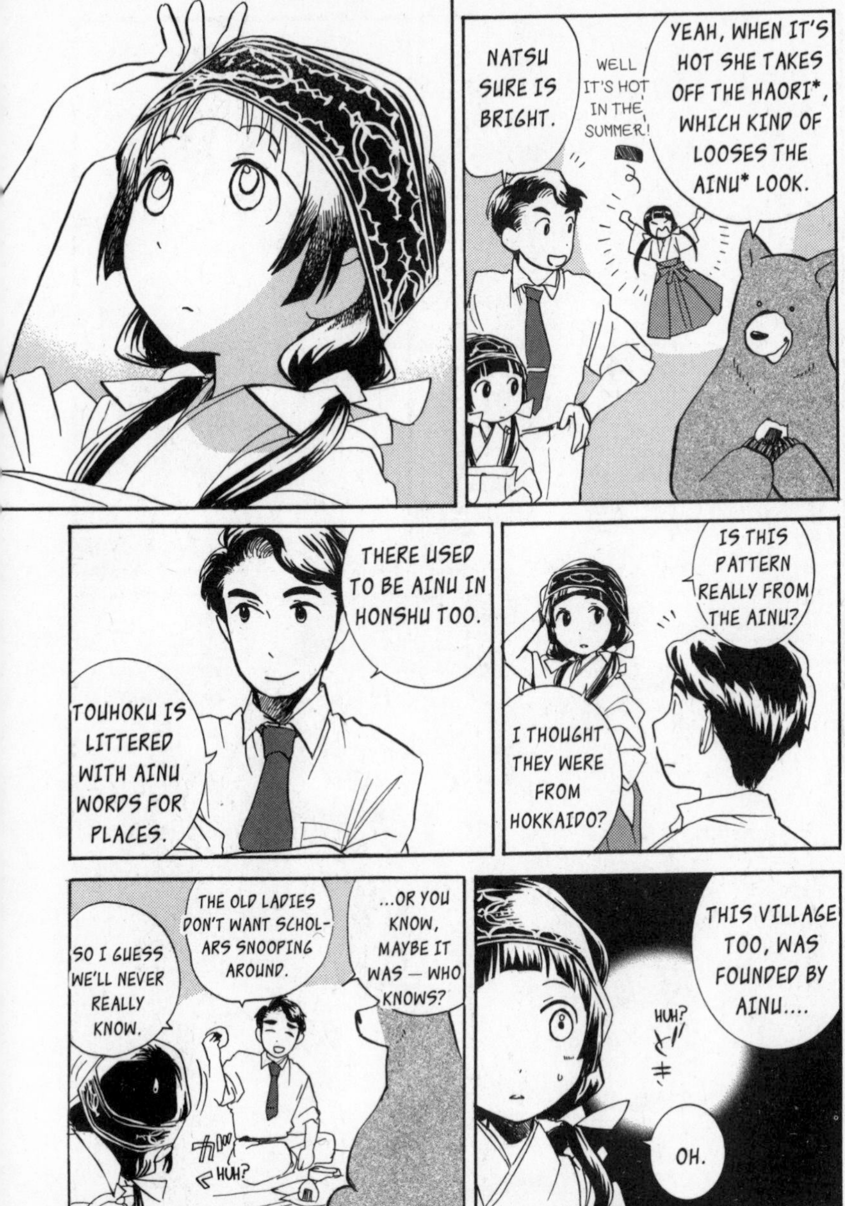
YEAH, WHEN IT'S HOT SHE TAKES OFF THE HAORI*, WHICH KIND OF LOOSES THE AINU* LOOK.
WELL IT'S HOT IN THE SUMMER!
NATSU SURE IS BRIGHT.
IS THIS PATTERN REALLY FROM THE AINU?
I THOUGHT THEY WERE FROM HOKKAIDO?
THERE USED TO BE AINU IN HONSHU TOO.
TOUHOKU IS LITTERED WITH AINU WORDS FOR PLACES.
THIS VILLAGE TOO, WAS FOUNDED BY AINU....
HUH?
OH.
...OR YOU KNOW, MAYBE IT WAS — WHO KNOWS?
THE OLD LADIES DON'T WANT SCHOL-ARS SNOOPING AROUND.
SO I GUESS WE'LL NEVER REALLY KNOW.
HUH?

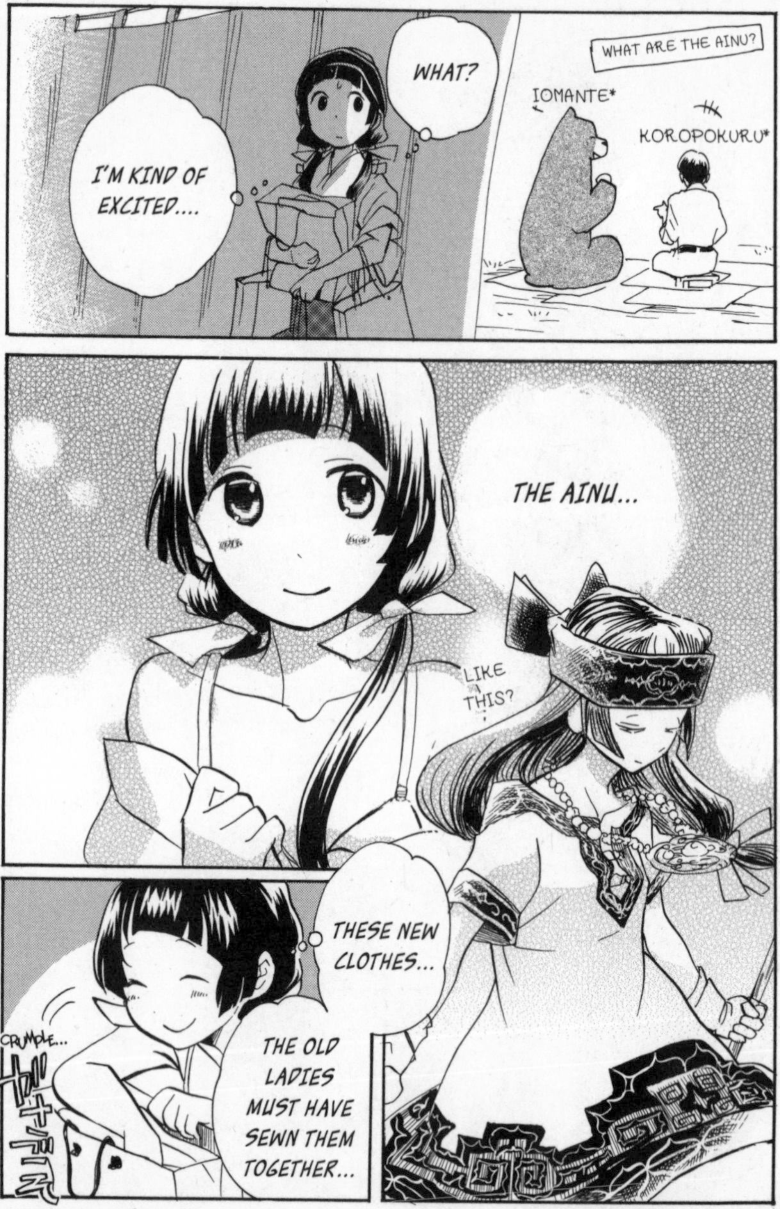
WHAT ARE THE AINU?
IOMANTE*
KOROPOKURU*
WHAT?
I'M KIND OF EXCITED....
THE AINU...
LIKE THIS?
THESE NEW CLOTHES...
THE OLD LADIES MUST HAVE SEWN THEM TOGETHER...
CRUMPLE...

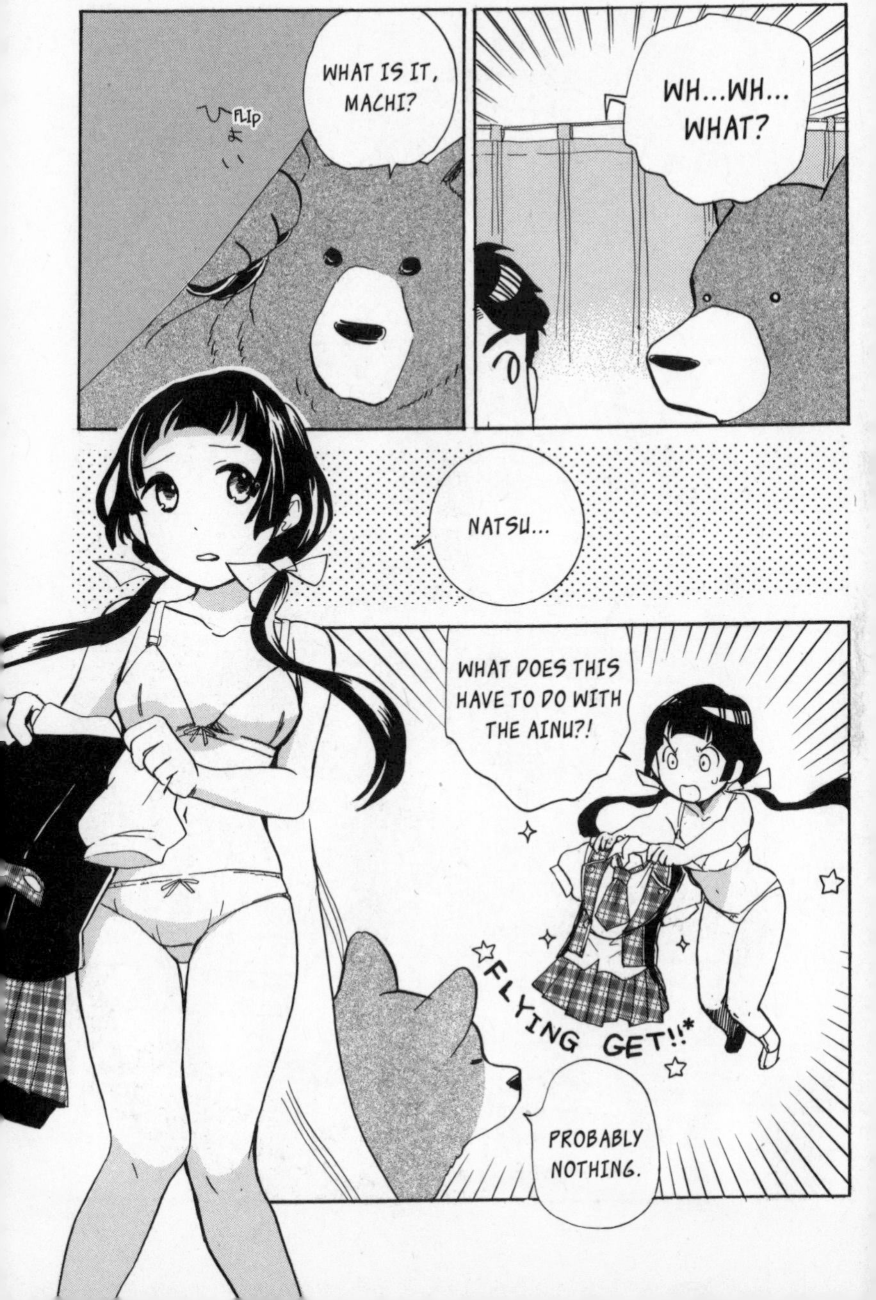
WH...WH... WHAT?
WHAT IS IT, MACHI?
FLIP
NATSU...
WHAT DOES THIS HAVE TO DO WITH THE AINU?!
FLYING GET!!*
PROBABLY NOTHING.

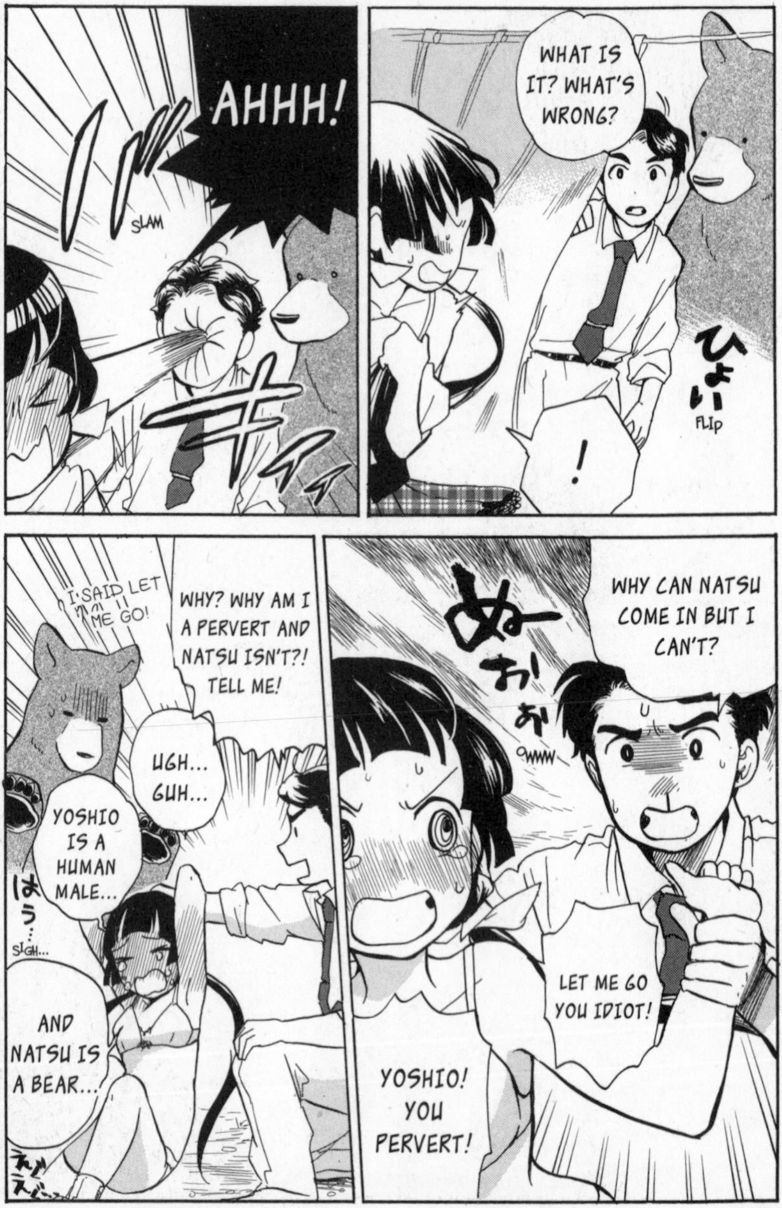
WHAT IS IT? WHAT'S WRONG?
ひょい
FLIP
!
AHHH!
SLAM
ぬおぉ
WHY CAN NATSU COME IN BUT I CAN'T?
LET ME GO YOU IDIOT!
YOSHIO! YOU PERVERT!
WHY? WHY AM I A PERVERT AND NATSU ISN'T?! TELL ME!
I SAID LET ME GO!
UGH... GUH...
YOSHIO IS A HUMAN MALE...
はう...
SIGH...
AND NATSU IS A BEAR...

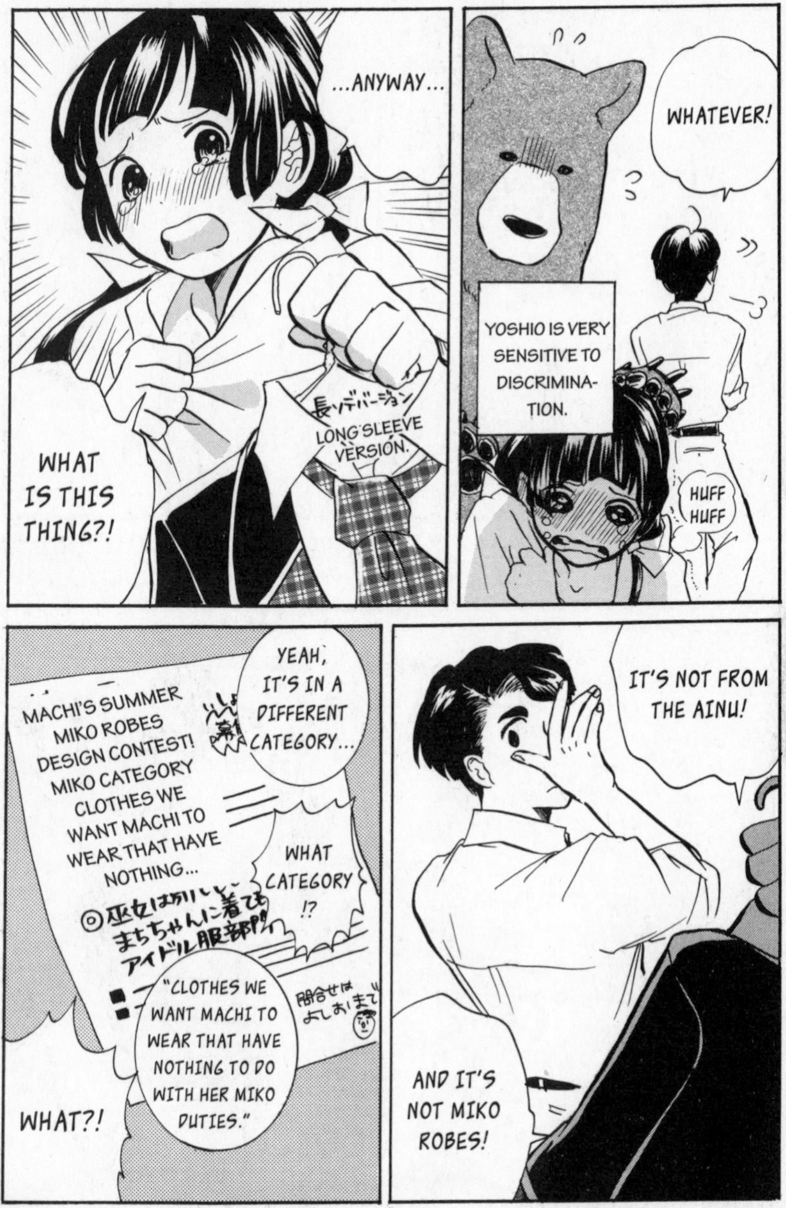

WHATEVER!
YOSHIO IS VERY SENSITIVE TO DISCRIMINA-TION.
HUFF HUFF
...ANYWAY...
WHAT IS THIS THING?!
長ソデバージョン
LONG SLEEVE VERSION.
IT'S NOT FROM THE AINU!
AND IT'S NOT MIKO ROBES!
YEAH, IT'S IN A DIFFERENT CATEGORY...
MACHI'S SUMMER MIKO ROBES DESIGN CONTEST! MIKO CATEGORY CLOTHES WE WANT MACHI TO WEAR THAT HAVE NOTHING...
WHAT CATEGORY!?
◎巫女は別にしても
まちちゃんに着ても
アイドル服部門
問合せはよしおまで
"CLOTHES WE WANT MACHI TO WEAR THAT HAVE NOTHING TO DO WITH HER MIKO DUTIES."
WHAT?!

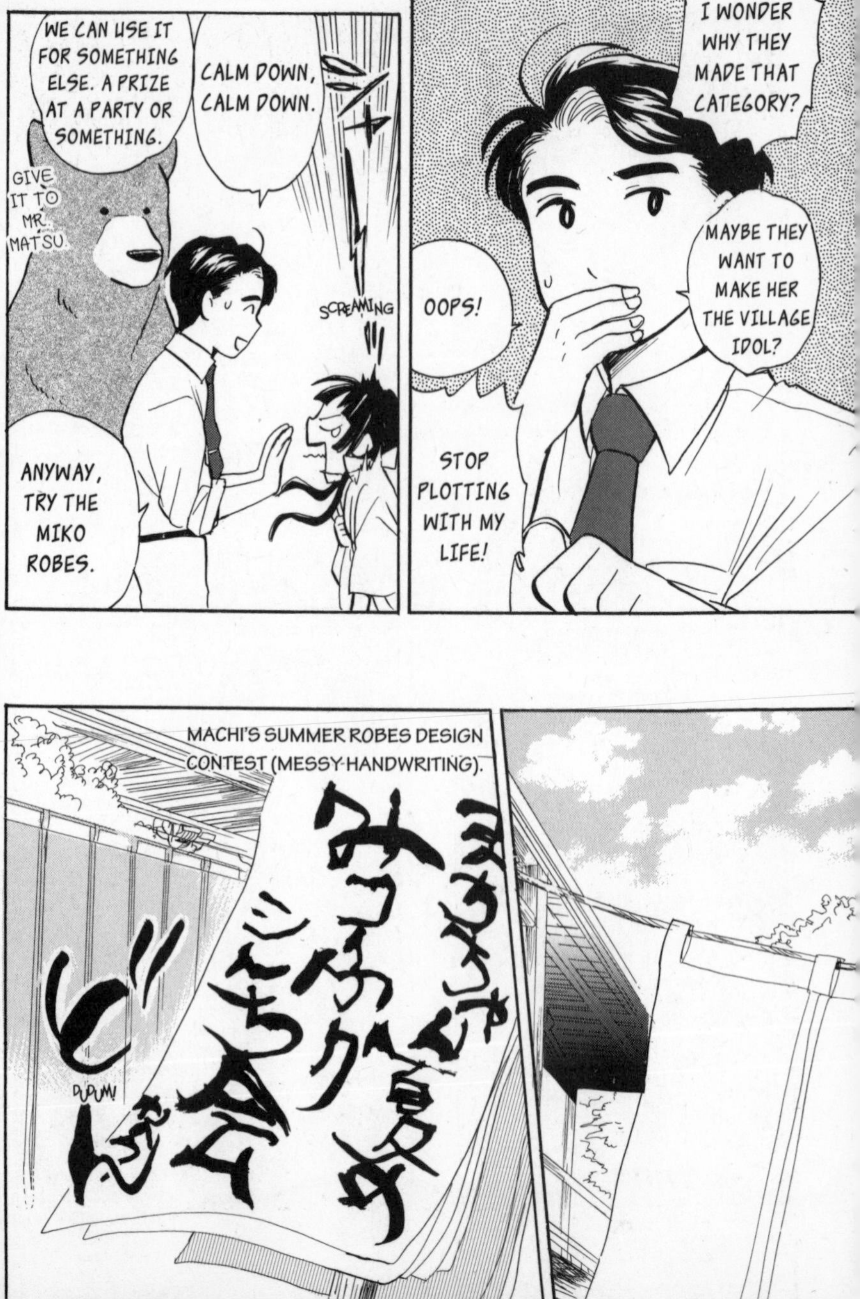
I WONDER WHY THEY MADE THAT CATEGORY?
MAYBE THEY WANT TO MAKE HER THE VILLAGE IDOL?
OOPS!
STOP PLOTTING WITH MY LIFE!
CALM DOWN, CALM DOWN.
WE CAN USE IT FOR SOMETHING ELSE. A PRIZE AT A PARTY OR SOMETHING.
GIVE IT TO MR. MATSU.
SCREAMING
ANYWAY, TRY THE MIKO ROBES.
MACHI'S SUMMER ROBES DESIGN CONTEST (MESSY-HANDWRITING).
DUDUM!

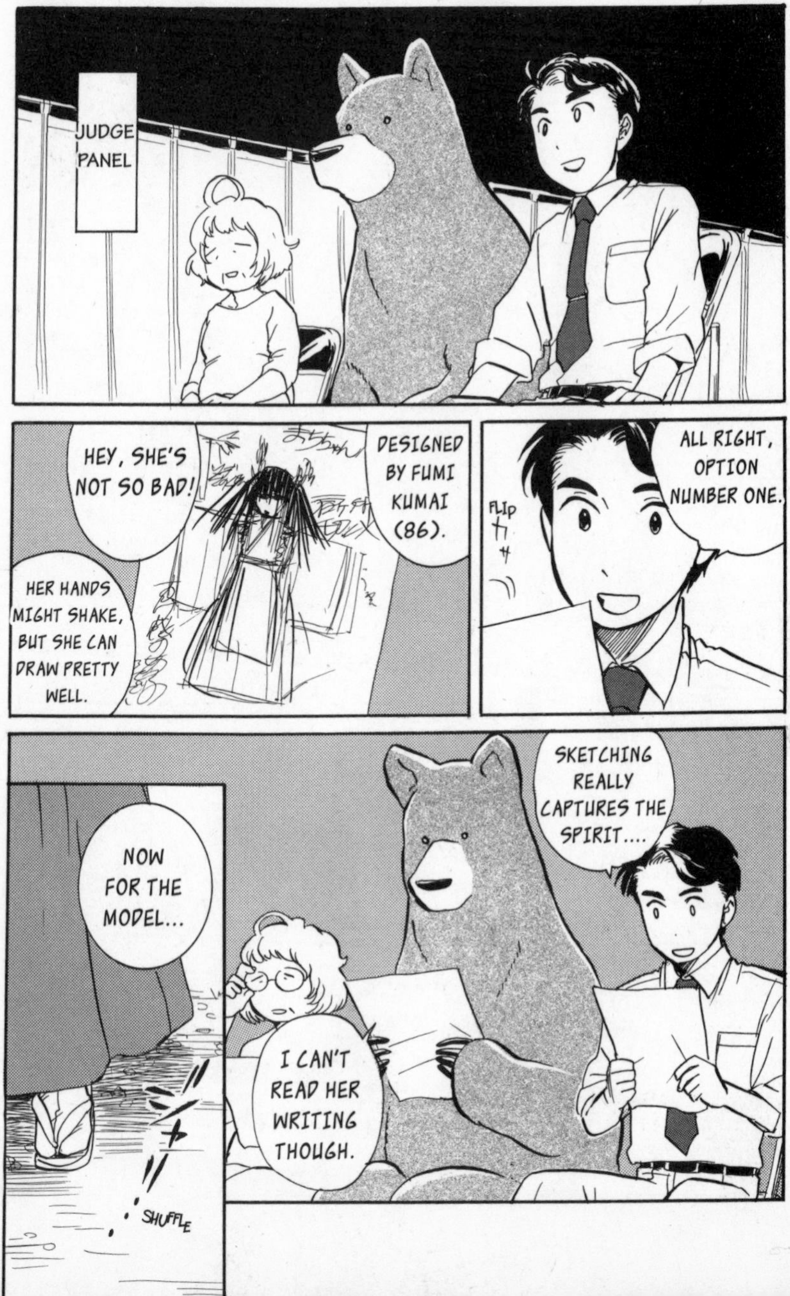
JUDGE PANEL
ALL RIGHT, OPTION NUMBER ONE.
FLIP
DESIGNED BY FUMI KUMAI (86).
HEY, SHE'S NOT SO BAD!
HER HANDS MIGHT SHAKE, BUT SHE CAN DRAW PRETTY WELL.
SKETCHING REALLY CAPTURES THE SPIRIT....
I CAN'T READ HER WRITING THOUGH.
NOW FOR THE MODEL...
SHUFFLE

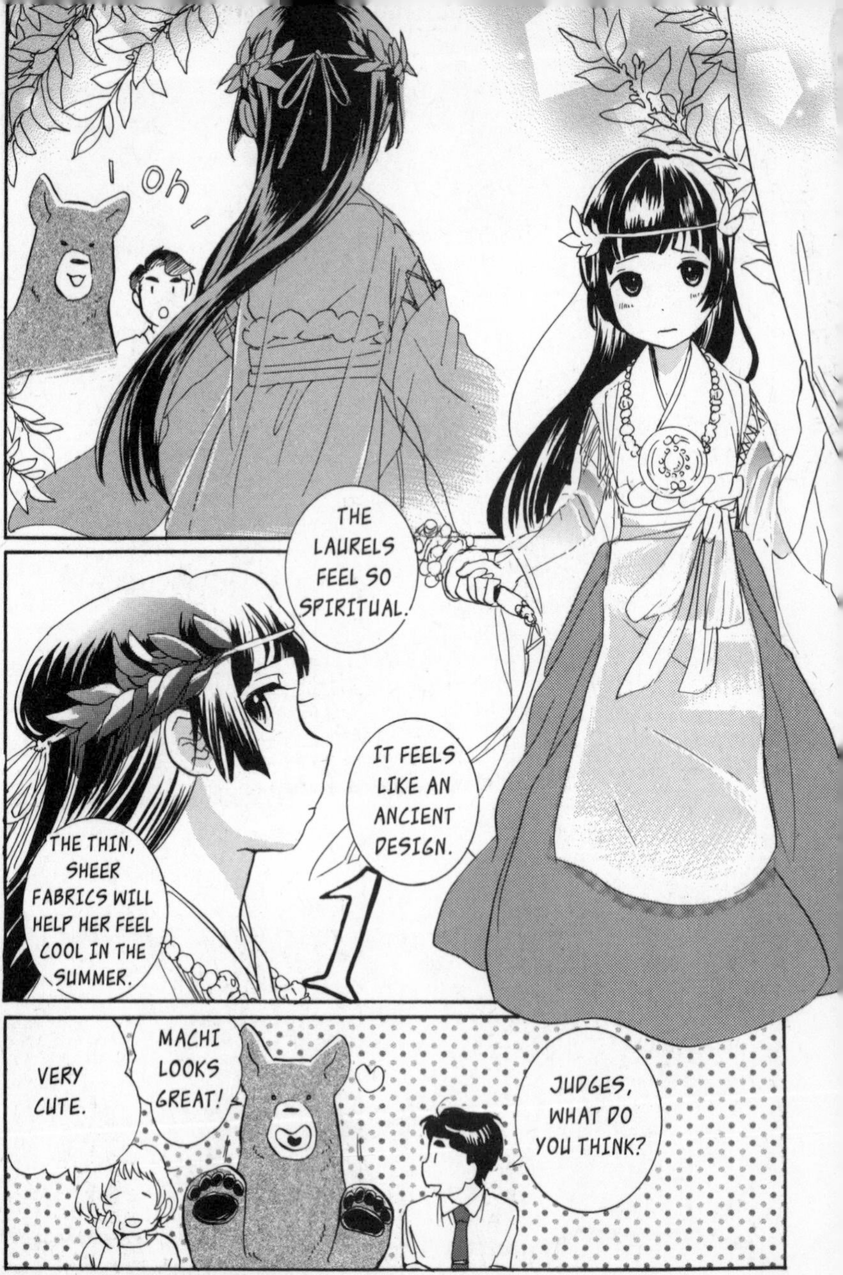
Oh
THE LAURELS FEEL SO SPIRITUAL.
IT FEELS LIKE AN ANCIENT DESIGN.
THE THIN, SHEER FABRICS WILL HELP HER FEEL COOL IN THE SUMMER.
JUDGES, WHAT DO YOU THINK?
MACHI LOOKS GREAT!
VERY CUTE.

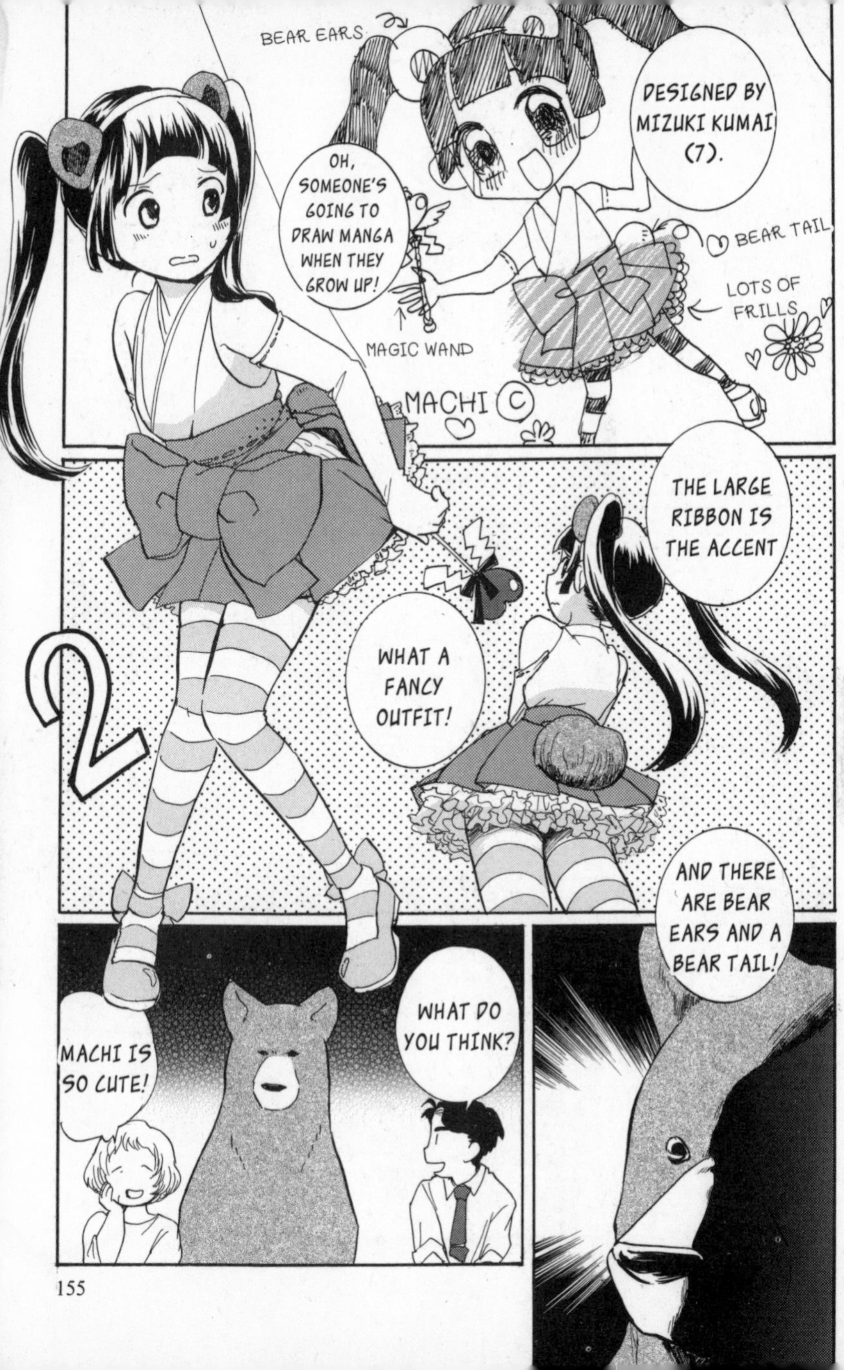
DESIGNED BY MIZUKI KUMAI (7).
BEAR EARS
BEAR TAIL
LOTS OF FRILLS
OH, SOMEONE'S GOING TO DRAW MANGA WHEN THEY GROW UP!
MAGIC WAND
MACHI ©
THE LARGE RIBBON IS THE ACCENT
WHAT A FANCY OUTFIT!
AND THERE ARE BEAR EARS AND A BEAR TAIL!
WHAT DO YOU THINK?
MACHI IS SO CUTE!

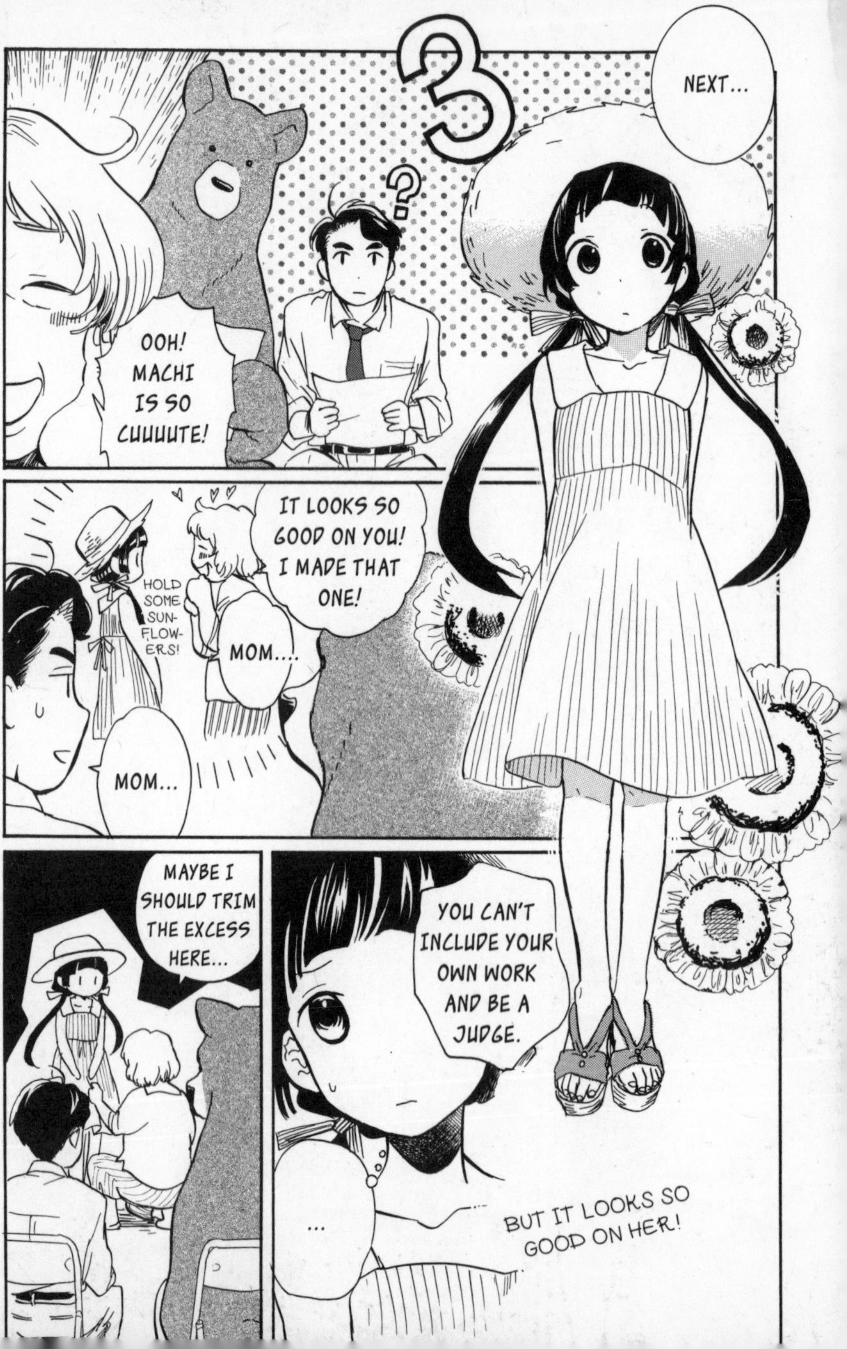
NEXT...
3
OOH! MACHI IS SO CUUUUTE!
IT LOOKS SO GOOD ON YOU! I MADE THAT ONE!
HOLD SOME SUN-FLOWERS!
MOM....
MOM...
YOU CAN'T INCLUDE YOUR OWN WORK AND BE A JUDGE.
...
BUT IT LOOKS SO GOOD ON HER!
MAYBE I SHOULD TRIM THE EXCESS HERE...

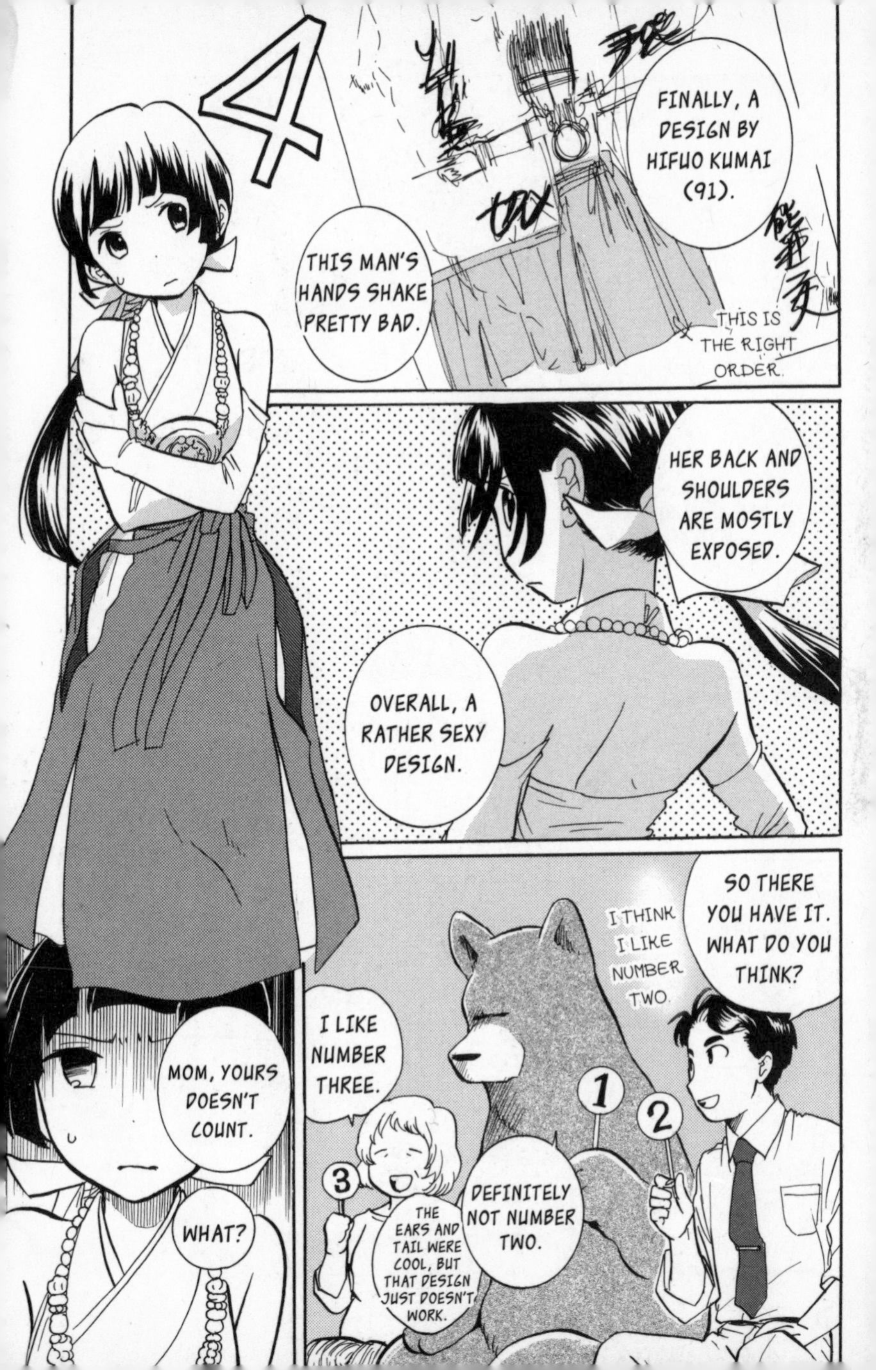
4
FINALLY, A DESIGN BY HIFUO KUMAI (91).
THIS MAN'S HANDS SHAKE PRETTY BAD.
THIS IS THE RIGHT ORDER.
HER BACK AND SHOULDERS ARE MOSTLY EXPOSED.
OVERALL, A RATHER SEXY DESIGN.
SO THERE YOU HAVE IT. WHAT DO YOU THINK?
I THINK I LIKE NUMBER TWO.
I LIKE NUMBER THREE.
DEFINITELY NOT NUMBER TWO.
THE EARS AND TAIL WERE COOL, BUT THAT DESIGN JUST DOESN'T WORK.
1
2
3
MOM, YOURS DOESN'T COUNT.
WHAT?

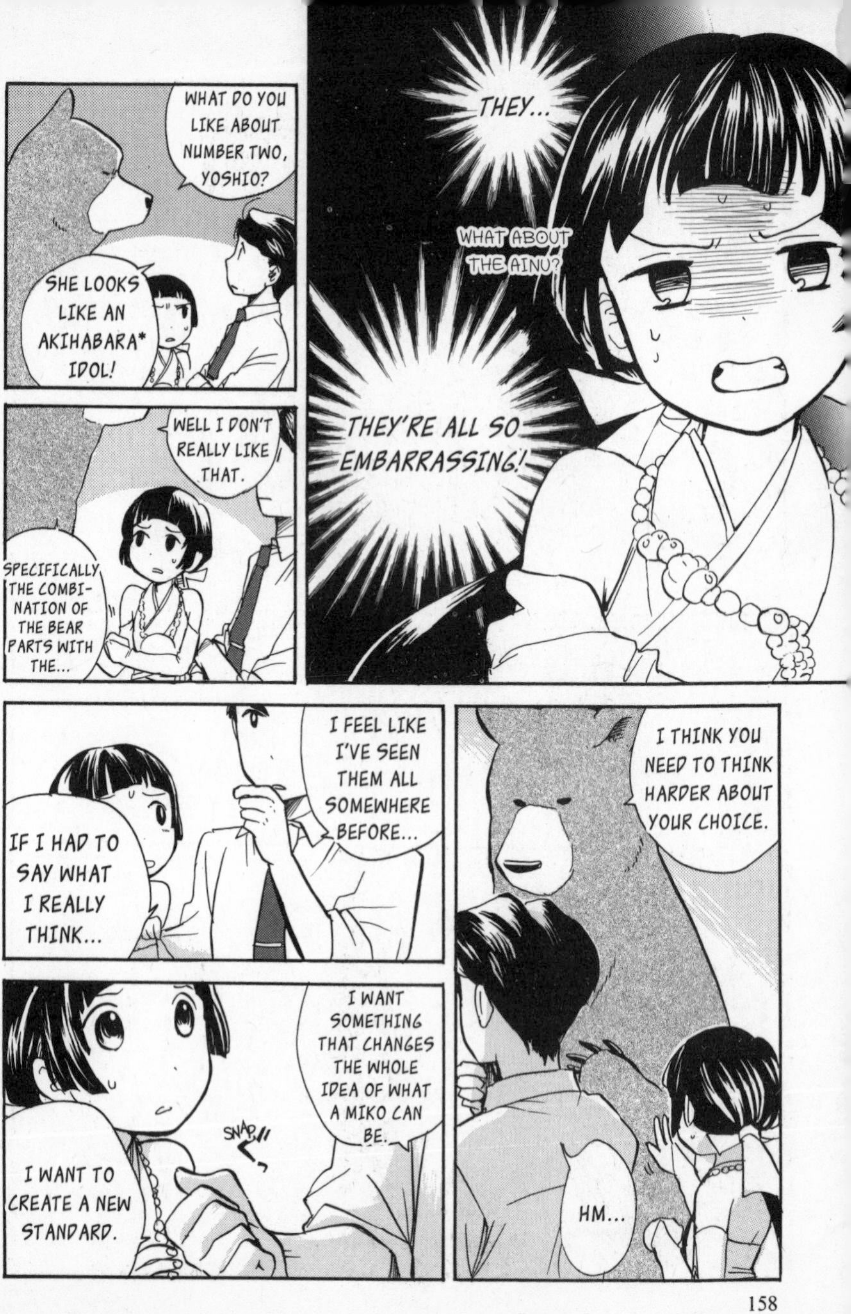
THEY...
WHAT ABOUT THE AINU?
THEY'RE ALL SO EMBARRASSING!
WHAT DO YOU LIKE ABOUT NUMBER TWO, YOSHIO?
SHE LOOKS LIKE AN AKIHABARA* IDOL!
WELL I DON'T REALLY LIKE THAT.
SPECIFICALLY THE COMBI-NATION OF THE BEAR PARTS WITH THE...
I THINK YOU NEED TO THINK HARDER ABOUT YOUR CHOICE.
HM...
I FEEL LIKE I'VE SEEN THEM ALL SOMEWHERE BEFORE...
IF I HAD TO SAY WHAT I REALLY THINK...
I WANT SOMETHING THAT CHANGES THE WHOLE IDEA OF WHAT A MIKO CAN BE.
SNAP!!
I WANT TO CREATE A NEW STANDARD.

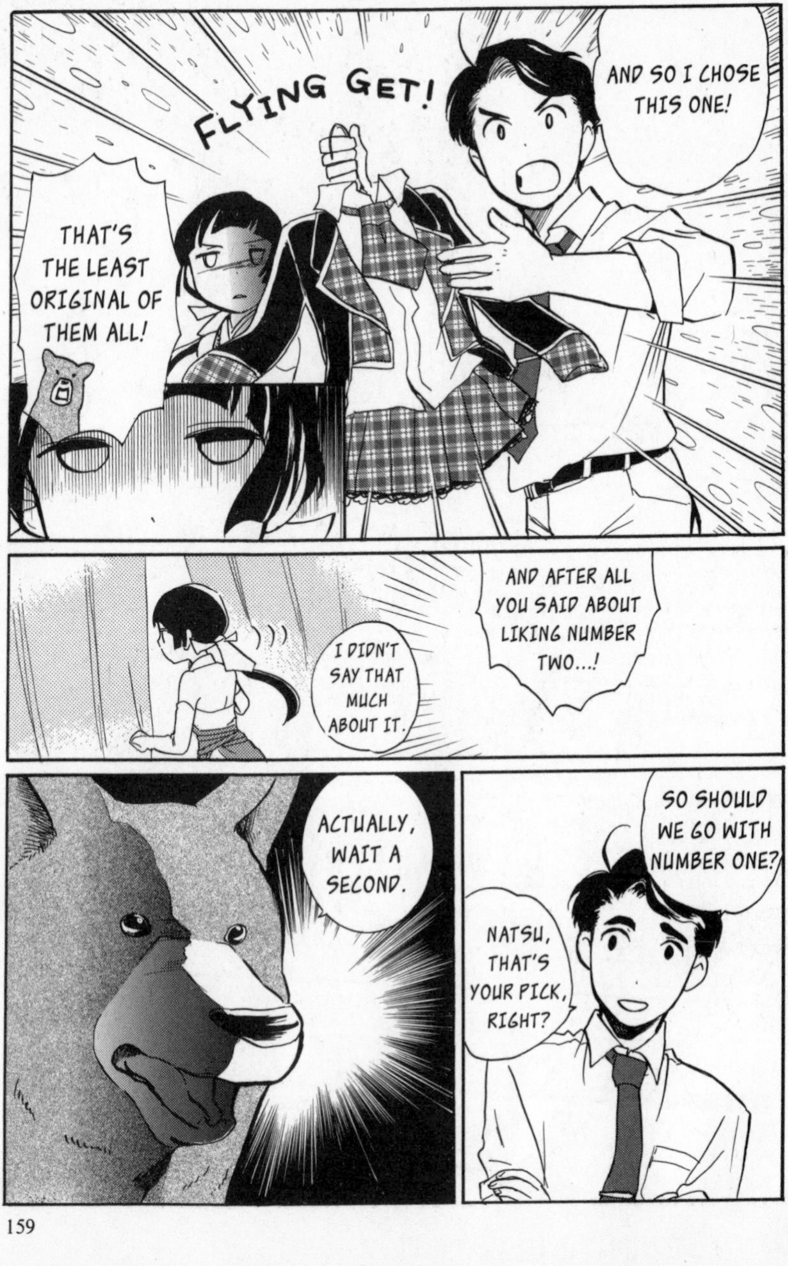
AND SO I CHOSE THIS ONE!
FLYING GET!
THAT'S THE LEAST ORIGINAL OF THEM ALL!
AND AFTER ALL YOU SAID ABOUT LIKING NUMBER TWO...!
I DIDN'T SAY THAT MUCH ABOUT IT.
SO SHOULD WE GO WITH NUMBER ONE?
NATSU, THAT'S YOUR PICK, RIGHT?
ACTUALLY, WAIT A SECOND.

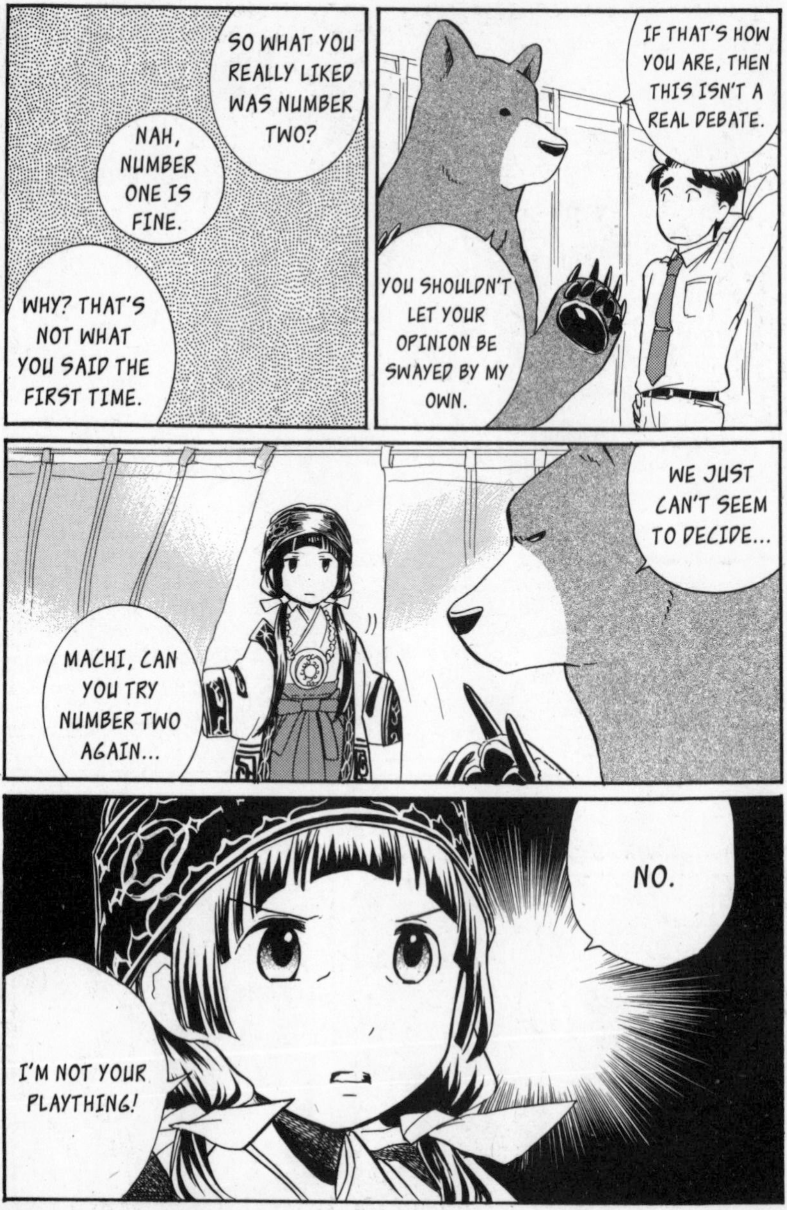
IF THAT'S HOW YOU ARE, THEN THIS ISN'T A REAL DEBATE.
YOU SHOULDN'T LET YOUR OPINION BE SWAYED BY MY OWN.
SO WHAT YOU REALLY LIKED WAS NUMBER TWO?
NAH, NUMBER ONE IS FINE.
WHY? THAT'S NOT WHAT YOU SAID THE FIRST TIME.
WE JUST CAN'T SEEM TO DECIDE...
MACHI, CAN YOU TRY NUMBER TWO AGAIN...
NO.
I'M NOT YOUR PLAYTHING!

● TO BE CONTINUED.

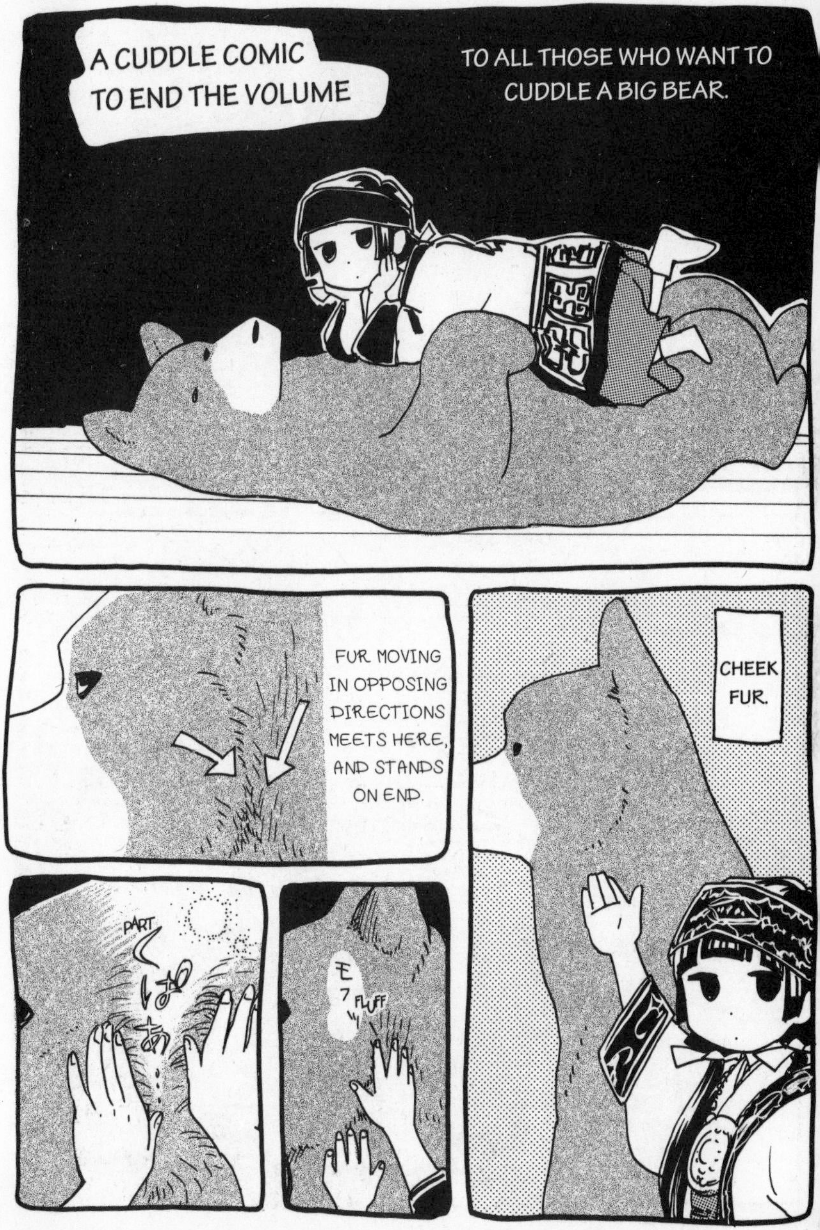
TO ALL THOSE WHO WANT TO CUDDLE A BIG BEAR.
A CUDDLE COMIC TO END THE VOLUME
CHEEK FUR.
FUR MOVING IN OPPOSING DIRECTIONS MEETS HERE, AND STANDS ON END.
モフ FLUFF
PART
くぱあ

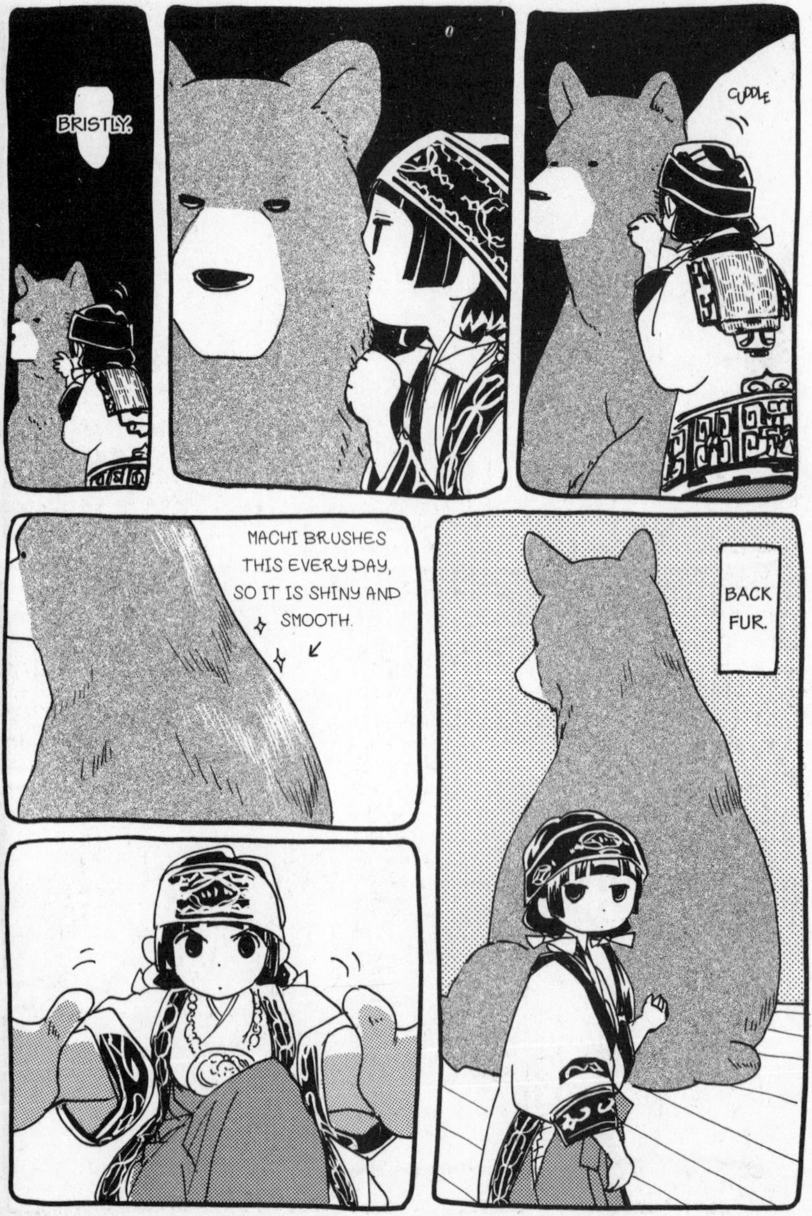
CUDDLE
BRISTLY.
BACK FUR.
MACHI BRUSHES THIS EVERY DAY, SO IT IS SHINY AND SMOOTH.

NECK FUR.

SHINY BECOMES MATTE.

NECK MEASUREMENT: ONE METER.

THE END.

HOPE TO SEE YOU

NEXT TIME.

...MM

MMMMMM.

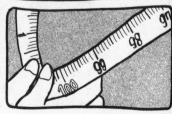

Fuji Apples are an apple hybrid developed in Fujisaki, Aomori, Japan. It is commonly believed that the best apples in Japan come from this region.

Mugi-cha, otherwise known as roasted barley tea, is a caffeine-free, roasted-grain-based infusion made from barley, popular in Japanese cuisine, especially as a cool drink during the summer months.

Haori is a traditional Japanese thigh-length jacket, worn over a *kosode*, a basic Japanese robe for men and women.

The Ainu are an indigenous people of Japan's northernmost island Hokkaido and, formerly, northeastern Honshu, Russia, Sakhalin, and the Kuril Islands.

Koropokuru are a race of small people in the folklore of the Ainu.

Iomante is the name of an Ainu ceremony and generally refers to the Ainu brown bear sacrifice.

Flying Get is the 22nd single by the Japanese idol girl group AKB48, a 130-member Japanese all young girl music and entertainment group named after the Akihabara area in Tokyo.

Akihabara is considered, in modern Tokyo, by many to be an *otaku* cultural center and a shopping district for video games, anime, manga, and computer goods.

Machi's notes:

A miko is traditionally a shrine maiden or a priestess. In modern Japanese culture the role is institutionalized.

A naginata is one of several different varieties of traditionally made Japanese blades in the form of a feudal period pole weapon.

Suica is a Romanization of the Japanese word for watermelon. Suica is also a name for the contactless smart card used as a fare card on train lines in Japan.

JR is the acronym for the Japan Railways Group, the center of Japan's railway network, operating a large proportion of the country's rail service.

OIOI is known as Marui Co., Ltd., a Japanese retail company that operates a chain of department stores in Japan. The company's logo is two circles, which are read "maru," in Japanese, each followed by a vertical line, which may represent the numeral 1, or the Japanese character い which is pronouced /i:/ in Japanese.

O ko Ichihara is a reference to a famous Japanese actress with a distinct voice, known for narrating a long-running anime series about Japanese folklore.

Kagura is literally translated as "god-entertainment" and is a Japanese word referring to a specific type of Shinto theatrical dance.

Kyary Pamyu Pamyu is a Japanese pop singer best known for the hit song *PonPonPon*. Her music is produced by Yasutaka Nakata of the electronic music duo Capsule.

Kuma Miko: Girl Meets Bear Volume 1

© Masume Yoshimoto 2013
First published by KADOKAWA CORPORATION in 2013 in Japan.
English translation rights arranged by One Peace Books
under the license from KADOKAWA CORPORATION, Japan.

ISBN 978-1-935548-53-9

Written and illustrated by Masume Yoshimoto
English Edition Published by One Peace Books 2016

Printed in Canada

1 2 3 4 5 6 7 8 9 10

One Peace Books
43-32 22nd Street STE 204 Long Island City New York 11101
www.onepeacebooks.com